Perceptions, Emotions,
Sensibilities

Perceptions, Emotions, Sensibilities

Essays on India's Colonial and Post-colonial Experiences

TAPAN RAYCHAUDHURI

OXFORD
UNIVERSITY PRESS

OXFORD
UNIVERSITY PRESS

YMCA Library Building, Jai Singh Road, New Delhi 110001

Oxford University Press is a department of the University of Oxford. It furthers the
University's objective of excellence in research, scholarship, and education
by publishing worldwide in

Oxford   New York
Athens   Auckland   Bangkok   Bogota   Buenos Aires   Calcutta
Cape Town   Chennai   Dar es Salaam   Delhi   Florence   Hong Kong   Istanbul
Karachi   Kuala Lumpur   Madrid   Melbourne   Mexico City   Mumbai
Nairobi   Paris   Sao Paolo   Singapore   Taipei   Tokyo   Toronto   Warsaw

with associated companies in

Berlin   Ibadan

ISBN 019 564863 3

Typeset by Guru Typograph Technology, New Delhi 110 045
Printed in India at Wadhwa Internationals, New Delhi 110 020
and published by Manzar Khan, Oxford University Press
YMCA Library Building, Jai Singh Road, New Delhi 110 001

For
LEELA LAKSHMI WIGNARAJA
to thank her for the pleasure of her company
and to
BHUNU, GANESH AND HASHI
for their roles in making this pleasure possible

Preface

This collection of essays is based on published and unpublished articles and lectures written between 1992 and 1997. They vary in nature as they are addressed to different audiences. Some are full-fledged research papers, others are popularizers meant for the educated reader without any specialized knowledge of Indian history. Some are what is sometime described as 'think papers'—the presentation of an idea which is yet to be worked out fully. The two articles on sensibilities belong to the last mentioned category. One of these and the essay on British rule are not annotated. The editor of the relevant volume for the latter did not ask for notes. On the other hand, for the essay on Europe in India's xenology published in *Past and Present*, the desk editor asked for notes even on matters familiar to everyone in India. Hence a footnote on *varnasrama* which may surprise the reader in India. It seemed sensible to leave these as they were when first printed, for some educated readers outside India may well not know the meaning of such terms of everyday usage in our country and other readers may not be interested in annotation. I am aware that some of these essays would improve if expanded, but there is something to be said for leaving them more or less as they were first published.

The essays in the first section are related one way or another to my current subject of research—the mental world of the Bengali *bhadralok* in the nineteenth century. The book based on that research, I hope, will go to press in the foreseeable future. Here I have to record my deep regret for failure to keep a promise. I had undertaken to do a Bengali version of that projected book for a series in Bengali of which my friend the late Professor Ashin Das Gupta was the General Editor. I could not keep to that promise in his life time, but do hope that the project will materialize and the volume will appear in due course in the series now edited by his successor.

Some of the essays in this volume were published in the shadow of a trauma—the destruction of the Babri mosque. For those of our generation who were nurtured by the values of India's inclusive nationalism and retained some faith in the nation state despite its many failures, it was an incredible and totally unacceptable event. The fact that the perpetrators of that crime, instead of serving time in prison, are now in positions of great authority in the central government of India, enhances one's sense of horror. Vivekananda, whom the Hindu communalists have tried to claim as their intellectual ancestor, actually shared our feeling of revulsion for all that these fanatics represent. One essay, 'Had He Been Alive Today', for the most part a series of quotations from the patriot prophet's writings, records his sense of horror at the values represented by Hindu chauvinism. I commend it to those who see him as a pioneer of Hindu revival. I am grateful to Swami Lokeswarananda and the Ramakrishna Mission Institute of Culture, Calcutta for the opportunity to present these articles and lectures at various seminars and conferences organized by them. The essay on Swamiji's construction of Hinduism was presented at a seminar organized by Dr William Radice at the School of Oriental and African Studies, London and first published in a volume edited by him. I am grateful for his permission to include it in this collection of essays.

My valedictory lecture at the University of Oxford, delivered in June 1993, on the eve of my retirement after more than two decades of service, is addressed directly to the rise of Hindu communal forces in Indian politics. I, among others, see in this phenomenon frightening affinities with the rise of Nazism in Germany though of course developments in two different cultures, in two very different time periods, can not be identical in nature. I am no specialist on contemporary Indian history and my data for this essay, as I have acknowledged, are derived largely from other people's research. But when all that one values is threatened, it becomes incumbent on one to use every skill at one's disposal to defend these. 'Shadows of the Swastika' is my modest contribution to the country-wide effort to fight the forces of communal hatred. Incidentally, the essay when first published in a different form, came in for criticism from unexpected quarters—western radicals interested in India. Some of them in their wisdom had greeted the rise of Hindu chauvinism as the emergence of the true face of Indian society, intrinsically hostile to the bourgeois values of democratic secularism, a view remarkably similar to the colonial projection of the Indian reality. Now that the Hindu chauvinists in power are singing secularist tunes to beguile the voters, these savants should be invited to take a second look at their interpretation of Indian society.

The essay on Indo–Pakistan relations, based on a lecture delivered at the invitation of a conference at Madison, Wisconsin, is also based on no academic expertise. It only expresses a sense of urgency which many others share in our two countries. It also embodies an old man's hope that some day our mindless conflict will come to an end and our peoples will try to work for a more positive relationship which we do need quite badly. At the moment, this sounds like a pipe dream.

The three essays on the Raj are all commissioned articles and have appeared or will soon appear in different volumes. The first of these, an assessment of British rule in India, was published in an abridged form in a volume edited by Professor Peter Marshall: he had asked for a shorter essay. The reader he had in mind is the educated non-specialist, especially British. The coverage of elementary information is explained by this concern.

This essay attracted unfavourable attention in a section of the press in U.K. though it was accorded only 3000 words in a sizeable and sumptuous volume. A famous colleague found it rather 'cool' in its assessment of British achievements in India, inadequately appreciative of what he likes to describe as the *imperium*. Another critic complained that I had not even acknowledged the wonders of the judicial system introduced by the Raj, something which the great K.M. Panikkar himself had recognized as one of the greatest gifts of Albion to India. It pleases me that in one essay in this volume—on Moon's *Divide and Quit*, I could cite the opinion of a famous British civilian on the 'excellence' of that gift. I hope that the critic in question stumbles on those remarks at some point.

These responses to my modest effort—of no academic significance, once more made me aware how absurd it was to expect objectivity in perceptions of imperial history in people who accept the values which sustained the empire. The failure or refusal to see the truth is not necessarily linked to one's ethnic identity. One of the critics incensed by my failure to admire the empire is of non-British origin. His sentiments are no different from those of an once unknown Indian and, in fact, are identical with those of my late revered mentor, Sir Jadunath Sarkar. On the other hand the quotation from Orwell which introduces the essay in question evokes a perception rooted in the British radical tradition. That perception appears to have receded into insignificance in both popular and academic discourse in Orwell's country.

If any historical discourse is badly in need of deconstruction, an unravelling of its ideological and social roots, it is probably British imperial history. These roots may be traced to vested interests who benefited most from the empire in the past, but the ideology they projected with great finesse and rare persistence have taken in a surprisingly wide variety of people ranging from persons who were actually victims of the colonial nexus to foreign academics who accept the views projected in colonial records at their face value. The subtlety and insidious nature of the indoctrination is truly amazing. Nirad C. Chaudhury, who, like many of his middle class contemporaries in India, suffered terribly from the absence of employment opportunities, remains convinced that he was a victim of his compatriots' malice and not the colonial nexus. An American historian, who was certainly not a propagandist for imperial glory, put on record his innocent belief that the prime concern of the British in India was the welfare of Indians. An English secretary who told me that at the end of the second World war her family lived on her mother's weekly income of fourteen shillings, was convinced nevertheless that the Empire was of benefit to all Britishers and that the raj had done a world of good to the benighted Indians. She received this wisdom from a tabloid which to her was an adequate substitute for the Holy Book. I cite this anecdotal evidence to draw attention to the need for serious work on perceptions of the imperial past. In its absence, the historical literature on the colonial period in India, with its vast omissions and almost subliminal falsifications, is of very limited use as indicator of what really happened.

Such analysis is also necessary to meet a wider need of our times. I have spent the last ten months in Germany where, very appropriately, the liberal intellectual is obsessed with the national sense of guilt over the holocaust. There is an on-going debate in that country as to whether one should feel guilty for the misdeeds of one's forefathers. I for one believe that guilt is not something one should inherit. But with one qualification: if one is in the business of glorifying a past from which one continues to benefit, then one should be made aware of the crimes integral to the relevant achievements. It is well to remember that the holocaust is only the most spectacular among crimes committed by people ruthlessly seeking power to control other people's lives. In the history of mankind, especially of European empires, there are impressive antecedents, ranging from the slave trade to systematic genocide, which should not be wiped off the record. The British school child who reads in his history text book of Lord Clive's wonderful achievements should also be told that the man was a criminal by any definition. Admiring accounts of Churchill's life should not omit his charming suggestion that Gandhi, bound hands and feet, should be trampled by the viceregal elephant or his extreme reluctance to send foodgrains to Bengal to help the victims of a famine which took some three million lives.

In my long sojourn in Britain, I have rarely come across an awareness that the imperial record contains actions and attitudes of which any decent human being should be ashamed. Admittedly, Britain has nothing as spectacular as the holocaust in its imperial past. But perhaps it would do the British psyche no harm if the persistent glorification of the empire and the Raj was at least a little counterbalanced by some knowledge of how the 'mutiny' was crushed, of what happened in the Punjab *after* Jallianwalabagh, how the non-violent salt satyagrahis at Dharsana were treated or the fact that in 1943, four years before the transfer of power, three million people starved to death in Bengal, mainly as a result of administrative bungling. Where there is any cognisance of such facts, they are nicely wrapped in explanations produced by masters in the art of explaining away. Criticism of the imperial past is not a growth industry in the UK. However deep your appreciation of Britain's many-splendoured civilization, if you are critical of the colonial record, you are anti-British. Any suggestion that imperialism and fascism are animals from neighbouring stables is still unmentionable heresy. A benign amnesia shrouds all imperial misdeeds and it permits academic and popular projections which distort truth beyond the limits of acceptability.

Philips Hutchins in his brilliant study of the imperialist psyche, *Illusion of Permanance*, pointed out the vested interest which the most reactionary element in British society had in the empire, especially the jewel in their crown and how their position in Britain was bolstered up by the imperial ideology. The influence which these elements still exert over all channels of communication—from the media to academic institutions, guarantees a permanent ambience of brainwashing. The techniques deployed range from sophisticated academic statements to the brash crudities of the tabloid press. Perhaps contemporary Britain could learn something from their fellow Europeans of Germany where, incidentally, the initial resistance to acknowledgment of responsibility for the holocaust was considerable. In Japan, the most hawkish element in society have apparently succeeded in their effort to brush under the carpet the horrors perpetrated by their countrymen during the Second World War. It is incumbent on the historian to resist such tendencies wherever one encounters them. Lest we forget.

British perceptions of the imperial past is not a central concern of the essays in this volume. Yet with some understanding of it, much of the on-going discourse on colonial India remains incomprehensible. Hence this lengthy digression.

Lastly, a word regarding the title of this volume, 'Perceptions, Emotions, Sensibilities'. Of course, it is more relevant for the first than for the second or third part of this collection. Yet, the essays in the second part are also about perceptions. Those in the third have much to do with all the three categories in question—the mutual perceptions of Hindus and Muslims, a coarsening of sensibilities which generates action informed with blind hatred and, of course, the sentiment of hatred itself. The concern of this volume is less with external facts and more with what goes on in the minds of men.

I can not acknowledge within any short space my gratitude to all the persons and institutions who have helped me to produce this volume. My wife's disapproval and my daughter's impatience with my ways finally made me abjure my habitual lethargy and get my act together. Generous grants from the British Academy, Social Science Research Council and the Leverhulme Foundation made possible the research on which some of these essays are based. The grand hospitality of the Woodrow Wilson Centre, Washington, D.C. and the Wissenschaftskolleg zu Berlin and a delightful spell in the Universities of Western Australia and Sydney provided ideal conditions for writing and then preparing these essays for the press. Dr Shalini Randeria helped me select the essays for the volume. In fact, but for her approval, I would have been very hesitant to send these to the press. Thus some of the blame for their publication should be shared by her. The rest falls on Rukun Advani and Bela Malik of the Oxford University Press, New Delhi and their anonymous reader. *Mea non culpa.*

Contents

I. PERCEPTIONS, SENSIBILITIES,
BELIEF

1 Transformation of Indian Sensibilities: The West
   as Catalyst   3
2 Europe in India's Xenology: The Nineteenth-century
   Record   22
3 The Pursuit of Reason in Nineteenth-century Bengal   49
4 Love in a Colonial Climate: Marriage, Sex and
   Romance in Nineteenth-century Bengal   65
5 Transformation of Religious Sensibilities in
   Nineteenth-century Bengal   96
6 Swami Vivekananda's Construction of Hinduism   111
7 Muslims and Islam in Swamiji's Vision
   of India—A Note   129
8 Had He Been Alive Today   136
9 Gandhi and Tagore: Where the Twain Met   141

II. THE RAJ CONSIDERED

10 British Rule in India: An Assessment   155
11 Historiography of India, 1858–1937   172
12 Re-reading *Divide and Quit*   188

III. COLONIAL LEGACIES:
POST-COLONIAL CONFLICTS

13 Shadows of the Swastika: Historical Perspectives on
   the Politics of Hindu Communalism   207
14 Indo–Pakistan Relations: In Quest of a Silver Lining,
   Even a Smudged One   230
   Index   241

I
Perceptions,
Sensibilities, Belief

1

Transformation of Indian Sensibilities: The West as Catalyst*

The present paper is an exploratory exercise trying to map the way in which Indian sensibilities, the way people felt about and reacted to things, developed in the nineteenth and early twentieth century. It focuses on the nature of the western impact and on a very small segment of the population, the one which has had some exposure to modern education, directly or indirectly. The reference group probably did not account for more than 1 per cent of the population, but this minute segment played a leading role in all major innovations in the life of the subcontinent.

The term elite has often been applied, somewhat loosely and inaccurately, to describe this segment which included scions of the old landed classes, industrial entrepreneurs, highly successful professionals as well as middle and low level functionaries in the apparatus of colonial government and often very poor schoolteachers, journalists, briefless lawyers, medical licentiates and preachers propagating the new religious reforms. The vast majority of such men and women had very little access to power or resources. Such status as they enjoyed derived from their position in the caste hierarchy and the respect, often reluctant and ambivalent, for their education and new occupations. I have introduced an imprecise description to identify the people I am talking about because I find none of the alternative labels—elite, middle class, colonial bourgeois, intelligentsia etc.—altogether satisfactory.

My central argument in this paper is that the contact with the west was a crucial factor in the transformation of modern Indian

*A version of this essay was circulated as a Working Paper by the Woodrow Wilson Center, Washington D.C.

sensibilities, but the term westernization is an inappropriate description of the changes in question. That term implies a pattern of change
which resulted in an approximation to western ways of thinking,
feeling and acting and an adoption of western cultural artifacts on
an extensive scale. The concept also accommodates the notion of
synthesis, i.e., a happy amalgam of western and local Asian or African
cultural traits. I do not suggest that such adoptions or synthesis did
not occur, but merely that the changes traceable to the contact with
the west were the end results of processes which went far deeper
than mere imitation, borrowing or amalgamation of disparate cultural
traits. The contact, to my understanding, was a catalyst: it triggered
off responses and reactions which acquired a life of their own. The
results, manifest in new ways of thinking, feeling and action, were
very different from their counterparts in the Indian past or the contemporary western experience. I shall limit the scope of this paper
to processes arising out of cultural and social contact, direct and
indirect, especially the meaning Indians read into such encounters.
Further, my paper is merely illustrative of my argument with reference
to three areas—intra-family relationships, social–political ideology
and religion—and I draw my examples mainly from Bengal and western India.

The western impact was mediated by three mutually overlapping
areas of social and cultural experience—over-all perceptions of western civilization, interpretations of colonial rule and responses to
western critiques of Indian life and culture. Each of these generated
emotional affects which informed attitudes and action. The relevant
documentation on this subject is vast and varied. The preoccupation
with the west is almost obsessive in the written record of Indian concerns during our reference period. And, of course, the thinkers and
writers did not speak in one voice.

Such diversity notwithstanding, one can extract certain dominant
themes in the Indian interpretation of the west. One authority on the
mutual perceptions of India and Europe, Halbfass, has suggested
that the Brahminical culture saw itself as universal and all other
civilizations as peripheral and irrelevant. Two Sanskrit texts produced in the nineteenth century touched upon the western presence
in passing. One noted with regret that the world, i.e., India had come
under the rule of the *sveta-mukhas*, people with white faces, a threat
to the ancient way of life and comparable to the mighty but evil demon
king, Ravana. The other, professing to predict the future, declared

that such a misfortune would come to pass and the holy land would be rescued by Kalki, the tenth and yet unborn incarnation of Vishnu.

Modern Indian perceptions of the west were sharply discontinuous with this older attitude in which the west, even as the ruling power, was a peripheral concern. From the early decades of the nineteenth century, an informed awareness of the west became an overpowering presence in the consciousness of educated Indians. Its content was determined by the education dispensed at the new institutions of higher learning where one studied western literatures, history, philosophy, politics and to a lesser extent science, encounters with Britishers and the institutions of government they had created and increasingly, travels in Europe.

There was a fairly universal recognition that the west was now dominant. A range of concerns followed from that recognition—attempts to understand the reasons for that triumph, to identify what India should or should not learn from the west, assessments based on moral judgements and comparisons between India and Europe. Values derived from the inherited culture and social institutions as well as those imbibed from the west or modified by the cultural encounter informed the relevant assessments.

Both the admirers and denigrators of the European civilization agreed on one point. An attitude to knowledge, fundamentally different from the one informing Indian civilization, was the key factor in the triumph of the west. For Europe, knowledge was a road to power over nature and over men; Indians had sought knowledge in order to achieve salvation with uncertain results. The western pursuit of knowledge had been systematic, persistent, experimental and based on uncompromising rationality. One Muslim observer further refined this argument and pointed out that the western intellectual tradition, unlike its Islamic counterpart, had abandoned Aristotelian logic in favour of inductive reasoning, a fact which was at the root of their scientific achievements.

A second key motif in this essentialist perception of the west was the centrality of the nation state in western political culture. Loyalty to the nation, the virtue of patriotism, was identified as a core value of western civilization, far more important than those ordained by the Christian faith to which the modern European was seen to offer no more than lip service. Actions considered heineous in any other context became sanctified if performed in the service of the nation-state.

A third dominant characteristic of the western civilization was its emphasis on material concerns, on an enjoyment of this life on earth. Many of the popular stereotypes concerning the west and western stereotypes regarding Indian perceptions of the west hinge on this particular perception. The intellectual discourse, however, was highly nuanced and marked by considerable sophistication whenever it touched on this theme. Swami Vivekananda described the core value of European civilization as *dharma*, the good life on earth lived according to high moral principles; western worldliness was in his eyes equivalent to the heroic quality of *rajas*, this worldly virtues suitable for the Kshatriya, the warrior caste, according to the Indian tradition; it was an appropriate step towards the highest quality accessible to man, *satva*, or spirituality. Contemporary Indians sunk in *tamas*, bestial inertia, could not hope to by-pass *rajas* on their journey to *satva*. The Europeans were the children of Virochana, the giant who, called upon to identify the self, *atman*, had pointed at his body. But the *danavas*, giants of Indian myths, were a mighty race who challenged the gods themselves and they were not devoid of moral or spiritual worth.

Still, in Indian eyes, modern Europe, in her pursuit of material wealth, had endangered her own survival. Combined with the emphasis on national interest and the much-lauded value of competition, so central to the new industrial civilization, western materialism was leading to patterns of conflict which might annihilate the entire culture. And the amoral quest for empire and wealth were utterly destructive for other peoples. It legitimized aggressive conquest and genocide. 'At the very scent of the European races, other races withered away.'

Finally, the materialism itself was but one expression of the fundamental value on which the totality of western civilization was based: individualism. At one extreme, Indian modernizers extolled its virtues. At another, it was described as nothing more than a rationalization and apotheosis of selfishness, an ideological offspring of the institution of individual property which the barbarian invaders had adopted from the Roman empire. Interestingly, the British historian, Macfarlane agrees with at least one part of this thesis.

The enquiry into the lessons of Europe's history and civilization which India should learn was closely linked to the exercises in comparison between the East and the West as well as ethical judgements on the relative value of the two civilizations. While there was a sharp awareness of the diversities contained within western civilization, the essentialist perception of Asian and European cultures appears to have been generally accepted. So was the simplistic dichotomy between the two. The comparisons frequently derived from Orientalist perceptions of Indian and Asian civilizations, often set out to stand the formulations of the western discourse on their head or to challenge them.

Certain *leitmotifs* emerge from the impassioned debate on the subject. At its most negative, the critique focuses on the alleged immorality of western civiliziation. Beyond doubt, the popular perception of the westerners in India saw them as a licentious people who also happened to be immoderate, shameless and unclean in their physical habits. Their ethical inadequacies were compounded by their arrogance and aggression. The sight of drunken British soldiers and sailors and the fact that the English in India could at times literally get away with murder enhanced such negative perceptions.

The intellectual discourse tried to modify such assessments but did not entirely reject them. Vivekananda invoked the principle of cultural relativism to assert 'we are all right and so are they': he explained that it was a mistake to judge other cultures in terms of one's own. Keshab Sen returned from Europe enchanted with the charms of English family life. The orthodox Radhakanta Dev complimented Bishop Heber on the quality of European social life so enhanced by the presence of educated ladies. Yet, the theme of European immorality, arrogance and violence recur over and over again in Indian comments on the west. The explanation is sought in history. There are repeated references to the barabarian origins of modern Europe as one explanation of the pervasive proneness to violence and unrestrained physicality. One conservative writer pointed out the marked difference between the conduct of the poor in India and that of their European counterparts. The latter in their fondness for drink, lewd language and violent quarrels showed unmistakable signs of their descent from the barbarian tribes who destroyed the Roman empire.

A related theme focused on the comparative merits of western and Indian religious traditions. Rammohan, the great pioneer of modern thought in India, wrote on and commended the precepts of Jesus as the ultimate in ethical ideals vouchsafed to man. But he questioned Christ's divinity and the Trinitarian principle and this started a bitter debate between missionaries and Indian intellectuals which died away only when the latter ceased to be interested in such issues. Western, especially missionary criticisms of the Indian social and religious traditions, were deeply resented even when some of the criticism was taken on board in programmes for social reform and all assessments of Europe's religious traditions were inevitably coloured by these reactions to mostly ignorant criticism. An intellectual tradition of high regard for Christ and his teachings co-existed with a certain contempt for the institutionalized religion of Europe. The latter was seen to be no less irrational than popular Hinduism and far more bigoted. Missionary attacks on the faith of a conquered people who were in no position to hit back was described as extreme caddishness. Besides, as noted, Europeans were seen to pay nothing but lip service to the Christian precepts for the only deity they really worshipped was the nation state. In matters of religion, India had nothing to learn from Europe.

The Orientalist discovery of the Indian past enhanced a pride in the religious tradition of the country. Following Orientalists that tradition was identified as India's real glory. The popular belief in the spiritual superiority of India, never projected in unqualified terms in the intellectual discourse, reflected this perception which was given a fresh boost by the Theosophists' tribute to the superior spirituality of the Hindus.

The discussion on the relative merits of the western and Indian social and political traditions was marked by a curious ambivalence. The British emphasis on the absence of nationhood and any patriotic tradition in India was resented yet implicitly accepted. It was sought to be answered along two lines. First, the paradigm of unity in diversity and the elements of cultural homogeneity in the Indian past were cited to prove that Indian indeed had a tradition of strong cultural unity. At another level, the limitations of nationalism as an ideal were underlined. Patriotism was seen to be a virtue, but one of a low order which precluded the allegedly Hindu ideal of universal love. It led much too easily to conflict and aggression. Besides, each civilization was seen to have its characteristic proneness. If the state was central to the evolution of western societies, India's emphasis had always been on society. The latter's goal was peace, mutual accommodation and universal well-being. As objectives these were not inferior to the pursuit of wealth, power or even intellect.

As the diversity in the assessments of Europe suggests, there was no intellectual consensus on what India should learn and adopt from the west. Nor is it valid to categorize opinions on this question simply as conservative, radical or moderate. The same individual or group could take up very different positions depending on the question at issue. The arch-conservative Radhakanta Dev, who resisted the British legislation for the abolition of suttee, was one of the pioneers of women's education in India. A person's evaluation of Europe underwent significant change over time. Bankim, a protagonist of romantic nationalism, once described modern European civilization as the acme of human achievement. Later he saw western science as an evil handmaid of war. Yet certain broad agreements and prescriptions emerge from this varied discourse.

The first generation of students at the centres of western learning in Calcutta and Bombay, especially the former, contained a highly vocal element who favoured a total rejection of tradition and an equally total adoption of western ways; but even among them only a handful practised what they preached. The unquestioning imitators of western ways became subjects of ridicule virtually in every part of India. They are a universal presence as figures of fun in modern Indian literature. Considered judgements prescribed a judiciously selected adoption of western ways and cultural artifacts and an equally firm rejection of much that the west had to offer. One conservative thinker summed up his advice as follows: 'We should learn from Europe only their skills in matters practical, and nothing else. It is better that we learn nothing else from the west.' For him the history of Europe was an object lesson in what mankind should avoid. If through the contact between the Indians and the British, the British and not the Indian character had undergone a change that, in his view, would have been for the best. But this was not to be hoped for. His positive recommendation that India should adopt from the west their knowledge of the external world, their technology and skill in social organization reflected a widely accepted opinion. There was however one outstanding exception to that rule in the early twentieth century—Mahatma Gandhi. For him the totality of modern technological civilization was Satanic, an adjective he borrowed from Tolstoy.

Others might subscribe to less negative views, but serious reservations about adopting western social mores were pretty universal. The continuity of the Indian extended family, so central to the social experience of all Indians and the associated value system, was seen to be threatened by the adoption of individualistic values and western consumerism. The boom city of Calcutta under the John Company had seen patterns of conspicuous consumption for which there are few precedents in the Indian past. Such consumption usually went with amoral conduct, a great deal of misery for the members of the family, especially the women, and eventual ruin. The educated Indian of modest means developed a fear and aversion for that pattern of behaviour which they associated *inter alia* with western-style luxury and vices. The less sophisticated saw in such conduct a threat to ritual purity. At a more elevated level, the intellectual discourse identified mindless imitation as subversive of identity and much that was best in the received tradition. On the other hand the model of the Victorian family with its alleged discipline and moderation, as projected by British publicists in India and Indian visitors to England, was admired as something worth emulating. However, the literature abounds in caustic portrayals of the novel-reading educated woman who imitated the memsahibs.

There was an element of shadow boxing in Indian critiques of the west: all the nuanced assessments, rejections and qualified acceptances went with a surrender in real life to much that was being criticized and questioned in the intellectual discourse and popular stereotypes. Individualism might be unacceptable in terms of values and familiar emotional responses, but the conditions of urban employment under colonial rule resulted in a reorganization of the family which increasingly privileged the individual. The new patterns of career aspiration led to similar consequences. The new education emphasized western learning. This inevitably meant a dilution of one's knowledge of the inherited culture, no matter what one's sentiments were concerning the latter. Ritual purity might be a desired object, but it required extra-ordinary discipline to maintain it in a colonial metropolis and few bothered to do so. The very vocal objections to western critiques of Indian ways were increasingly based on very poor knowledge of the tradition.

More important, the fact of defeat was a part of one's daily experience. The triumph of the west was manifest in the limited access to career opportunities and material resources. That triumph was interpreted, however reluctantly, as a token of western superiority in popular consciousness. The intellectuals' argument that the conclusion did not follow from the fact was of little consolation. Overtly or otherwise, the educated Indian began to see no choice but an adoption

of western ways—in education, means of livelihood, family organization and even the construction of a social ideology—as his only
route to a reasonable existence. This existential compulsion was in
deep tension with the felt need for cultural self-assertion and genuine
attachment to a whole range of inherited values and ways of life. An
anxiety to resolve such tensions and to find answers which self-consciously precluded a surrender to the West or at least protected
one's cultural self-esteem left its mark on modern Indian sensibilities.
The encounter with the West in the context of colonial rule initiated
tortured processes of change full of complexities, uncertainties and
ambivalences.

This is particularly evident in the changing sensibilities associated
with family life. We do not know to what extent the extended family
in which several generations and siblings with their progeny sharing
a home was the modal fact of Indian life at any time. But the values
which go with such an arrangement certainly were dominant over a
very extensive social space. The great reformer Vidyasagar who did
admire the individualistic values of the west mentions with pride
that his great grandfather presided over such a home and made no
distinction between his own children and the children of his brothers,
nephews and nieces. Yet Vidyasagar himself arranged for his brothers to live separately so that the tensions characteristic of an extended family were avoided. But he did not fail to provide for all his
siblings even though they had incomes of their own. The novelist
Bankimchandra bitterly resented the endless demands his feckless
brothers and spendthrift father made on him. But he could at no
point bring himself to say no and, with some anguish, continued to
pay for the worship at the ancestral chapel even after his father's
death. One publicist drew attention to a peculiarity of the new British
Indian law which obliged people to provide for their wives but not for
their mothers. Popular cartoons caricatured the value system underlying such decrees: the western educated Babu was portrayed as
carrying his wife on his shoulders while dragging his parents with
halters round their necks. Whatever the practice, the notion that
one's primary responsibility was to one's wife and children and not
to one's parents remained unacceptable. The Gujrati novelist, Govardhan Tripathi, maintained a Victorian style diary where he poured
forth his angst at having to suffer the impositions of feckless scro-
unges. He saw no chance of his own talent flowering so long as he

had to share his home with thirteen others. But eventually he reconciled himself to this misery in terms of his personal interpretation of Vedanta. Or did he?

The nuclear home of the new professional men and state functionaries in the urban areas seldom remained nuclear. Distant relations, fellow villagers and caste men and even people who were in no way connected with one came to live in such homes to study, look for jobs or just to pass the time. One was not supposed to turn such people away. It is far from clear that most people wanted to. The Maharashtrian publicist D.D. Karve describes how he and his friends with their spouses replicated the extended family arrangement in a Bombay tenement. He too was a believer in the values of individualism, a theme very central to the modernist discourse in Maharashtra. It is far from clear if any significant section of the Indian literati ever went through a restructuring of their sensibilities with regard to the demand of the extended family and the kinship group. In some, individualistic preferences in such matters merely intensified their angst and contributed to a measure of social isolation. Bankim acquired a reputation for stand-offishness because he preferred to be on his own at least part of the day.

Inter-generational conflict was probably no part of the Indian life-experience in pre-modern times and the dominant values emphasized the supreme importance of filial piety. Parents were gods on earth. The nineteenth-century memoirs document a remarkable survival of the emotional affects associated with such beliefs. These affects hightened and complicated the tensions generated by the ideological stances of the younger generation. The emphasis on rationality imbibed from western education had led to a questioning of received beliefs, a theme to which I shall return later.

The departure from orthodoxy at times went with patterns of action informed by the Victorian ideals of moral courage and principled behaviour, terms which occur frequently in the Indian pronouncements of the period. Parents and relations lived in great fear that their educated children would accept Christianity or Brahmoism, the new reformed doctrine or be involved in the movement supporting widow remarriage. Any such action might involve excommunication, i.e., loss of caste for the entire family. The reforming youth went through experiences which could be far more traumatic than any social persecution. We read of a young man from Orissa who had become a Brahmo howling in misery as his father dashed his bleeding head against a wall. The poet Michael's mother pined away when he converted to Christianity. One had to be exceptionally strong and committed to risk the pain of such confrontations. No wonder that the reforms had only very limited success. Filial piety and family ties were a more powerful influence on modern Indian sensibility than any ideological commitment to social change.

Western views on Indian society were particularly critical of the way Hindus treated their women. The indigenous questioning of tradition was also deeply involved with the same issue. The debates on suttee, widow remarriage, child marriage, polygamy and women's education were central to the nineteenth-century programmes of reform. The relevant agendas were partly prompted by the desire to set one's house in order in response to western criticism. But their origins are also traceable to the new concern for rational and humane social conduct and introspection induced thereby, in short, to sensibilities of western derivation. The intense passion evident in these debates reflect the depth of such sensibilities.

But these were in no way clones of their western counterparts. Indian perceptions and attitudes in such matters were marked by the co-existence of strangely contradictory elements. To take one example, R.C. Dutt, civilian and scholar, saw through the apparent freedom of Victorian women and noted that their entire upbringing was geared to one objective, namely catching a husband. He found this a form of servitude and suggested that the only way to ensure the freedom of women was to open all careers to them. Yet the heroine in one of Dutt's romantic novels is a girl of twelve. More than one nineteenth-century Bengali reformer sang the praises of child marriage as an arrangement suffused with tender emotions.

What they meant by the latter is very different from an old pundit's fond remembrances of marital bliss, the delicious nights he spent with his eleven year old wife at the age of twelve. The reformed Hindu was too Victorian to talk of such things, but even the members of the very advanced and highly sophisticated Tagore family took sub-teen agers as wives and according to one insider's assessment, they did live happily ever after. The Age of Consent Bill prescribing fourteen as the minimum age of marriage for girls aroused great opposition among orthodox Hindus. The reformist Hindu was of course in favour of the measure, but in practice the age of marriage for girls did not move up to the prescribed level until the nineteen twenties. R.C. Dutt's description of his twelve-year old heroine as a budding flower is perhaps an apt illustration of his generation's romantic sensibilities. Interestingly, in the first edition of Tagore's famous novel, *Gora*, the highly precocious heroine is a girl of thirteen or so. Later editions moved her age up to seventeen, evidently a concession to altered sensibilities. Possibly, generations of conditioning had rendered Indian men susceptible to pre-teen age charms, a susceptibility which could co-exist with very advanced social views. The objections to child marriage were grounded in considerations of health and eugenics, a feeling that it was a bad idea to impregnate twelve year olds. But romance with a nine year old was not perceived to be child abuse or in any way ludicrous. Resonances of the older pattern of preference are found even in some twentieth century writings.

Nirad C. Chaudhuri, among others, has written about the yearning for romantic love generated by the Indian youth's exposure to western literature. Bankim mentions that every college student knew by heart the balcony scene in Romeo and Juliet. The fact that social conditions did not favour the fulfilment of such yearnings outside a very small section of Indian society imparted a quality of pathos and frustration to conjugal relationships. But not always so. Realistic expectations do not appear to have included romance as a part of one's life experience. Besides, both in fictional representations and real life, we have instances of romantic love in and outside marriage, though the disappointed lover rather than requited love is the more typical and convincing image projected in nineteenth-century writings. Marriage, an arrangement between families rather than individuals, remained in most cases a matter of fact business. Only in a small number of instances do we find it flowering into romantic love.

The educated husband often assumed the role of a teacher to his child bride. Communication was not always easy. Bijay Goswami having explained to his bride that the Deity was formless asked if she had understood what he had said. She replied that she had and added that God was round in shape. The reformer recalled this in his old age with affectionate amusement rather than exasperation.

An apparent revolution in sensibility is reflected in the role assumed by the educated brides in supporting their reforming husbands in times of social persecution. The instances are many but it is not clear whether the values at work here were old or new ones. Jotiba Phule's wife fulminates against the orthodox and acknowledges gratefully that she owed all her wisdom to her lord and master. Mrs Ranade, the second wife of the great reformer who had married her under parental pressure when she was only eleven, had been educated by her husband. She wrote a memoir, she tells us, only to fulfill his wishes. The more it changed, evidently it changed not. Yet there were interesting nuances in these nouvelle vogue marriages. Kisori Mitra's wife talks of her loving and learned husband as a person who was at her feet. She went along with his questioning of received belief, but refused to deviate from the demands of Hindu ritualism for she did not want to be cut off from the kinship group.

The western impact induced some curious mutations in the emotional affects of man-woman relationship. Sex, as distinct from sexual excess, was probably never associated with any sense of guilt in India. Resonances of this older attitude are to be found in the explicit references to their extra-marital love life in the writings of Bharatendu Hrischandra, Narmad and Nabin Sen, authors who wrote in Hindi, Gujrati and Bengali respectively. By contrast, a number of Bengali memoirs records the authors' deep anguish over their sexual fantasies. One unfortunate tried to divert his sinful thoughts by meditating on his mother until, to his horror, he had sinful thoughts about his mother herself. The ideal of Brahmacharya, celibacy, acquired a new meaning in the context of modern sensibilities. The old belief that it was a road to spiritual power was now harnessed to more secular ends—physical and moral excellence to combat the western accusation that Indians were weak, degenerate and lecherous. An ideal which was traditionally relevant for young students preparing for the life of a householder or for the ascetic, was now appropriated into the marital context as well. One famous and extreme example of this was Gandhi's doctrine of married celibacy which he did impose on some of his followers. We have a curious instance of this in the lives of a Bengali couple whose joint memoir, *Aghorprakash,* written by the husband enshrines the belief that they had indeed merged into one personality. After the birth of their fourth child who was later to become a famous doctor and the chief minister of west Bengal, they decided that there should be no more children. And the way to achieve that end was to conquer sexual desire. The effort led to even higher things. One night they kissed and in the name of God the Truth, satyam, vowed not to touch each other again below the neck and more, try and conquer desire. Eventually they felt that they had achieved their high ideal and celebrated a spiritual wedding with the wife bedecked as a Buddhist nun, her head duly shaven. I have not encountered in my reading instances of such sensibility in the modern western tradition or in traditional India. I do not suggest that it was modal in the modern Indian tradition either, but at least some contemporaries considered the couples' achievement highly laudable.

Indian religious sensibilities in the nineteenth century are generally supposed to have been deeply influenced by the West. The brahmo reform movement, with its emphasis on monotheism, the more popular Arya Samaj with its invocation of a single authoritative text as the source of India's religious tradition, the reformed Hinduism of the late nineteenth century are all supposed to have appropriated elements of the western Christian tradition, especially non-conformist Protestantism. This perception certainly is valid up to a point for one particular movement, the Brahmo movement in its later phase. Keshab Sen used the language of Protestant Christianity and even accepted Christ as saviour, though not as Divinity. The Sadharan Brahmo Samaj adopted the institution of Sunday School where the moral lessons dispensed were very much those of Victorian non-conformity.

Yet, one has to probe only a little below the surface to realize that the peculiar tensions of the colonial experience, with its unlikely interpretations of the indigenous tradition coloured by that tension, produced affects which had no counterparts in either western or older Indian religiosity. Keshab, the most self-consciously pro-Christian among the Indian reformers, was deeply disappointed by his encounter with the Christian west because he did not find there the intensely emotional spirituality he associated with his adoration of Christ, something he had almost certainly imbibed from his Vaishnava background. In the final phase of his *vita religiosa* he took to a Vaishnava style *kirtan*, devotional singing of hymns, to celebrate his faith in the Deity. He also professed an aggressive universalism which was no part of either the Indian or the Western tradition, though the former did contain a recurrent statement of faith in the validity of all religious beliefs. On his death bed he was found repeating a most unusual prayer, 'Oh Mother of Sakya, oh mother of Buddha, vouchsafe me nirvana.' This is a prayer without antecedents in any tradition.

A feature of this new religiosity was self-denial, at times for its own sake. The famous preacher, Sibnath Sastri wrote of his intense resolve to surrender to God in every way. He stopped eating meat, not out of pity for living beings, but because he had an excessive fondness for meat-eating. To quote his words, 'Earlier, I could not concentrate on my studies if I heard a goat bleat.' This self-torture for the love of God evidently mobilized two very different traditions, the Hindu one of penance for spiritual realization and the old Christian practice of self-mortification to exorcise evil instincts. In the nineteenth-century Indian context, mortification of self appears to have been a way of proving to oneself one's capacity for dedication to God.

Modern Indian reform was to a large extent structured around religious issues for a number of reasons. The line of demarcation between religious belief and other areas of social concern is very thin in the Hindu tradition: observation of ritual purity is a religious as well as a social obligation; caste is lauded in the Gita and is very much a part of one's social existence. The intense debates in the nineteenth century on such issues of social reform as abolition of suttee or widow remarriage invariably invoked scriptural authority in support of mutually opposed positions. Missionary criticisms of Hindu belief and practice induced efforts to answer them as well as deep introspection.

A preoccupation with the religious traditions, which was taken for granted by the vast majority, became a central feature of the educated Indians' awareness in the nineteenth century. In the latter decades of that century we find school students debating the nature of the Deity—whether he was formless or not. One supreme argument in favour of the former view was that since he was acknowledged to be all pervasive, one would have dashed into him if he had any form. This concern manifested itself in a pervasive and intenese religiosity among the youth in the latter decades of the century. It might assume many forms such as ostentatious observance of the ritual prescriptions as acts of Hindu self-assertion, the highly emotive devotionalism of the neo-Brahmo movements or, as among the followers of Ramakrishna, youthful renunciation of the world in quest of God. But in its intensity and pervasiveness it harked back to the Chaitanya movement of the sixteenth century. Only, it subsumed elements of personal quest, multi-faceted questionings, that one does not encounter in the earlier movements. It may not be simplistic to suggest that it was also fuelled by the material and ideological frustrations of the colonial era, a loss of faith in the regenerative potentials of British rule. One expression of this new religiosity was an active assertion of a faith in the truth and validity of all religious traditions. This was indeed a restatement of an Upanishadic doctrine and the mediaeval syncretic faith, but in the nineteenth-century context, it underlined messages of tolerance and spiritual hunger which expressed both the impassioned longings of that period and had obvious resonances of an emerging concern to forge a nation out of diverse ethnic elements.

Nationalism and modern political ideas are the areas of Indian life where, next to industrial technology, borrowings from the west are most obvious. The colonial discourse never tired of emphasizing the absence and impossibility of nationhood in multi-ethnic India with its history of political disunity. And nationalism certainly had no antecedents in the Indian past. Yet contingent factors, interacting with the particular experience of colonialism and the Indian social–cultural realities, gave a measure of distinctiveness to the political sensibilities of modern India.

These were determined by multiple tensions—a sad acceptance of the colonial perception that the Indians were a weak and degenerate people, the need to work out the psychological problems associated with the fact of subjection to alien rulers, an anxiety to recover a glorious past, often in terms of the discoveries of Orientalism and attempts to evolve agendas for national regeneration and the construction of a nation. New conflicts arising out of colonial rule, especially between Hindus and Muslims, also overshadowed the agendas for reconstruction.

The self-perception of decay and worthlessness, fairly ubiquitous in nineteenth-century Indian writings, was an element without precedent in Indian history. Perhaps it would be true to say that it took a sustained mass agitation to exorcise this particular ghost from Indian consciousness. Indian political sensibility was long informed by this negative belief and much of the effort at national reconstruction was an attempt to emerge out of the alleged degeneration and weakness. The cultural self-assertion of the late nineteenth century was largely a reaction to the same negative belief.

The belief in an Indian nationhood as a historical fact was no doubt based on western models; but it was also an emotionally charged reply to the rulers' allegation that India never was and never could be a nation. The vocabulary of early Indian nationalism has often been described as mere rhetoric by historians who have explored the interest-based roots of modern Indian politics. Whatever the truth of that line of analysis, it by-passes the strong emotional overtones of the efforts at national reconstruction. These were inspired both by the rulers' contempt and an awareness that creating a sense of nationhood in a highly diversified population was a daunting task. There was a selective appeal to history to recover elements which would validate this larger identity. Hence the anxiety to underline the unifying elements of the Indian religious traditions, mediaeval syncretism and the strand of tolerance and impartiality in the policies of Muslim rulers. India came to be perceived in the words of the national poet as the one great ocean into which all races and cultures had merged over the centuries. A carefully nurtured feeling for that unique identity had to combat an alternative view, derived from the colonial representation of Indian history which presented the Indo-Islamic past as a record of Muslim tyranny. The early nationalist reconstruction of mediaeval Indian history had projected the conflicts of the Turkish and Afghan chieftains with their Rajput and Marhatta counterparts as the story of Hindu struggle for independence. This particular construction of history continues to feed the political sentiments now described as Hindu communalism. The more inclusive historical perception soon appropriated the anti-colonial sentiment to project the conflicts between Indian princes and the English East Indian Company as Indian struggles for independence. It is largely in these terms that the rebellion of 1857 became the First Indian War of Independence. In short, the specifities of the colonial experience interacting with the special problems of imagining a nation in a multi-ethnic context engendered particular myths and constructs. The political sensibilities of Indian nationalism were deeply involved in this highly atypical act of imagining.

Two other features of Indian political development are particularly relevant to this discussion. First, there is the well-known fact that the Indian national consciousness developed initially alongside a great enthusiasm for British rule in India. The colonial projection that the British conquest was the best thing that had ever happened to India was widely accepted until the 1890s. Yet the daily experience of this wonderful development was fraught with a great deal of humiliation and frustrations. The theoretical perception of British beneficence and the objectively positive role of colonial rule had to be reconciled with the pragmatic experience of injustice and racism, which inspired a strong measure of xenophobia. Thinkers who saw no end to British rule in the foreseeable future devised agendas of self-help or, like Vivekananda, projects for the spiritual conquest of the West. In terms of sensibility, the underlying tensions imparted a quality of hopeless cynicism to Indian political consciousness. The British rule might be praised out of fear or worse, but it was increasingly an intolerable experience. And there was no light at the end of the tunnel. The sense of liberation which the Gandhian movement brought to the politicized Indians has to be understood in that context. Whether *swaraj* would come in one year or not, the act of defiance was a welcome deliverance from decades of wordy inaction. Gandhi's description of the Raj as satanic also summed up what generations of educated Indians had come to believe but dared not say. Militant anti-colonialism in the Indian case was the end product of a long and tortured history. Hence the ambiguities and complexities which informed it. Rajendraprasad, who had spent years in prison in British India described Britain's colonial record as one of exceptional humanity on the night of India's independence.

Finally, it is important to remember that the Indian intelligentsia in their encounter with western political thought and institutions had a wide choice of models. They selected out of that extensive repertory ideas which were highly unlikely from the perspective of an extremely hierarchical society. At one end, the emphasis was on the long struggle for political liberty, in England, Ireland, Greece and throughout Europe in the nineteenth century. At another, it was the egalitarian ideals of revolutionary Europe which had wide appeal. Rammohan expressed this new enthusiasm as early as the 1820s as did the students of the Hindu College. In short the enthusiasm was for something absent from their indigenous social experience as well as the colonial regime which surely did not encourage freedom or egalitarianism.

As nationalist consciousness crystallized, the inconsistencies between such ideological preferences and the realities of middle class political aspiration became apparent. The attempts to resolve the programmatic incongruities by taking the concerns of the dispossessed on board belongs to the late twenties of the present century. But the awareness that exploitation was something the politicized classes were as guilty of as the colonial ruler goes back to the very beginning of modern political consciousness in India. The nineteenth-century Indian literature is permeated with feelings of guilt. If one is to look for the psychological roots of India's allegedly socialistic leanings in recent times, this is where one should perhaps concentrate.

In this long and somewhat rambling paper I have tried to show that the modern Indian sensibilities were the products of a particular history which made it different from its counterparts in the Indian past and the contemporaneous west. The emotional affects and values associated with the family could not remain unaltered because the material environment, the very means of livelihood were changing. These could not replicate western models because *inter alia* individualism based on a universal system of private property, had limited relevance in the Indian case. The immense power of the inherited religious traditions resisted Christianization, partly because the protagonists of the rulers' faith were arrogant in their criticism of cherished ways. But the feelings for the latter underwent curious mutations in response to the new ideas as well as the psychological compulsions of the colonial era. The new political ideologies were of course of western derivation. But the patterns of selection and construction were determined by the exigencies of the Indian experience. And the sensibilities which informed them were marked by characteristics one does not encounter elsewhere, at least in that combination. Perhaps this could be best illustrated with reference to the emotional affects of Gandhian satyagraha which I have not included in my discussion. Christian in inspiration, here was an attempt to bring political action within the fold of spiritual and ethical quests for which there are no precedents. Its emotional affects recorded by Gandhi's many followers also had a unique quality.

2

Europe in India's Xenology:
The Nineteenth-century Record*

In nineteenth-century India we come across two distinct components
in the valuation of Europe. One embodies the world-view and value
systems of the old civilizations, unaffected by the encounter with the
west. The other reflects the complex, varied and highly nuanced
evaluations by people whose outlook had been altered profoundly
through the catalytic impact of the same encounter. The sharp discontinuities between these two sets of perceptions had no clear
chronological boundaries. They pertained to the mental world of nineteenth-century Indians.

I

The tradition of Hindu xenology has been described as one 'of silence and evasion'. The *mlechchha,* the impure foreigner, was the
object of 'utter disregard and radical exclusion', a 'faint and distant
phenomenon', a negative and abstract 'otherness' posing no concrete
cultural or religious challenges.[1] This tradition persisted in colonial India, though evasion was no longer possible. The Sanskrit text
Sarva-devavilāsa, written in Madras *circa* 1800, refers to the seizure
of power by despicable foreigners, *śveta-mukhás* (the 'white-faced').
Their rule, a threat to the sacred systems of *varna* and *asrama,*[2] is
compared to that of the mighty but evil demon Ravana.[3] The undated

Published in *Past and Present,* November, 1992.

*The relevant literature on modern Indian perceptions of Europe is vast
and varied. This article is based on material drawn mainly from western
Indian and Bengali sources, but the themes and ideas they cover have a representative character. The discussion embraces one eighteenth-century work,
Siyar Mutaqqherin, and Gandhi's *Hind Swaraj,* published in 1909, because of
their thematic relevance.

Bhaviṣyapurāṇa, claiming to predict the future, associated the advent of the Europeans, *gurundas* (cow-killers), with the final phase of the dark age, *Kaliyuga.* India would be rescued from the abomination of *mlechchha* rule by Kalki, Vishnu's last and as yet unborn *avatāra* (incarnation).[4]

This perception of the foreign presence may well be one more statement of Brahminical self-universalization and self-isolation, an assertion that the alien is only a threat to the identity of traditions. But it echoes in a significant way more popular perceptions which ascribed non-human identity to the aggressor, expressing deep-seated fears and resentment shared by the old élite and the masses. We learn from the Anglophile Mirza Lutfullah that around 1810 the people of central India believed that the 'abominably white' Europeans had no skin and ate everything, including human flesh, when driven to extremity, but were 'perfect in magical art'.[5] Francis Buchanan discovered that the Nayars of Malabar had persuaded their womenfolk that the Europeans were a species of hobgoblin, with long tails used for sexual union.[6] The peasantry in Bengal described the oppressive indigo-planters as 'blue monkeys'.[7] *Lal bandar* ('red monkey') remains the popular racist pejorative for a European in Indian languages.

In general, however, the traditional Hindu showed a remarkable lack of curiosity about foreigners, particularly Europeans. A classic example of such indifference is the multi-volumed diary of J.-F. Dupleix's Tamil *dubash* (interpreter), Ananda Ranga Pillai, which offers no assessment or description of western ways, even though the author had a fair knowledge of events in Europe.[8]

Indo-Islamic culture, with its concern for an understanding of Hindu civilization, had a fairly developed tradition of xenology going back to al-Bīrūnī.[9] The Indian Muslims' encounter with Europeans revived this established tradition, producing some interesting results. Though they were aware of the differences between the various European nations, Europe was often perceived as a single culture. Her people, 'speaking the same language and possessing the same religion',[10] were seen to be distinguished from the people of Asia by the colour of their skin, their Christian faith and their habit of wearing hats. At times the comments on the English have a wider relevance, though this fact is not always spelt out. The English continued to represent Europe even to those Indians who acquired a sophisticated understanding of the west. The terms 'British' and 'English' remained for the most part surrogates for 'European', except where a more specific meaning was stated clearly.

The eighteenth-century historian Ghulām Hussain, in his classic account of the British conquest of Bengal, praised the courage, military skills and worldly wisdom of the British, but regretted their apathy and indifference to the welfare of the local people 'groaning' under their dominion. He criticized as senseless violence the continual conflict between European nations. The French and the English, for instance, had been engaged in mutual massacres for centuries. They laid down their arms just to 'take breath . . . in order to come to blows again and to fight with as much fury as ever'.[11] Hussain's French translator read into his text 'a subterraneous vein of national resentment'. This resentment provides an element of continuity between 'pre-modern' responses to western dominance and the consciously nationalistic assessments of a later epoch.[12]

Close encounter with Europe and Europeans did not significantly alter traditional perceptions of the west. We have more detailed information from Indian Muslim visitors to Europe such as Abu Talib and Lutfullah, but no fresh assessments. The inherited system of values spelled out the criteria for judgements on the 'other' culture.

The sense of 'otherness', however, does not always come through very strongly in these writings. The aristocratic Abu Talib wrote of his pleasure in the cleanliness and elegance of Europe's cities, her delicious viands, exquisite wines, the beauty of her women and the music which 'charmed his senses'. He graded cities according to their standards of excellence, placing London at the very top. He found Europe—both nature and what man had created—much more attractive than India.[13] But the preference simply expressed a sense of enhanced pleasure, not any value judgement. This is in marked contrast to the westernized Babu's[14] preference for European ways as something inherently superior in terms of taste and sensibilities.[15]

A second yardstick used in judging Europe was concerned with 'virtues' or moral excellence as understood in the Indo-Islamic tradition. This again contrasts with the 'English-educated' Indians' acceptance of new ethical standards which questioned the inherited system of values, as well as their mood of self-assertion which tried to justify these traditional values in terms of preferences acceptable to or at least understood by westerners. Courage, honour, benevolence (especially in the matter of liberal hospitality), courtesy, physical vigour and sexual restraint were among the chief virtues which the two observers had evidently been brought up to admire. They graded the social cultures they encountered with reference to such criteria. The Irish, for instance, in Abu Talib's opinion, surpassed the English in 'bravery and determination, hospitality and prodigality, freedom of speech and open-heartedness', but, being 'deficient in prudence and judgement', they were impoverished by their very generosity, so that they failed to achieve either the comfort and elegance of the English or riches and honours like the Scots. Moving in high society in London, he concluded that hospitality was 'one of the most esteemed virtues of the English'.[16] Lutfullah, who consorted with the less affluent, saw selfishness as 'the general character of John Bull'.[17]

Abu Talib stated that the Europeans had certain advantages over the Indians. Anticipating later writings, he traced these to the cold climate, which rendered men 'vigorous both in mind and body'. It obliged them to take exercise, which hardened the constitution and inspired them with valour. The climate also encouraged a steady pursuit of knowledge, for European youth were not 'led away by the flights of fancy'. Tight clothing helped because it was 'troublesome to take off'. The youth of Europe were thus prevented from spending their daytime in indolence, while their nights passed in innocent sleep.[18]

Cultural relativism, however, was no part of the value system to which these two observers subscribed. Western social mores were criticized from a strictly ethnocentric standpoint. Men's clothing in Europe was obscene, because it failed 'to screen such parts as the law of modesty has taught men to conceal'.[19] The whirling ballerinas let 'their short gowns fly up to the forbidden heights', thus violating the laws of decorum.[20] Despite their Christian faith, the Europeans in effect worshipped images, and 'most absurd of all . . . they attributed to the Almighty God as having wife and children'. Both Abu Talib and Lutfullah deplored above all 'the freedom granted to women' and the mischief arising from this 'unreasonable toleration'. Lutfullah, aware of the arguments in favour of monogamy, found the Islamic prescription of limited polygamy preferable in every way.[21] Abu Talib, however, saw through the 'apparent liberty' of English women, and praised the wisdom of the English lawgivers in 'confining them in strict bondage'. Happily, 'by the laws of England a man may beat his wife'.[22] The sense of otherness informs Lutfullah's concluding remarks. The English might be 'ingenious, civil and active', but their language, customs and manners were 'entirely different from our own'. The destiny of his 'sweet native land' was now in the hands of that strange people.[23]

II

The modern Indian intelligentsia, shaped by their experience of colonial rule and exposure to western thought, developed structures of thought and feeling marked by jagged discontinuities with earlier patterns of perception and, to some extent, even emotions. Raja Rammohan was a contemporary of Abu Talib and senior by several years to Lutfullah. All three shared the cultural experience of a Perso-Arabic education. But in their comments on Europe as in their views of the world they appear to belong to two very different ages, separated by centuries. The nineteenth-century Bengali novelist Bankim Chatterji remarked that what he and his contemporaries wrote would have been incomprehensible to earlier generations, however one might try and translate it. European civilization in all its variety and complexity was assessed and categorized with varying nuances in the context of these new patterns of thought and feeling.

It has been suggested that the orientalist self-definition of Europe as a distinct, clearly definable entity in relation to an equally definable 'other', the Orient, which was quintessentially homogeneous and, in the scale of universally valid systems of value, somehow inferior, was accepted by the collaborating classes in India. The result, it has been claimed, was partly the end-product of often self-conscious programmes initiated by the colonial state for the consolidation of political control. According to this line of analysis, pedagogic and evangelical efforts without any formal links with state power served similar purposes and contributed to the same object.

The system of education, with its emphasis on all that was best in Europe's—especially England's—literature and philosophy, projected an image of benign excellence. This subtle appeal to the imagination helped divert attention from the unacceptable face of conquest and colonial rule. The collaborating classes, whose vested interests were closely linked to the survival of colonial rule, actively espoused this ideology.[24]

The complex and highly sophisticated thesis of which the above is a somewhat simplistic summary no doubt contains a solid core of truth. But it tells us only part of the story. It does not accommodate other facts and nuances which would seriously modify the thesis in question. For one thing, the orientalists did not see the civilizations of Asia exclusively as Europe's other, nor did they de-emphasize altogether the shared inheritance of mankind.

The debate on orientalism is perhaps not relevant to the present context. Some of its resonances, however, are, for to read into Indian assessments of Europe in the scale of civilizations any simple reflection of Europe's self-projection as a superior culture would be an oversimplification of a complex, and frequently autonomous, structure of perception. Contact with the west and the experience of colonial rule are two analytically separable historical categories, though of course the impact of the two overlapped and interacted in multiple ways. The social groups who perceived western civilization as a high point in human achievement, in many ways superior to the Indian record past or present, were not simply conditioned by the fact of their vested interest in the continuation of colonial rule. Even the most ardent loyalists among them were often sharply critical of the colonial regime, and did not accept the latter's self-assessments without serious qualifications.

Admiration for the west was at no point unqualified. The qualification had multiple sources: inherited systems of value; the negative experience of colonial rule; nationalistic self-assertion in response to western criticism of Indian mores; and, increasingly, assessments informed by the values of liberal humanism—tests based on western criteria which nineteenth-century Europe frequently failed to pass. In short, one rarely encounters an ingenuous acceptance of western superiority, especially as projected by the colonial masters. Indian admiration for Europe was highly selective at all times.

Yet underlying much of the nineteenth-century Indian discourse on the west was a basic concession of superiority. It is doubtful if this simply reflects the new relations of power, because the fact of political subjection was, with rare exceptions, resented even by those who considered British rule providential. The process by which the conquest was achieved was described over and over again as immoral and unacceptable. The English, as the most accessible representatives of Europe's high civilization, were admired in spite of the perceived immorality of conquest and the unacceptable face of colonial rule, not because of them.

The admiration as well as criticisms were informed by a system of values which was in no way a clone of Europe's cultural norms and mores. We have here a historical process of selective adoption, in many ways akin to the acceptance of a religious ideology originating in a different culture. In the process of transmission the beliefs and practices are accepted selectively and often undergo fundamental alterations. This was also true of the values of western Enlightenment and liberal humanism in their transition to India. The new Indian way of looking at things was more than a simple synthesis of western and Indian traditions. It represented something new, a product of a specific historical experience of cultural encounter which had a cata- lytic impact on the perceptions and preferences of the Indian literati. The ways of thinking and feeling around which it was constructed were very different from their counterparts both in the Indian past and the European present. Modern Indian assessments of Europe reflected some of this distinctiveness in the intellectual and emotional make-up of the new intelligentsia.

The assessments were informed by diverse ideologies, ranging from the assertion of orthodox Brahminical values to a new univers- alism emphasizing the fundamental unity of all cultures. Yet they are marked by a surprising continuity of concerns. The same themes keep recurring over and over again: the reasons for Europe's success, especially her intellectual achievements; her core values and their distinctiveness *vis-à-vis* the Indian traditions; nationalism; what India has to learn from the west, and the like. While the later assessments have clear overtones of nationalism, no clear chronology is discer- nible in these judgements. The following discussion is therefore struc- tured around the main themes in the discourse and the identifiable sources of specific evaluations.

Rammohan Roy, generally considered the pioneer of modern thought in India, stated in unequivocal language that he found the Europeans with whom he associated 'more intelligent, more steady and more moderate in their conduct' when compared to Indians, a fact which reconciled him to British rule in the hope that it would lead 'to the amelioration of the native inhabitants'.[25] It was the 'con- soling and rational conversation' of his European friends which com- forted him in his days of conflict with Brahminical orthodoxy.[26] He agreed with his friend John Digby that 'in point of view of vices' Hindus were no worse than the generality of Christians in Europe and Ame- rica, yet he found the former lacking in patriotic feeling and, owing to their obsessive addiction to ritual, 'incapable of undertaking any

difficult enterprise'. He was convinced that close contact with educated Europeans would lead to an all-round improvement in Indian
character and intellect.[27]

Such concessions of superiority were based on very clear and
selective criteria. In Rammohan's opinion, Europe's ascendancy
derived from her high achievements in the 'useful sciences', while
the products of Indian thought were comparable to medieval schol-
asticism, the pre-Baconian stage of western science and literature.[28]
Rammohan's Maharashtrian contemporary, Jambhekar, wrote in
similar language of the 'disproportionate intellectual advancement'
in Europe and Asia owing to the Asiatic philosophers' inattention to
useful arts and sciences, and their evident view that knowledge was
useful only in religion and 'in no way was connected with the common
purposes of life'.[29] The argument was spelt out, in an idiom very
similar to Macaulay's, in Akshay Datta's famous treatise on Indian
religious traditions: 'Errors, imagination and superstitions pervade
every area of Sanskritic learning. Those well-versed in English,
French and German have little to learn from Sanskritic studies by
way of genuine knowledge'.[30] Datta noted a peculiar deficiency in
the Indian intellectual tradition—failure to pursue a line of scientific
enquiry beyond its initial stages. The sage Kaṇāda had propounded
a theory of atoms, but it went no further. The same theory was refined
and fully developed only in the fortunate clime 'which gave birth to
Bacon, Comte and Humboldt'. Ancient India had possessed her fair
share of great thinkers, 'born with well-nourished seeds of shining
intelligence'. Had they followed the correct path of scientific enquiry,
then India too would have been transformed like Europe into a 'heaven
on earth'. Perhaps, Datta concluded in a mood of unrelieved pessimism, the Indian climate was incapable of generating the type of superb
intellect which revolutionized man's knowledge of the universe
through fundamental discoveries and startling inventions; 'Perhaps
such achievement was a monopoly of Europe', 'the mother of gems'
(*ratna-garbhā*). Europe's triumph, then, was the triumph of pure intellect (*viśudhha buddhi*), uncluttered by fanciful ideas and irrational
beliefs. To Datta and the generation of young Bengalis profoundly
influenced by his writings, this ultimate supremacy of pure intelligence was represented by two European thinkers, Francis Bacon
and Auguste Comte.[31] Unlike these thinkers, the seers of ancient
India, when they hit upon some intuitive truth, went on to embellish it

with fanciful notions, instead of enquiring systematically into the laws of nature; 'They needed some one to show them the way. They needed but one Bacon, one Bacon, one Bacon'.[32]

Datta's pessimism was not shared by all his contemporaries. His mentor, Rammohan, had put his faith in an educational agenda which would bring the benefits of Europe's scientific knowledge within the grasp of educated Indians.[33] Jambhekar reminded his readers that 'knowledge is not confined to a particular country; and that human nature is the same everywhere'. The fact that, less than a millennium ago, England was less advanced than nineteenth-century India 'in science as well as in literature' was a reason for hope.[34] In Jambhekar's view, the inhabitants of Europe had achieved 'pre-eminent superiority . . . over the rest of the world, in almost every department of science, and . . . most of the Arts' through the selfless dedication of intrepid individuals to the pursuit of knowledge for its own sake. Their disinterested labours added to the stock of human knowledge, and promoted 'the good of man, by discoveries and inventions which enlarge his powers, or augment the means of his usefulness to his fellow creatures'.[35] Bankim Chatterji, the poet and prophet of romantic nationalism, in his early writings returned repeatedly to the theme of Europe's superiority and the core factors which both embodied and explained it. To him Europe represented the 'more perfect type of civilization', while the Indian record provided material for a study of arrested development. In particular the superiority of the English as a people—in power, civilization and knowledge—was beyond doubt. The civilization of Europe since the Renaissance was in his eyes the highest level of achievement yet attained by mankind, way beyond anything ever imagined possible in earlier ages and other cultures.[36] Bankim identified the inductive method, the scientific culture of systematic observation and experiment, as that 'correct way' which explained Europe's intellectual victory. Following Datta, he elaborated the theme of contrast between India and Europe with reference to Aryabhatta's early discovery of the diurnal rotation of the earth and the annual motion of the sun, which yet failed to lead up to the next logical step, the heliocentric theory. In Europe, Copernican theories led to the discovery of Kepler's laws. Knowledge in the western tradition was geared to the quest for power. In India, the quest was for salvation, escape from life's pains, which generated the ideal of life-denying asceticism, as had happened in Europe during the Middle Ages. The revival of classical learning reversed the trend and thereby unblocked the channels of intellectual enquiry. If Europe's intellectual history was comparable to physiology, the Indian counterpart was similar to pathology.[37]

Such concessions of superiority often extended to matters where Europe's advantage might be open to question. The comments of the reformer Iswarchandra Vidyasagar, a great Sanskrit scholar, on the relative merits of the two philosophical traditions, are an instance in point. As principal of Calcutta's Sanskrit College, he had devised an agenda for popularizing western thought in the vernacular through a body of young scholars well versed in English as well as Sanskrit. The ideal intellectual diet for these pioneers, he opined, should provide correctives to *Vedānta* and *Sānkhya*,[38] because it was 'no more a matter of dispute' that these were false systems of philosophy, though highly regarded by the Hindus. The false systems would be taught in the Sanskrit course, but were to be opposed by 'sound philosophy' in the English course 'to counteract their influence'. Berkeley's ideas were to be excluded because they corroborated those of the false Hindu systems, and hence might increase rather than diminish the students' reverence for the latter. In the circumstances, the one indispensable study was that of Mill's *Logic*. We have here an example of a very selective ideological conversion, focusing on a particular tradition of rationalism.[39]

Vidyasagar's writings also provide some indirect evidence as to what he considered superior in European culture besides its rationalist tradition. Among his numerous publications for the instruction of school children was a collection of biographical sketches based on Chambers' *Biographies*. These sketches project the achievements of sundry Europeans who through hard work and sustained effort rose from humble circumstances to heights of success. These 'improving' examples were evidently meant to inculcate a system of bourgeois values which converged with the traditional Hindu goals of material success to be achieved through sustained effort, especially acquisition of knowledge.[40] The reformer was actually criticized for prescribing role models drawn exclusively from European life.[41]

III

In the intellectual tradition of nineteenth-century India the selective admiration for Europe focused frequently on elements absent from the Indian experience. The ideals of liberty and political justice were identified as crucial to the perceived excellence of public life in the west. Yet from the very beginning of this high regard for democratic ideals the Indian intelligentsia showed an awareness that the battle for liberty and political justice had not yet ended in any secure victory. On receiving the 'unhappy news' that the Neapolitan revolution had failed, Rammohan felt 'obliged to conclude' that he would not live to see liberty 'universally restored to the nations of Europe' and even less to the latter's Asian colonies. While he felt sure that 'enemies of liberty and friends of despotism' would never be ultimately successful, he saw quite clearly that even Europe had a long way to go before the ideal of freedom was fully realized.[42] Even the very modest First Reform Bill was in his eyes a part of the struggle between liberty and tyranny throughout the world. The aristocratic opposition to the Bill in his view showed the aristocrats' want of political principle, and was part of their strategy to continue their unscrupulous exploitation of the masses.[43] His contemporary Jambhekar expressed similar sentiments, but added a cautious caveat that it was difficult to judge from a great distance what was desirable for a country like England.[44] Rammohan showed no such hesitation in his ideological assessments of the west, its failure to live by its professed values. He was shocked to note that civilized Englishmen saw nothing wrong in denying emancipation to their Catholic fellow subjects and were 'indifferent about their political degradation'.[45] The institution of monarchy itself was in his eyes an incongruous anomaly in a polity based on the principle of liberty. He noted with contempt that to enter France, a country 'blessed above all by the possession of a free constitution', express permission was necessary, a practice unknown even in Asia, China excepted.[46]

Modern Indians acknowledged Europe's civilization as superior mainly with reference to the humane rationality which they saw as the dominant feature of its system of values. The self-projection of superiority failed to impress whenever marked departures from these professed values were noted. Such basic criticisms of Europe, often formulated in terms of western values, came not from disgruntled nationalists seeking evidence to counterbalance their sense of inadequacy in relation to the 'pace-setters of civilization', but from intellectuals who in their overall assessment conceded undoubted superiority to the west without hesitation.

One area of western life which failed to pass muster in evaluations based on the criteria of rationality and humane tolerance was its

institutionalized religion, especially the methods adopted for its propagation. Rammohan, in pioneering modern religious reform among
the Hindus, was undoubtedly influenced by the ethical doctrines of
Christianity, and put on record his deep reverence for the teachings
of Jesus in his *Precepts of Jesus in* 1820.[47] But his refusal to accept as
true any version of the Christian dogma provoked the missionaries,[48]
and in his subsequent writings he drew attention to what, in his opinion, were the unfortunate features of Christian practice and belief.
He deplored the fact that the enlightened British had departed from
their earlier practice of non-interference in the religious life of their
Indian subjects, and allowed the missionaries the freedom to abuse
Hinduism and Islam without restriction. Since the turn of the century,
missionaries had published tracts full of scurrilous attacks on Hindu
and Muslim religious beliefs and converted poor people through
the promise of material benefits. Rammohan conceded that there
was something heroic in preaching the Christian faith in countries
not under Christian control, but he found the attack on the beliefs of
a weak and conquered people in no position to hit back downright
indecent. He compared the missionary attack on the Hindu religion to the idolatrous Romans' gibes at the monotheistic faith of the
conquered Jewish people.[49] Some seventy years later Swami Vivekananda, in his speeches in America, vehemently criticized the missionaries' work in India again on the ground that they presented to
the world a grotesquely distorted picture of Indian society.[50]

Christian intolerance, sectarianism and narrowness of vision are
themes which keep recurring in Indian perceptions of Europe. In his
controversy with the missionaries cited above, Rammohan underlined
the irrationality of the Christian attacks on the belief in the miraculous
among followers of other religions alongside the acceptance of mira-
cles described in their own scriptures as revealed truth. One comes
across similar statements at times from unexpected quarters. The
industrialist Jamsetji Tata, in a journal of his travels in Palestine,
summed up his impressions after a heated debate with a European
on matters concerning the Christian faith: 'when arguing against the
religious beliefs of a man why should you beg of him to have faith in
all your absurdities while denying him the same privilege with regard
to his own?'[51] Keshab Sen, the one Indian reformer who accepted
the Christian faith almost entirely, was highly critical of its division
into many denominations.[52]

But the strongest criticism of Europe's religious beliefs focused on their departure from the principles of rationality. Rammohan, who found Unitarianism perfectly acceptable, attacked Trinitarian beliefs as contrary to all rational thought. In this respect he found even the Hindu legends of gods and goddesses to be superior to Christian dogma, because the former explicitly described the myths as imaginary tales meant to help the ignorant conceive their deity and induce virtuous conduct, while the latter attributed human characteristics to the Infinite in a literal sense.[53] He saw such beliefs 'with their stress on mystery and mystical points' as a means to delude the masses supported by 'wealth, power and prejudice' in their battle against 'reason, scripture and common sense'.[54] The rationalist Datta described the suprarational dogmas of all religions as allegories, but added that institutionalized religions, including Christianity, had caused more misery and bloodshed than anything else.[55] Keshab, in a speech delivered in London, appealed to Christians to come to India in the spirit of Christ, adding 'but pray, spare me the infliction of antiquated and lifeless dogmas', 'the stereotyped phrases and outward rites'.[56] Rammohan failed to understand how the 'honourable and learned men' of the Anglican Church could continue to adhere to the Thirty-Nine Articles, which were far from self-evident truths, unaffected by their studies or communications with other modes of thinking. He found it astonishing that no single member of so numerous a body, studying the relevant issues all their lives, ever differed from the prevailing dogma. 'It might be unfair to doubt their sincerity', he concluded, 'yet how else to account for such a uniformity of opinion'?[57]

If Christian values were acknowledged as one valid basis for Europe's claim to be a superior civilization, the realities of her life often failed to measure up to the standards expected. Keshab found that the English he admired so much had Christian virtues, but were 'not yet a Christian nation'.[58] He did not find among them the approach to God 'in a simple and living way' which to him was the hallmark of Christian life.[59] Their hearts were as full of selfishness and conflict as were those of men who had not embraced Christianity. People were still a long way from being Christian in spirit.[60] Western Christianity, which offered prayers to God that thousands of men might be slaughtered, was too hard and muscular, 'more materialistic and outward than spiritual and inward', to live up to the precepts of Jesus.[61]

Europe's record of continual mutual violence and colonial aggression was cited as evidence of rejection in practice of all Christian principles. One author commented that the great propensity to violence modern Europe had inherited from the barbarian tribes was modified to a small degree by her acceptance of Christianity, but as the victorious barbarians learnt their faith from the defeated Romans who, in their turn received it from an alien and subject people, the Jews, European regard for their religious ideology was limited—often no more than lip-service. The patriotic ideal, Graeco-Roman in origin, was Europe's real religion. Acts considered immoral at the level of the individual were legitimate in a patriotic cause. The nation state was the Europeans' true God, and crimes performed in its service were equated with heroism. European civilization, judged in terms of this unwholesome ideology, had to be branded inferior.[62] Keshab, in his admiration for Europe, would not go so far. But he did conclude that the gentle faith of Jesus was more in tune with the peace-loving traditions of Asia than with Europe's violent past and present. R.C. Dutt perceived a very different element of weakness in western Christianity. Most reputed thinkers, he noted, had lost their belief, and disbelief was gradually filtering down to lower levels of society. Those who continued to believe did so because they had been brought up in their religion, but had never seriously reflected on the subject.[63]

Europe's failure to live up to her professed ideals was seen to be quite pervasive. The reality seldom seemed to match the vaunted norms said to inform her high civilization. Dutt noted with admiration the political power effectively wielded by the common people in England: 'the will of the people is the law of the land'.[64] He admired too the spirit of independence, the sense of dignity possessed by servants and labourers, and the absence of flattery and cringing. Yet English society was flawed by the strong demarcation between classes, based not on any functional need but inherited prejudice manifest in the mindless homage paid to the aristocracy.[65] Keshab saw this as no different from India's caste system, which he loathed.[66] Vivekananda described western political democracy as a sham, 'a feast of bribery, robbery in broad daylight'. European politics were controlled by the rich and the powerful, 'the band of thieves who sucked people's blood in every European country'.[67] The condition of the poor in urban England, with its misery, drunkenness and prostitution, and the habitual cruelties within the family, were considered unworthy of a Christian country. Legislation and state policy, Keshab noted with horror, actually encouraged the drink habit and traffic in women. 'Your rich people are Brahmins, and your poor people are Sudras', he said in his farewell speech to his English friends.[68]

Even the condition of women in Europe, generally regarded by the modernizing intelligentsia as far superior to its Indian counterpart,[69] was found to be far from ideal in terms of the new values of freedom and equality. The education of a young lady, Dutt observed, had but one purpose—to make her pleasing to men so that she might fascinate a suitor. 'To suppress all strong and independent expressions of thought, to ignore all emotions except the kindly emotions of pity or love . . . to affect a delicacy of feeling where perhaps none is felt', such were the degrading arts of deception, 'the fair candidate for marriage in England had to acquire'. As a result, a youth in Europe knew as little of the true character of his lady-love as the Indian boy did of his betrothed. The artificiality of conduct attributed to the English, despite their habitual candour and independence, was a necessary consequence of the hypocritical conduct imposed on their women by a false system of values. Justice required that all careers should be open to women, but most Englishmen felt that their society required no change, no improvement: 'It was the old story of the orthodox Hindus over again'.[70]

IV

The new elements in the value system of the modern Indian intelligentsia in terms of which they assessed Europe were not derived exclusively from the west. Their perceptions and norms reflected *inter alia* a pattern of self-awareness in which social mores and emotional responses taken for granted in the older society acquired the status of cherished values. Inevitably Europe was found wanting in terms of such criteria, which formed no part of the neo-Hindu self-assertion. The warmth and openness of a face-to-face society, the close interpersonal relationships of rural life which survived even in the urban and metropolitan complexes, came to be recognized as life-enhancing features of India's traditional society. Their perceived absence from European life was seen as an element of impoverishment. While admiring the abundance of public charity in England, Dutt found it lacking in 'tenderness and affection'. It was charity 'measured by rule and compass', very different from the impulsive flow of compassion which owned no law he had known in his own land.[71] Measured against the pleasure of modest comfort and uninhibited sociability so dear to them, the Indian intelligentsia found the pomp and circumstance of western high life, its codes of good manners, more than a little ridiculous. The Parsi reformer Behramji Malabari noted in his diary that he had stopped dining with his English friends because he could no longer cope with 'the bowing and smiling to order, and the laughing over stale jokes', the feigning of pleasure over every dish and every glass. 'All this is too much for a heathen like myself', he concluded.[72]

Preferences rooted in inherited ways of life were restated as high ideals across a broad spectrum in nineteenth-century India. This unself-conscious exercise may have been prompted partly by the need for psychological security in the context of western dominance. But as these ideals were projected mostly by people who were quite uninhibited in their admiration of the west, one must take them as genuine preferences articulated in a modern idiom as transcendent values. European civilization appeared to be a very flawed product in terms of such criteria. Western consumerism appears to have really repelled a person like Keshab. The plethora of shops and the absurd claims of the advertisements, 'the art of puffing' as he called it, were too much for that simple man.[73] The ascetic Vivekananda wrote approvingly of the sophisticated pleasures of Parisian life, but described the logical climax of western consumerism, the American obsession with 'satisfaction of appetites', 'their true God', as utterly meaningless. Western man was seen to be incapable of contemplation and obsessed with action. Materialism in the eyes of such observers was not an abstract description to rubbish the west, but an almost palpable sickness of the soul which they found truly disgusting. In their view the factory industry on which the whole structure of consumption was based reduced the worker to a mindless automaton and the consumer to an equally mindless slave of habit. A life-destroying uniformity was engulfing the west, reducing men to machines. And when men became machines, a civilization did not survive for long.[74]

Negative assessments of Europe at a much less elevated level were an unavoidable component of the colonial encounter. Slanging matches, often provoked by sneering comments on the general backwardness and low morality of Indians, were very much a part of the 'cultural exchanges' of the nineteenth century. Dadabhai Naoroji's little-known tract, *The European and Asiatic Races,* provides a classic example of such exchanges.[75] John Crawfurd, F.R.S., read a paper before the Ethnological Society in London expounding the mental inferiority and low morality of Asiatics. Naoroji quoted *in extenso* the responses to this statement of a Parsi gentleman long resident in London. The latter talked at length of the sharp business practices he had encountered in England, the dishonesty of artisans, the number of immoral haunts in London, unfaithfulness in domestic life, the perversity of crimes detailed in police reports, corrupt practices in elections and so on—in short the whole gamut of evils one could discover in the shadier areas of European life. But such negative images were not merely part of a defensive response to western criticism. Vivekananda summed up in a famous passage the ethnocentric and highly negative perception of Europe commonly found in India in his day: 'Intoxicated by the heady wine of newly acquired power, fearsome like wild animals who see no difference between good and evil, slaves to women, insane in their lust, drenched in alcohol from head to foot, without any norms of ritual conduct, unclean, materialistic, dependent on material things, grabbing other people's land and wealth by hook or crook . . . the body their self, its appetites their only concern—such is the image of the western demon in Indian eyes'.[76]

The development of nationalist consciousness and the associated quest for agendas which would restore past glory induced more serious enquiries into the nature of European civilization and the possible ways in which India could relate to it. These exercises, while genuinely appreciative of many features of British rule, were at the same time informed by a pervasive resentment of foreign domination. That resentment strained the conscious efforts at objectivity in nationalist assessments of Europe.

Bankim Chatterji, in his review of Dutt's anonymously published *Three Years in Europe,* stated quite clearly that Indians needed to feel superior to Europe at least in some respects in order to regain their national self-confidence, but that claims to superiority had to be based on sound reasoning. In his later years, the writer modified much of his earlier enthusiasm for the achievements of modern Europe which he had once described as the highest level ever attained or even imagined by mankind.[77]

Self-consciously nationalist assessments of Europe had two explicit concerns: first, to discourage mindless imitation of the west; and secondly to weigh carefully what India could learn from Europe and establish which elements of western life must be rejected as harmful to her future. Comparisons between Indian and western civilizations provided a framework for these enquiries. Despite the effort to achieve objectivity, the end result of such sophisticated analysis was often simply a reasoned denigration of western culture alongside a recognition of its many points of strength.

Bankim did not entirely repudiate his earlier admiration for Europe, but qualified it with the statement that even nineteenth-century Europe with all her achievements was still an immature stage in the evolution of human society. Western science, the height of man's achievement in his eyes at one time, was now seen to be a handmaid of war, a producer of weapons of mass destruction. Its other product, the machine, instead of serving man, had in effect become the object of worship. Patriotism, the ultimate virtue in western eyes, had acquired horrendous features leading to aggression and genocide to serve the interests of one's own people. Nations of Europe fought over the spoils of conquest like pariah dogs. Her international law, which recognized the right of conquest, might as well recognize the right of theft. Bankim contrasted this pervasive immorality of western life with what he projected as the Hindu ideal. The latter was in fact a synthesis of ideologies derived as much from Utilitarianism and Comte as from the Hindu scriptures.[78]

In the most extensive analysis of European civilization attempted by any Indian, Bhudev Mukherji's *Samajik Pravandha* (Essay on Society),[79] the author started from a relativist position, stating that different cultures were not comparable because different civilizations did not pursue identical aims. Evaluation of their varied ideals in terms of some universally acceptable criterion could be the only basis for comparison. And that criterion had to be the gradual expansion of man's capacity for love. Focusing first on one's self, it had spread out to encompass the family, community, nation, mankind and finally the entire universe. In western culture it had stopped at the level of the nation. Compared with the Hindu ideal of universal love, this was an inferior goal for mankind. The apotheosis of the nation state was the end product of Europe's history, with its endless conflicts between and within nations. The characteristic virtues of European life—solidarity, discipline, obedience to the leader and self-sacrifice in the national cause—were the necessary products of this long record of conflict. To these were added ideologies born of love of money and an excessive concern for property rights. Their ultimate embodiment was individualism, which relieved the individual of all responsibility to look after his kith and kin and was in effect an apotheosis of selfishness. Pervasive selfishness undermined all potential for beneficence in western civilization. The machine, instead of making life easier for man, had become a tool for the enslavement of working people and contributed to the ceaseless quest for markets and monopolies leading in turn to wars, conquest and genocide. Europe's egalitarian ideals, a reaction to this ideology of greed and rapine, were themselves polluted, for they could provide nothing better than violence for the solution of man's problems. Of all the peoples of Europe, the English were the most selfish, but there was a quality of innocence in their selfishness. In their total infatuation with self-interest they believed that whatever was to their advantage was of benefit to others, and that all subject peoples eagerly welcomed their rule. Indians had nothing to learn from the west except its skills in practical matters. It would be better if they learnt nothing else. If through the contact between the English and the Indians the English rather than the Indians underwent a change in character, that would be for the best. But this was an unlikely outcome.

The above bald summary of Bhudev's highly complex arguments built on a wealth of data focuses on the author's main concern that India should not lose her faith in her inherited values. His rejection of western values and, consequently, of Europe's claim to superiority, was not simply an attempt to compensate for a sense of inadequacy. His responses reflected a system of values structured into the social system and life-habits of the Brahminical Hindu. The aggression, consumerism and even the intense activity characteristic of nine-teenth-century European life could be genuinely repellent to a person conditioned by such values. This is evident from the writings of the poet Rabindranath Tagore, whose world-view was far more universalistic than Bhudev's. In his essay on eastern and western civilizations Tagore cited Guizot in describing modern European culture as unique in one respect.[80] The poet accepted entirely this ascription of uniqueness. Every culture in history, he argued, had been characterized by a single central concern, a dominant tendency around which all its efforts were built. Modern Europe was the one grand exception. There was no precedent nor parallel for its immense complexity and variety, the turbulent co-existence of mutually incompatible elements, temporal and spiritual power, monarchy, republicanism and theo-cracy—in short, every conceivable stage in the evolution of human institutions. Iron discipline coexisted with a reckless love of independence; societies based on deep mutual trust and co-operation accommodated an urge towards uncompromising individualism. Like the universe itself, modern European culture was infinitely varied, its energies expressed in multiple directions. A culture was usually located in one country, but European civilization had already en-compassed three continents, and was evidently poised to absorb the rest of the world. Such were the indicators of its unique greatness.

Tagore's sense of awed admiration for this marvellous pheno-menon was, however, strictly qualified. And his reservations were in many ways similar to those of other thinkers whose ideas have been discussed above. Underlying Europe's variety of purpose and effort he found one common denominator—the protection of national inte-rest. All differences disappeared when these interests were threa-tened and people stood together 'single-minded, mighty, cruel'. The dominant objective of any civilization, Tagore commented, was deter-mined by history, but when pursuit of that goal destroyed some higher purpose the destruction of the civilization itself could not be far off. Europe was fast approaching that point of no return. The old slogans of equality and fraternity were treated as a joke. Chauvinistic nation-alism with its totally amoral outlook had cast its shadow even over religion and literature. The fact that the Indian past had no record of nationalism had become a cause for shame to modern Indians. But in India's ideology liberation occupied the place which freedom did in Europe's. The fact that people had fallen from it did not dimi-nish the glory of the ideal. But one need not take the nation as the ultimate stage in the development of civilizations. Nationalism as an ideology was steeped in lies and injustice, and marked by ruthless cruelty. Unlike Europe, Indian culture had emphasized society, rather than the state.[81] There was no reason for shame in the fact.

The poet identified another basic difference between the two cultures, and in developing his argument revealed his culturally deter-mined preferences. Indian civilization, with society as its central fo-cus, was, in his opinion, concerned more with the general well-being of all concerned than with the pursuit of self-interest—the quest for wealth, status and power through ruthless competition. Modern Indians, as taught by the English, saw in this absence of competition the root cause of India's sorry state. In firmly rejecting this view, he pointed out how the great nations of Europe had come to the brink of mutual destruction in their competition for wealth and power, and asked if peace, mutual accommodation and universal well-being were not better objectives than wealth, power and even intellect. There was no need, he repeated, for anyone to feel inferior; 'The one who flies has strong wings and weak legs, the one who runs, has strong legs but no wing'.[82]

Gandhi's *Hind Swaraj* (India's Independence), written in 1909, invoked the supposed ideal of India's self-sufficient 'village republics' in rejecting the civilization of modern Europe, but was in fact inspired by a particular strand in western thought.[83] The authorities cited by Gandhi included two Indian writers, Naoroji and Dutt,[84] but their works discussed India's impoverishment through colonial rule, not the evil inherent in modern civilization, the central theme of *Hind Swaraj*. The inspiration for the theme came from Tolstoy, Ruskin, Mazzini *et al.* 'This huge sham of modern civilization' was Tolstoy's phrase, quoted by Gandhi. He described Europe's civilization as Satanic long before he applied that epithet to the British government in India. People, like the English caught up in the throes of this civilization, should be pitied rater than hated: 'India was being ground down not under the English heel, but under that of modern civilization'.[85] All its products were evil. Railways spread plague and impoverished the poor; lawyers aggravated quarrels; doctors encouraged indulgence rather than self-control; the large cities were a snare. The object of this godless civilization was to propagate immorality. Machinery, its symbol, was the great evil. Unlike other Indian critics of the west, Gandhi saw nothing worth praising in its modern civilization. His prescription was that Indians should reject it totally and fall back on the tradition of India's primordial villages and its highly moral ideals.

Vivekananda, steeped in the tradition of Hindu mysticism, had, by contrast, a very positive view of modern Europe. His position, like Bhudev's, was relativist in inspiration. 'They are all right, so are we, but goodness manifests itself in a variety of ways'.[86] It was a mistake, he wrote, to judge others in terms of one's own values, and hence one must look at Europe through its own eyes. He too talked of the central concerns of each civilization, its dominant tendency. And he devised several paradigms drawing on Hindu cultural idioms to conceptualize the character of European civilization. What Hindus described as *dharma*, the good life on earth lived according to the principles of morality, was in his opinion the central motive of European culture; India on the other hand had set salvation as her goal. This basic difference was manifest in every aspect of the two cultures, including daily habits. The concept of three *gunas* or elements in the human personality provided the basis for another paradigm. Europe, weak in spiritual qualities or *satva*, excelled in *rajas*, manly virtues and enjoyment of life on earth; this explained her marvellous achievements. India, despite her spiritual or *sātvika* ideals, had fallen into a state of *tamas*, brutish inertia and self-indulgence, and must learn the lessons of *rajas* from the west. A third paradigm drew upon the caste system, and projected the history of mankind as the successive domination of the four *varnas*. The age of Brahmins or the priestly caste and the warrior *Kshatriyas* had given place to the domination of Europe's *Vaishyas*, the merchant caste. Their sway, the power of money and capital, excelled that of all others. Finally, he drew upon the myth of *asuras*, demons, and *devas*, gods. To him, the gods were the peace-loving settled populations of ancient Asia, while the *asuras* were the nomadic pastoral races who migrated to Europe and transmitted to the Europeans their warlike courage, energy and endurance. Aggression, so pervasive a feature of western culture, derived from this source.

While as vehement as any other Indian nationalist in his condemnation of European aggression and her record of international conflict, Vivekanand made some distinctive contributions to the way India perceived Europe. Popularly he is seen to be one of the formulators of the simplistic stereotype—materialistic west and spiritual east. But in his Bengali writings western materialism was projected as a highly laudable embodiment of *rajas*, a quality India had to emulate to escape from her current state of overpowering *tamas*. He preached a fair exchange of cultural wealth leading to a grand synthesis. He saw elements of this synthesis in the history of past encounters between Asia and Europe, in the growth of the ancient civilizations around the Mediterranean, the migrations from Asia's steppes, the contributions of Islam to the growth of modern Europe and, according to his belief, of India to the growth of Christianity. Nationalistic self-assertion in one form or another is almost marginal to his grand vision of a cultural synthesis which would usher in a spiritual millennium for all mankind. Though he visited continental Europe only for a few months, he was also the first Indian to discuss at any length the distinctive features of Europe's national cultures, especially the vast difference between the more advanced European nations, like the English, French and Germans, and their poor relations in the Balkans and eastern Europe.

Locating Europe in the scale of civilizations was a recurrent concern in colonial India. This concern was no doubt influenced by the experience of colonial rule. The stock of ideas produced by this interest had elements derived from western self-projections as well as responses prompted by a sense of inadequacy and the psychological need for cultural self-assertion. But there was a great deal more to this intellectual and polemical enterprise. Above all it acquired almost from the very beginning a measure of autonomy and originality which allowed it to transcend the familiar compulsions of a colonial context. The value system which informed the appraisals had appropriated the more radical components of liberal humanism—uncompromising rationality, the ideal of liberty, and, in some instances, equality between social classes as well as between men and women. A self-conscious appreciation of certain features of Indian life, perceived to be absent in the industralized societies of Europe, also figured prominently in the preferences of the modern Indian literati. Warmth and spontaneity in interpersonal relations, uncalculating generosity of a people very poor by western standards, and preference for a simple life-style were prominent among the newly discovered merits in the inherited social tradition. Nationalism inspired the quest for models in the European experience which India could emulate. But European nationalism came to be seen for the most part as something negative and dangerous. Selective admiration for western achievements was moderated by a rejection of much that Europe valued. The latter's claims to excellence were questioned in terms of professed western norms. The Indian discourse on Europe was a complex web of ideas. It was not a simple reiteration of Europe's complacent self-projections. Nor was it a set of exercises in denigration prompted by envy.

Notes

1. W. Halbfass, *India and Europe: An Essay in Understanding* (New York, 1988), ch. 11, esp. pp. 172–6, 187, 194–5.
2. *Varna*, one aspect of caste, refers to the ideal division of society into four groups on the basis of occupation. *Asrama* means the four stages of life prescribed in Brahminical scriptures.
3. *The Sarva-Deva-Vilasa* [The Pleasure of All Gods], V. Raghavan (ed.) (Adyar, n.d.).
4. Halbfass, *India and Europe*, pp. 187–95.

5. *Autobiography of Lutfullah, a Mohamedan Gentleman*, E.B. Eastwick (ed.) (London, 1857), pp. 35–6.
6. Francis Buchanan Hamilton, *A Journey from Madras through the Countries of Mysore, Canara, and Malabar*, 3 vols (London, 1807), ii, p. 514.
7. Satischandra Mitra, *Jasohar–Khulnar Itihas* [History of Jessore and Khulna], quoted in Suprakas Ray, *Bharater Krishak Vidroha o Ganatantrik Samgram* [Peasants' Revolts and Struggles for Democracy in India] (Calcutta, 1966), p. 400.
8. The *Private Diary of Ananda Ranga Pillai, Dubash to Joseph Francois Duplex*, J.F. Price (ed. and trans.), 12 vols (Madras, 1907–14).
9. Al-Bīrūnī (973–1048), born in Khwarezm in central Asia, accompanied the Turkish conqueror Mahmud of Ghazni to India, and wrote in Arabic his famous account of Indian civilization which has been described as the first objective account ever made of a foreign culture.
10. Ghulām Husain Khān Tabaṭāba'ī [Ghulam Hussain], *Seir Mutaqharin: A Translation* [into English by Muṣṭafā], 2 vols (Calcutta, 1789), ii, p. 223 n.
11. Ibid., ii, p. 759.
12. Ibid., i, pp. 22–3.
13. *The Travels of Mirza Abu Talib Khan in Asia, Africa and Europe during the Years 1799, 1800, 1801, 1802 and 1803*, C. Stewart (trans.) (London, 1810), pp. 64–5, 114–15, 136, 161–2.
14. 'Babu', a Bengali word for gentleman, often had a pejorative connotation in Anglo-Indian vocabulary. In the latter context, the word referred to low-level functionaries, perceived as weak and cringing.
15. Bankimchandra Chattopadhyay [Bankim Chatterji], 'Aryajatir Sukshma-silpa' [The Fine Arts of the Aryan Race], in *Bibidha Pravandha, Bankin Granthabali* [Miscellaneous Essays of Bankimchandra Chattopadhyay], centenary edn., S. Das and B. Bandyopadhyay (eds) (Calcutta, 1938).
16. *Travels of Mirza Abu Talib Khan*, pp. 136, 138, 161–2.
17. *Autobiography of Lutfullah*, p. 387.
18. *Travels of Mirza Abu Talib Khan*, pp. 260–5. For very similar ideas, see *Autobiography of Lutfullah*, pp. 26, 339 ff.
19. *Autobiography of Lutfullah*, pp. 36, 41.
20. Ibid., pp. 220, 406, 434–5.
21. Ibid., p. 407.
22. *Travels of Mirza Abu Talib Khan*, pp. 260–5.
23. See above, n. 20.
24. G. Viswanathan, *Masks of Conquest* (New York, 1989; London, 1990), chs 1, 2.
25. *Rammohan Rachanavali* [Collected Works], Ajitkumar Ghosh (ed.) (Calcutta, 1973), pp. 448–50, Raja Rammohan Roy to Mr Gordon, 1833. Questions have been raised regarding the authenticity of this auto-biographical letter, but there is little reason to doubt the information it contains.

26. Ibid., p. 461, Rammohan to John Digby.
27. Ibid., pp. 462, 468, Rammohan to John Digby, 18 January 1828; Rammohan to J. Crawford, 18 August 1818.
28. Ibid., pp. 433–6, Rammohan to Lord Amherst, 12 April 1809.
29. *Bombay Durpun* [Mirror of Bombay], 24 August 1832.
30. Akshaykumar Datta, *The Religious Sects of the Hindus; Bharatvarsiya Upasak Sampraday*, 2 vols (Calcutta, 1870), II, p. 32.
31. Ibid., pp. 20–1, 33, 51.
32. Ibid., p. 52.
33. *Rammohan Rachanavali*, p. 434, Rammohan to Amherst, 12 April 1809.
34. *Bombay Durpun*, 2 March 1832.
35. Ibid., 13 July 1832.
36. Bankim Chattopadhyay, 'Jativaira' [Racial Animosity], in *Bibidha Pravandha*, pp. 344–5; Bankim Chattopadhyay, 'The Study of Hindu Philosophy', in his *English Works*, J.C. Bagal (ed.) (Calcutta, 1983), p. 142.
37. Chattopadhyay, 'Study of Hindu Philosophy', pp. 146–7; Bankim Chattopadhyay, 'Bangadesher Krishak' [The Peasants of Bengal], in *Bibidha Pravandha*, pp. 260–1.
38. Two of the six systems of Indian *darśana*, loosely translated as 'philosophy'. *Vedānta* projects the monist doctrine according to which the supersoul, *brahman*, is the only reality. *Sānkhya* traces all creation to *prakṛti*, nature, and ascribes a passive role to the male principle, *purusha*.
39. *Vidyasagar Rachanavali* [Collected Works of Vidyasagar], T. Datta (ed.) (Calcutta, 1984), pp. 670–5, Iswarchandra Vidyasagar to F.J. Mouat, 7 September 1853.
40. Iswarchandra Vidyasagar, 'Charitavali' [Life Sketches], ibid., pp. 1327–66; Iswarchandra Vidyasagar, 'Jivan Charit' [Biography], ibid., pp. 1421–46.
41. Mukundadev Mukhopadhyay, *Bhudev Charit* [Biography of Bhudev], 3 vols (Calcutta, Bengali year 1324 [1917]), i, pp. 178–9.
42. *Rammohan Rachanavali*, pp. 454–5, Rammohan to J.S. Buckingham, 11 August 1821.
43. Ibid., pp. 457–8, Rammohan to Mrs Woodford, 27 April 1832; Rammohan to W. Rathbone, 31 July 1832.
44. *Bombay Durpun*, 6 January 1832.
45. *Rammohan Rachanavali*, pp. 460–1, Rammohan to ? (n.d.).
46. Ibid., pp. 484–5, 486–8, Rammohan to T.H. Villiers, 22 December 1831; Rammohan to minister of foreign affairs, France (n.d.).
47. Rammohan Roy, *The Precepts of Jesus* (n.p., 1820).
48. *Rammohan Rachanavali*, pp. 470–2, Rammohan to Rev. T. Belsham, 1821.
49. Rammohan Roy, 'Brahman Sevadhi/Brahmunical Magazine', ibid., pp. 241–2, 245–9.
50. T. Raychaudhuri, *Europe Reconsidered*, 2nd edn. (Delhi, 1989), p. 289.
51. 'Mr Tata's Journal during his Travel in Palestine, 1873', in F.R. Harris,

Jamsetji Nusserwanji Tata: A Chronicle of His Life, 2nd edn. (Bombay, 1958), pp. 289–97.

52. Keshub Sen [Keshab Sen], 'Religious and Social Liberty', in his *Diary, Sermons, Addresses and Epistles*, 3rd edn. (Calcutta, 1938), p. 291.

53. Rammohan Roy, 'Brahman Sevadhi', p. 241; *Rammohan Rachanavali*, pp. 455–6, Rammohan Roy to J.B. Estlin, 7 February 1827.

54. Rammohan's speech before the Unitarian Association, London, in *Rammohan Rachanavali*, p. 567.

55. Datta, *Religious Sects of the Hindus*, i, pp. 92–3, 102–3.

56. Keshub Sen, 'Religious and Social Liberty', p. 291.

57. *Rammohan Rachanavali*, pp. 471–2, Rammohan to Rev. T. Belsham, 1821.

58. Keshub Sen, 'Christ and Christianity', in Keshub Sen, *Diary, Sermons, Addresses and Epistles*, p. 242.

59. Keshub Sen, 'Religious and Social Liberty', p. 291.

60. Keshub Sen, 'Christ and Christianity', p. 235.

61. Keshub Sen, 'My Impressions of England', in Keshub Sen, *Diary, Sermons, Addresses and Epistles*, pp. 487–8.

62. Bhudev Mukhopadhyay [Bhudev Mukherji], *Samajik Pravandha* [Essay on Society], in J. Chakravarti (ed.) (Calcutta, 1981), pp. 39–41; first published in *Education Gazette* [Calcutta] (1875–6).

63. [R.C. Dutt], *Three Years in Europe: Being Extracts from Letters Sent from Europe by a Hindu* (Calcutta and London, 1873), p. 26. These letters, written by R.C. Dutt between March 1868 and September 1871, were published anonymously.

64. Ibid., pp. 17–18.

65. Ibid., pp. 53–5.

66. Keshub Sen, 'Impressions of England', p. 483.

67. Swami Vivekananda, 'Pracya o Pascatya' [The East and the West], in *Swami Vivekanandar Vani of Racana* [The Sayings and Writings of Swami Vivekananda], 6th edn., 10 vols (Calcutta, 1982), vi, pp. 161–2. This essay was first published in the journal *Udbodhan* [Awakening] (Bengali years 1306–8 [1899–1901).

68. [Dutt], *Three Years in Europe*, p. 57; Keshub Sen, 'Impressions of England', pp. 483–4.

69. The reformist Maharashtrian writers of the nineteenth century, such as Agarkar, Lokhitavadi and the novelist Harinarayan Apte invoked repeatedly the ideal of womanhood in modern Europe as the one India should emulate. Like their counterparts in Bengal, they were the objects of ridicule by social conservatives such as Tilak who broke with Agarkar on issues such as these.

70. [Dutt], *Three Years in Europe*, pp. 87 f., 91.

71. Ibid., pp. 61–2.

72. D. Gidumal, *The Life and Work of Behramji M. Malabari* (Bombay, 1988), p. 291.

73. Keshub Sen, 'Impressions of England', p. 483.
74. See Raychaudhuri, *Europe Reconsidered*, ch. 4, for a detailed discussion of Vivekananda's views on the west.
75. D. Naoroji, *The European and Asiatic Races: Observations on the Paper Read by John Crawfurd, Esq. F.R.S., before the Ethnological Society on February 14th 1866* (London, 1866).
76. Vivekananda, 'Pracya o Pascatya', pp. 149–50.
77. Raychaudhuri, *Europe Reconsidered*, pp. 198 ff.
78. Ibid.
79. Bhudev Mukhopadhyay, *Samajik Pravandha.*
80. Rabindranath Tagore, 'Pascatya o Pracya Sabhyata' [Western and Eastern Civilizations], in *Bharatvarsa, Rabindra-racanavali* [Works of Rabindranath Tagore], 27 vols (Visvabharati, Bengali years 1341–73 [1939–66], iv, pp. 416–24.
81. Rabindranath Tagore, 'Baroyari-mangal' [Public Welfare], in *Bharatvarsa, Rabindra-racanavali*, iv, pp. 424–40.
82. Ibid., p. 429.
83. M.K. Gandhi, *Hind Swaraj* [India's Independence] (first published serially in *Young India*, November 1909–March 1911), in *Collected Works of Mahatma Gandhi*, 91 vols (New Delhi, 1958–88), x, pp. 2, 20–1, 24–5, 26, 33, 35–7, 38, 58.
84. Dadabhai Naoroji, *Poverty and Un-British Rule in England* (London, 1901); R.C. Dutt, *India in the Victorian Age: An Economic History of the People* (London, 1904).
85. Gandhi, *Hind Swaraj*, p. 24.
86. See above, n. 74.

3

The Pursuit of Reason
in Nineteenth-century Bengal*

Causality and verification of intuitively perceived 'truths' in the light of rational argument were not unknown to the intellectual traditions of India. In Bengal, the inheritance of the Brahminical high culture was manifest most powerfully in the cultivation of two disciplines, *nyāya* and *smriti*. Of the two, the former was a highly technical and sophisticated system of enquiry into the nature of philosophical categories and their intellectual validation. The tradition of Islamic education to which sections of both the Hindu and Muslim literati had access also subsumed techniques of rational argumentation. In short, rationality and rational enquiry into questions of interest to mankind were not alien to the mental world of the social groups who came into contact with the western intellectual traditions in nineteenth-century Bengal.

Yet, it would be probably correct to say that the average educated person in pre-modern Bengal was not preoccupied with the pursuit of reason in any sphere of his life. His or her actions and beliefs in day to day life were determined by inherited codes. These were not questioned, except very rarely by religious sects seeking paths to salvation unrestrained by the rules of orthodoxy. Even such rejections were in terms of intuitive faith and not any rational questioning of received wisdom. As to intellectual concerns, the educated were at best familiar with Sanskrit, Bengali and Persian literary products and perhaps with the religious texts of the sect they belonged to. The specialist scholars were the only exceptions to this general pattern. Rational argument or enquiry was no part of this literary culture. And there is no indication in the evidence of any tradition of assessment of social needs or enquiry into natural phenomena in the light of rational thought untrammelled by scriptural authority.

*Reprinted from Rajat Ray (ed.), *Mind, Body and Society.*

Rational assessment of current needs and received traditions, both indigenous and alien, became the hallmark of Bengali thought in the nineteenth century. Arguably, this development marked a total discontinuity in the history of the region. A product of the colonial encounter, it was a development with explosive potentialities which acquired a measure of autonomy. Its ramifications went way beyond the limits of the colonial experience. The non-realization of its potentialities was due to specific historical circumstances only partly related to the colonial relationships of power.

Raja Rammohan Roy is by common consensus regarded as the pioneer of modernization in India. Arguments based on reason were among the most powerful instruments he used in the furtherance of causes—social, religious and political—which he espoused, though these were by no means the only ones. Appeals to emotions as well as scriptural authority were equally potent instruments in his armoury. And whatever his personal predilections, he was reluctant to repudiate the scriptural prescriptions beyond a point. Since he was willing to risk his life in defending highly unpopular causes like the abolition of *sati*, it is perhaps a fair conclusion that his regard for the Śāstras was prompted by genuine faith rather than any fear of public opinion. Like many intellectuals in all parts of the world in all ages, his rationality conceded a space to beliefs which reason could not sustain.

His allegiance to reason, however, predates his encounter with the West. The first treatise he wrote, at the age of sixteen and in the Persian language, was an attack on idolatry. The text is no longer available. But his *Gift to the Monotheists*, written in Persian with an introduction in Arabic, probably before he had any deep knowledge of western thought (the book was published in 1804), shows a remarkable capacity for sustained reasoning without any appeal to authority. The following is a typical example of his style of argument in this book:

In mundane matters men do not accept one phenomenon as the cause and another as the effect unless they have knowledge of the causal relation between the two. But in matters of religion or religious belief they do not hesitate to accept one thing as cause and the other as its result even when there is no causal relationship. For instance, when one believes that he has secured redress from his misfortune or recovered from illness only through prayer without any struggle or attempt at remedy, there is no causal relationship between the one and the other. In such mysterious matters . . . leaders of religion . . . offer explanations which suggest that reason has no place in matters of religion and faith . . .

It seems extremely unlikely that in the latter half of the eighteenth century such lines of thought were common among the Bengali literati or that many sixteen-years-old Brahmins felt distressed enough by the Hindu practices of polytheism and image worship to attack them and incur the risk of being disinherited. Almost certainly we have in this man a unique personality who responded to one particular strand in western thought and life in his days and in so doing, facilitated its impact on the emerging concerns of his own social class.

It would be superfluous to recount here Rammohan's many-faceted thought and activities familiar to all students of modern Indian history. It is only necessary to note that all his initiatives were inspired by a liberal and humane ideology plus a belief in man's right to freedom which brought him very close to the political radicalism of his day. But his propagation of the desired cause was almost always in terms of reason. His classic statements against the practice of sati do cite scriptural authority, but the clinching arguments anticipate the idiom and stances of contemporary feminism. He rejected the prevailing view that women, being of limited intelligence and naturally fickle, were likely to go astray if allowed to survive as widows. '. . . When have you tested the intelligence of women that you describe them as stupid without hesitation? . . . You have never given them any access to knowledge or wisdom, then how do you decide that they are without intelligence?' As to fickleness, he asked for a head count on the number of unfaithful husbands adding that the Hindu, at the time of his marriage, accepted his wife as half his body (*ardhāṅginī*), but in practice treated her worse than an animal.

A similar concern for rational thought informed with humane values marks all his pronouncements on socio-cultural as well as religious issues. His famous plea for state support to western instead of oriental education seeking an enlightened system of instruction 'embracing mathematics, natural philosophy, chemistry and anatomy with other useful sciences', the tracts on Christianity questioning the Trinitarian doctrine, the letters defending the freedom of the press in India, are all inspired by a faith in reason and are couched in terms of rational argument.

But while his tract on monotheism and the precocious critique on image worship might represent a lone voice among late eighteenth-century Bengali Hindus, his concern for rational thought and conduct as manifested in the statements mentioned above was surely shared by many Bengalis of his social class. Influential members of Bengali society, men like Dwarkanath Tagore and his associates, evidently shared his beliefs. The memorial presented to Dwarkanath by the citizens of Calcutta when he went to England in defiance of customary taboo suggests that by the early forties a substantial body of public opinion was committed to rational thought. Such commitment was, however, not confined to supporters of social reform. Even Rammohan's staunch opponents did not simply evoke scriptural authority in defence of their conservative position. As is well known, the argument against prohibition of sati by law, an action to which Rammohan himself was at first opposed, emphasized *inter alia* the undesirability of state interference in matters religious or social. Radhakanta Dev, the leader of that agitation, as well as several other orthodox stalwarts of Hindu society who were bitterly opposed to Rammohan, were among the founders of the Hindu College, the first institution of western higher learning in Asia imparting such useful knowledge as Rammohan wanted for his countrymen. Radhakanta's objections to the Anglicist position in matters of educational policy were not those of a bigoted Hindu who saw no merit in western education. He pleaded instead for a diversified programme with an emphasis on mass education with the vernacular as medium, and focused on the vocational needs of the producing classes. With rare foresight, he anticipated in the 1830s the dangers of an educational system which would end up producing an army of educated unemployed seeking non-existent clerical appointments. The critics of Rammohan and his supporters denounced each other's ideology, yet spoke in a language very similar to their opponents'. Reason and rational argument were central to their world of shared discourse.

Reason, certainly, was central to the system of education introduced through the Hindu College and later emulated at the other institutions of higher education set up on the same model. A well-known yet inadequately emphasized fact should be noted in this context. Western education, as introduced in Bengal, was and remained exclusively secular and no alternative or complementary systems modified the consequent exclusion of religious instruction from the curricula. The Christian missionary colleges and the few institutions set up by the Brahmos did provide for the study of scriptures, Christian and Hindu respectively. But such study had no roots in the belief system of the majority of the students. The strong rationalist bias of the rest of the curricula and the mode of instruction ensured that religious faith could not be structured around intellectual persuasion for the bulk of the modern Bengali intelligentsia. Their education, perhaps uniquely in the nineteenth century, remained exclusively secular. Neither customary ritual observance, nor such limited knowledge of the indigenous religious traditions as one acquired from the home environment could counteract the overwhelming power of the reason-based knowledge acquired through the formal system of education.

The supremacy of reason in the new system of education was in a way symbolized by the young Eurasian professor of Hindu College, Henry Louis Vivian Derozio. A student of Drummond, a product of Scottish Enlightenment philosophy, Derozio lectured on Hume and Kant. More important, he encouraged his students to think for themselves. When charged with leading them astray from the Hindu way of life, he replied that he was guilty of nothing beyond the encouragement of independence in thinking. If such encouragement had led his pupils to hate 'everything Hindu'—and, according to the college governors, violate caste taboos and indulge in sodomy and fornication—of course he was not to blame. Derozio's scholarship and enthusiasm might have been the most potent influence in moulding the attitudes of Young Bengal. But post-enlightenment rationalism, rather than any religious faith, appears to have been the dominant ideology of the college faculty both during and after his time. His famous successor, Captain Richardson, was certainly a free thinker and allegedly a free liver. The persistent emphasis on rational thought induced a contempt for 'everything Hindu'. But it did not inspire any corresponding reverence for 'things Christian' as proselytizers like Rev Duff had hoped. Hume, Tom Paine and Gibbon were favourite authors and the chain of argument which undermined belief in Hindu dogma also acted as a 'cordon sanitaire' against Christian influence. What the young western-educated Bengali questioned was not any particular religious tradition, but the tradition of belief without rational argument itself. The resulting tensions may have focused attention temporarily on the nature and content of what one could believe, leading to the familiar debates about Brahmo versus orthodox Hindu practice. But so long as the primary allegiance was to reason, the social compass pointed relentlessly in the direction of agnosticism. As Duff noted with regret, some evil miscreant had imported one thousand copies of the *Age of Reason*, and the book sold out in Calcutta at five times the original price.

There was, however, something lacking in this pursuit of reason and 'useful knowledge'. The list of natural sciences which appear in Rammohan's famous letter to Lord Amherst were peripheral to the courses of study in the new temples of learning. The emphasis primarily, if not exclusively, was on the humanities, and social philosophy. Even when science was taught—and physics and mathematics were compulsory subjects at least by the 1830s—the instruction was purely theoretical, with hardly any access to laboratories. As one well-informed critic pointed out, western education in India lacked the central glory of western knowledge, namely the experimental method and the scientific spirit; scientific education was thus reduced to a half-comprehending acceptance of the words of European authors. Basically this was no different from memorizing Sanskrit or Arabic grammar. The enquiry into the nature and causation of social phenomena could be based on rational arguments, despite this limitation. But the same was certainly not true of studies relating to nature. Arguably, the exclusive emphasis in nineteenth-century Bengali thought on analysis of social issues and philosophical questions was due not to any propensity inherent in the culture (the culture subsumed very little in the line of social analysis), but largely to the absence of facilities for scientific education. Popular journals of the period abound in scientific essays, based on western popular science, but the same journals contain contributions on social and philosophical questions which are incomparably superior in intellectual sophistication and their content of knowledge.

The establishment of the Calcutta Medical College was a landmark in the development of scientific education in Bengal. The lectures were open to the public and, it appears, these were well attended. The amateur audience included in the early years of the college a very remarkable person, Akshay Kumar Datta, a school drop-out (not by choice, but because of extreme poverty) and an autodidact who became a major influence on the intellectual development of nineteenth-century Bengalis. A friend of the famous reformer, Iswar Chandra Vidyasagar and editor of the Brahmo periodical, *Tatvabodhinī Patrikā*, he wrote several didactic works of which one, *Bāhyabastur Sahit Mānav Prakritir Sambandha Bichār* (The Relationship of Human Nature with External Objects) based on a curious tract propagating vegetarianism, George Combe's *The Constitution of Man* (1828), expressed and helped shape the ideology of an entire generation.

The reason for the extraordinary influence of Datta's tract are not difficult to understand. The work went way beyond the issue of vegetarianism, the main concern of Combe's book. Datta merely picked up from the original its central argument that there were strong links between external objects and the human constitution, both body and mind. He substituted and supplemented Combe's data drawn from the European experience with evidence nearer home. More important, he developed from the original's meagre argument regarding the character of natural law a grand cosmological theory. Without denying the existence of God, he sought arguments in its favour in the great book of nature itself. Above all, the Divine Law was declared to be written in that book alone and nowhere else. It hence became the duty of men to peruse it with care and live by the commandments written clearly in that supreme text. Man was but a part of the sentient world and the latter integral to the created universe subsuming the living and the non-living, both bound by the same set of laws. Human morality, individual and personal, consisted in observing the laws manifest in the book of nature. Sin or crime were but excesses which undermined the body and mind, individual or social. Man's duty was to study carefully the natural sciences to understand the Divine Laws manifest in nature and to live according to these.

The negative dimension of such constructs was a respectful denial of validity of all institutionalized religions. Rammohan before him had asserted that 'every rite has its derivation from the allegorical adoration of the true Deity'. Datta built on that argument to paint institutionalized religions in somewhat lurid colours: 'It is doubtful if anything has caused more destruction and bloodshed in this world than religion. All religions are tarnished by hatred. Religious preachers addicted to power are enemies of reason, blind in their wrath and bereft of good sense.' This view, stated in his treatise on Indian religious sects, *Bhāratvarshiya Upāsak Sampradāy*, encompasses a statement of total rejection. All religions are described as bundles of error (*bhrāntibhār*). It is the unfortunate duty of the historian to write about these because his concern is with falsity as much as truth.

In the latter book one can almost hear him chuckle when he contemplates the likely discomfiture of the neo-Hindu stalwarts if they only knew that all the six systems of Indian philosophy were basically atheistic or agnostic. He noted with the same impish delight, 'There is no reason to doubt that all our [ancient] seers and savants were beef-eaters. In this respect there is nothing that distinguishes Vasishtha and Viswamitra, kings among sages, from Reverend Wilson and

Sheikh Waliullah.' The writer, incidentally, was himself a vegetarian following God's laws as written in the book of nature and interpreted by George Combe.

Anticipating some of his arguments, Rammohan had written some decades earlier that 'the reasoning faculty, which leads men to certainty with regard to things within its reach, produces no effect on questions beyond its comprehension.' Datta expressed the same sentiment in more acerbic language: 'The nature of the Deity is beyond the realm of words or the human mind. Then what can one do if even adults play childish games and derive childish pleasure from imagining his physical or mental attributes?'

In discussing the six systems of philosophy, he expressed his appreciation of the Kanāda and Vaiseshikā systems because of the attention they paid to natural phenomena and the atomic theory (*paramanu-vāda*) which traced the origin of the universe to the conglomeration of atoms for reasons unknown. He underlined the fact that this theory has no reference to God or any creator. He also noted that the ancient Indian philosophers were 'born with well-nourished seeds of bright intellect'. But unfortunately, their investigations into the phenomenal world proved to be stillborn. They discovered some truths intuitively and then embellished them with imaginary theories which were utterly fictitious. 'They were in want of someone to lead them. They were in need of one Bacon, one Bacon, one Bacon.' Lacking such a leader, they lost their way in the wilderness of ignorance, despite their occasional glimpses of scientific truth.

The moral of this tale is stated with great clarity: 'Man owes his humanity to his access to intellect and morality. Pure intelligence is the only road to knowledge. To enquire into truth without intellect and conscience is like trying to hear and see without the help of eyes or ears.' Devotion to truth implies a relentless journey in the direction where pure intelligence and reason, untrammelled by superstition, took one. That alone is beneficial for mankind which is discovered by pure reason.

A prescription follows: The seeds of truth failed to germinate in India. Perhaps the climate was to blame. Whatever the reason, the salvation of India could come from only one source—the pursuit of knowledge and reason as developed in Europe. An appreciation of this fact was Rammohan's true glory. Sanskritic learning, however precious, had to be the concern of the few. The educated Indian had to concentrate on European languages, English, German or French, and the stock of knowledge to which they gave access. There was no other way out of the state of degradation into which the country had fallen.

Datta's appeal lay in the fact that he offered a satisfactory solution to the intellectual dilemma encountered by the western educated Bengalis. Western education had shaken their faith in the received tradition without providing any acceptable alternative. The debates on religion, between Hindus and Christians and between Brahmos and Hindus, had created a psychological necessity for a conscious choice in matters of faith. In a tradition replete with theistic belief pure agnosticism or atheism was not a real choice to many. Brahmoism as propounded by Rammohan left too many questions unanswered for the rational mind, and the mystical propensities of the new leader, Devendranath Tagore, did not help. Western criticisms of the established practices had also generated a tendency towards self-assertion. Formal acceptance of Brahmoism implied an agreement with those criticisms. Datta, while a Brahmo himself, interpreted Brahmoism in terms of untrammelled rationality. Acceptance of his ideas involved no formal act of renunciation of the ancestral faith. His Deity was a God of reason, not faith. His theism bordered on agnosticism, if not atheism. He preached an orientation of attitudes rather than a system of belief. To individuals brought up exclusively in the school of reason his prescription was entirely acceptable. The nineteenth-century phenomenon known as reformed Hinduism which had no clear codes but combined a measure of latitudinarianism with humane practices, undefined beliefs and a formal tolerance of ritual requirements, could live with it without undue discomfort. Very probably, *Bāhyavastu* was a major influence in moulding the attitudes underlying reformed Hinduism. Rationality without compromise, in belief if not in practice, was its core value.

The pursuit of reason led in several directions in the second half of the nineteenth century. Datta like many of his contemporaries was greatly attracted to the philosophy of Auguste Comte and his Religion of Humanity. Hardly any Bengali intellectual remained unaffected by Positivist philosophy around this time. If for some, its appeal lay in its emphasis on pure reason and love of mankind, others like Bhudev Mukhopadhyay and Bankim Chandra Chattopadhyay in his later days, were also appreciative of its innate conservatism and the adulation of the priestly class, especially the Brahmins of India. Such admirers, however, rejected the absence of a Deity in Comte's religion.

The social philosophy which proved to be nearly as influential as

Comte's ideas was Utilitarianism. Spencer and John Stuart Mill were compulsory reading for anyone with intellectual pretension. But the very pursuit of reason which attracted one to Utilitarianism also blocked its acceptance beyond a point. Social philosophy in nineteenth-century Bengal was invariably geared to a clear purpose, namely, an enquiry into the needs and possibilities of contemporary Indian society. Rationality in such a context could not be value-free. And the values of the extended family, the abnegation of self for the greater good of others which constituted its norm whatever the reality, was generally assessed as something superior to the apotheosis of individualism at the heart of Utilitarian doctrine. The appeal of Mill had more to do with his egalitarian and libertarian preferences than with the specifically Utilitarian aspects of his thought. Organismic theories of society were invoked to justify the preference for the extended family. Bankim identified the Indian family system as the one source of cohesion in a society without any traditions of unity. But one is left with a strong impression that such theoretical justifications were but rationalizations of a preference rooted in the social psychology of the classes in question.

Rational enquiry could as well lead one in the direction of scientific theories towards pseudo-sciences. While Darwin was read and discussed extensively, Social Darwinism conceding ultimate evolutionary excellence to Europeans was also widely accepted. Theories regarding the influence of climate on historical evolution, pointing towards similar conclusions, especially as developed by Lecky and Buckle, were also much in vogue.

The attraction of the sciences and pseudo-sciences lay not so much in their intellectual content as in their claims to explanatory power *vis-à-vis* the development of human civilization and their consequent relevance to programmes for national progress. Outside the movements inspired by the impulse to cultural self-assertion and their most extreme expression, Hindu revivalism, there was general agreement regarding two basic assumptions. First, no one appears to have been in any doubt as to the decadent character of Bengali society—its insignificance in the eyes of the civilized world, physical and moral weakness and the total absence of worthwhile achievement. While this fallen state was often contrasted with a glorious Hindu past, the most influential leaders of society had serious misgivings about that past itself. Rammohan, while reading into the *Upanishads* a tradition of monotheism from which later Hindus were supposed to have departed, spelt out in his letter to Lord Amherst the utter futility of much that was central to the ancient Hindu civilization. In 1853, the great reformer, Iswar Chandra Vidyasagar, expressed similar sentiments, describing *Vedānta* and *Saṃkhya* as 'false systems of philosophy' which, if taught, should be opposed by sound philosophy in the English course 'to counteract their influence'. Bishop Berkeley's *Inquiry*, which had affinities with the said systems should hence be excluded from the syllabus. On the other hand, the study of Mill's work was indispensable 'in the present state of things'.

The Bengali modernizers in general had little doubt regarding the overall superiority of western civilization. Rammohan repeatedly emphasized the benefits likely to flow from contact with civilized Europeans representing a higher state of civilization. His plea in favour of colonization of India by European settlers whose energy and enterprise would rejuvinate a languishing economy was founded in this faith in European superiority. Akshay Kumar Datta, as noted, saw in the modern European tradition a unique concern for reason and truth which had led to a systematic unfolding of nature's mysteries, while the genius of India had lost its way in superstitions and imaginary conceits despite occasional glimpses of truth. As a result, Europe had become 'a heaven on earth' while India wallowed in misery and disgrace. So great was his sense of cultural inferiority that despite his firm belief that British rule had resulted in an all-round decay in Indian life, he saw no alternative to British leadership and intervention for his country's uplift.

Statements such as the ones cited above express impressionistic notions and are not generally presented as conclusions emerging from sustained enquiry. But in the last three decades of the nineteenth century a number of influential writers analysed systematically the relative advantages or otherwise of European civilization to identify features from which India could learn in her effort at national reconstruction. The most influential among these writers was Bankim Chandra Chattopadhyay, though his passionately patriotic writings probably had greater impact on modern Indian consciousness than his reasoned comparisons between Indian and European civilizations.

A younger contemporary of Akshay Kumar Datta, he developed a line of thought which has remarkable similarities with that of his older contemporary. He too identified reason and rational enquiry as the source of Europe's greatness. Knowledge in Europe was sought as the ultimate source of power whereas in India its primary object was salvation. Europe had achieved success in her pursuit of power through knowledge, especially power over nature. India had lost out in this world, while her success in the next was at best a matter of conjecture. Rational enquiry in Europe was based on experimentation and the willingness to pursue the intuitively perceived hypothesis to its legitimate conclusion. He described Torricelli's experiments to test the validity of his hypothesis and how Pascal took the barometer to the Puy de Dome to test his conclusion that atmospheric pressure bore an inverse relation to altitude. 'A Hindu philosopher in Torricelli's place would have contented himself with simply announcing in an aphoristic *sutra* that the air had weight. No measure of the quantity of its pressure would have been given; no experiment would have been made with mercury; no Hindu Pascal would have ascended the Himalayas with a barometric column in his hand.'

Bankim Chandra Chattopadhyay illustrated the long-term difference between the two cultural traditions with other examples as well. The Hindu discovery of the diurnal rotation of the earth, the apparent fixity of the heavenly bodies and the annual motion of the sun did not lead to the next logical step, the heliocentric theory and thence to further laws of the universe. The Copernican theory on the other hand led to the discovery of Kepler's laws and eventually to the law of gravitation. In India Aryabhatta's remarkable announcement rendered certain that nothing further would come of it. The emphasis here is on a perceived deficiency in the indigenous culture. The message for the nation is quite explicit. If India was to measure up to the standards set by the advanced western nations, reason and rational enquiry had to be the basis of social and individual life. Even faith had to have a rational basis. And the same was true of family life.

This application of reason to questions of belief was central to the religious controversies of the nineteenth century. The Brahmos adjured their faith in revelation as the source of the Vedas after a careful scrutiny of the texts based on expert knowledge. The first split in the movement, on questions of ritual observances such as the sacred thread, also resulted from an appeal to rationality. Significantly, the editor of *Tatvabodhinī Patrikā* did not see Brahmoism as a particular dogma or institutionalized religion, but simply as a system of rational belief derived from an understanding of natural laws. The final split, while it was triggered off by Keshab Chandra Sen's departure from the rule regarding the minimum age of marriage he himself had laid down, represented a deep cleavage in which one party, the founders of the Sadharan Brahmo Samaj, rejected the new emotionalism in matters of faith introduced by Keshab Chandra. The new Samaj, which had close affinities with Christian nonconformity, was inclined to reject everything inconsistent with reason and came remarkably close to Akshay Kumar Datta's notion of a *dharma* based entirely on reason.

The quest for reason in matters of religion went further when the first and only community of followers of Comte's Religion of Humanity with its full paraphernalia of man-oriented rituals was established in the city of Calcutta. The acceptance of a religion which had no place for a Deity was the natural conclusion of a purely rationalistic quest. But for many votaries of reason this was pushing things too far. Those who were attracted by Comte's innate conservatism and adulation of Brahmins, stopped short of accepting the Religion of Humanity precisely because the latter had no place for God. The uncompromising Positivist was necessarily an agnostic or atheist.

The defenders of the Hindu belief systems and rituals were not necessarily opposed to rationality. In fact two of the most powerful defenders of the received tradition, Bhudev and Bankim, constructed complex structures of reasoning to justify their positions. In an extremely erudite critique of western civilization, the former underlined selfishness, personal and national, as a motive force of European history. Individualism, the core value of nineteenth-century civilization, was shown to be an apotheosis of selfishness arising out of the long-term tendencies of western civilization. A somewhat idealized picture of Hindu belief and practice was projected by way of contrast and a clear message derived from this complex exercise: Hindus had nothing to learn from the West except their knowledge of the external world and their skill in practical matters. 'It is better that they learn nothing else.' Adherence to received traditions was justified again on historical grounds. The English derived their strength from their steadfast loyalty to tradition and so should the Hindus. Bankim built an elaborate system which he described as quintessential Hinduism, the future basis for national regeneration. But in fact it drew heavily on the western social philosophies—the doctrine of culture as expounded by Mathew Arnold, as well as Utilitarianism and Positivism, which had attracted him since his early youth. Interestingly, the cruder defenders of popular Hinduism, including its evidently superstitious beliefs, also invoked pseudo-scientific arguments rather than the authority of scriptures. By the latter part of the nineteenth century, it was no longer possible to debate any issue in Bengal without an appeal to reason and rationality, however contrived the arguments might be. Some of the crudest tracts against the legalization of widow remarriage justify their position in the light of two sets of arguments: scriptural authority and the dictates of reason. The latter might contain bizarre statements such as the belief that women's sexual instinct was eight times as strong as that of men. Nevertheless the authors recognized the need for justifying their position rationally.

Rationality of course remained a powerful element in the intellectual tradition of modern Bengal. But in the last two decades of the century and in the aftermath of the anti-partition agitation it yielded its position ,of supremacy to something more powerful. A profound emotionalism informed all social initiative and religious quests in the closing decades of the century. Bankim Chandra's reasoned arguments in his numerous essays and ideological constructs proved to be less influential than his passionate appeals to patriotic fervour and his fictional invocation of the motherland as the mother goddess, the ultimate object of worship. Hindu revivalism in its crudest form also had its roots in an emotionally charged cultural self-assertion. Keshab Chandra Sen turned the rationalistic Brahmo movement into a vehicle for intense devotionalism, redolent of the Vaishnava tradition in which he was brought up as a child. The cult which developed around Ramakrishna was marked by the same intensity of religious fervour. A variety of Guru cults flourished in this congenial climate. Rabindranath Tagore described in one of his most powerful novels, *Chaturanga*, how one time rationalists surrendered their will to gurus in this new atmosphere.

As in Bankim Chandra's *Ānandmaṭh*, so in real life a passionate religiosity linked to an equally intense patriotic fervour became the modal attitude of the idealistic young by the turn of the century. The prophet of this new nationalism was the young Cambridge-educated scholar and journalist, Aurobindo Ghosh. He and his associates prepared the ground for the emotionally charged political outburst following Curzon's decision to partition the province of Bengal. The appeal of their irredentist nationalism lay *inter alia* in the fact that they expressed in the most powerful and cogent form the attitudes and concerns of a generation.

I have described rather than tried to explain this shift in emphasis from reason to emotion in the social-political culture of nineteenth-century Bengal. It would of course be a mistake to exaggerate the implied dichotomy. The passion in Rammohan's pleas supporting the abolition of sati is too evident to be ignored; and Aurobindo's editorials in the *Bandemātaram* asserting man's birthright to freedom are built around a hard core of reasoned argument. Yet the shift in mood is unmistakable. The accumulated frustrations and humiliations of the colonial experience were no doubt one major factor behind the new emotionalism. One has hints of a growing perception that alien rule was the root evil in Indian life. Its eradication was the most important task facing the nation. Social reconstruction, the agenda offered by two generations of thinkers who either accepted the fact of British rule or saw no hope of an early end to it, could wait if the new diagnosis was correct. The corollary of such perceptions was a programme of immediate action involving great risks, and ideology of self-sacrifice. That ideology could be erected only on a foundation of intense emotions. Rational discourse was an inadequate impetus to martyrdom.

BIBLIOGRAPHICAL NOTES

The works of Raja Rammohan Roy are available in a variety of editions. I have used the edition edited by Ajitkumar Ghosh and published by Haraf Prakasani, Calcutta (1973). His *Tuhfatul Muwahhidin* was originally published in 1804. The Bengali translation by J. Das appears in the collected works, pp. 717–29. For his arguments against sati, see 'Sahamaran vishaye pravartak o nivartaker samvad' and 'Sahamaran vishaye pravartak o nivartaker dvitiya samvad'. For his letter to Lord Amherst, 11 December 1823 see pp. 433–6. Also see his 'Views on Settlement of Europeans', ibid., pp. 529ff. For his view on image worship cited in this paper, see 'Bhattacharyer sahit vichar', pp. 107ff.

Akshay Kumar Datta's two major works cited here are *Bāhyavastur Sahit Mānav Prakritir Samvandha Vichār*, 2 vols, 1774 śaka (AD 1852) and his *Bhārat Varshiya Upāsak Sampradāy*, 2 vols, first published in *Tatvabodhinī Patrikā* in 1848 and later as a book in B.S. 1289 (AD 1882).

The best account of the education and social concerns of the Bengali intelligentsia in the nineteenth century is Sibnath Sastri, *Rāmtanu Lahiri o Tatkālin Vanga Samāj*, Calcutta, 1903. Also see Alexander Duff, *India and Indian Missions . . .* Edinburgh, 1840 and Alok Ray, *Alexander Duff o Anugāmi Kayekjan* for the responses to Christianity. For the social and political ideas of the Bengali intellectuals, see Bimanbihari Majumdar, *History of Political Thought from Rammohan to Dayananda (1801–84)*, Calcutta, 1934 and Amit Sen, *Notes on the Bengal Renaissance*, Calcutta, 1946.

For the writings of Iswarchandra Vidyasagar, I have used the most recent edition of his works, Tirthapati Datta (ed.), Calcutta, 1987. For his articles on child marriage, widow remarriage and polygamy see pp. 678–1088. For his letter to the Secretary, Council of Education on the syllabus for Sanskrit College, see pp. 670–5.

For a detailed exposition of the ideas of Bankim Chandra Chattopadhyay and Bhudev Mukhopadhyay, see T. Raychaudhuri, *Europe Reconsidered, Perceptions of the West in Nineteenth Century Bengal,* Calcutta, 1988. Bhudev's *Sāmājik Pravandha,* originally serialized in the periodical, *Education Gazette,* was published as a book in 1892. The most important works of Bankim for his ideas on religion are *Krishnacharitra,* 1885 and *Dharmatatva,* 1888. For his ideas on rational discourse, see *Sāmya,* 1879 and *Bididha Prabandha,* 2 vols, 1887 and 1892. I have used J.C. Bagal (ed.), *Bankim Rachanābali,* Calcutta, 1983. *English Works,* Calcutta, 1983. His patriotic novel, *Ānandamath,* first serialized in *Bangadarśan,* was published as a book in 1882.

For an account of the development of Positivism in Bengal, see G.H. Forbes, *Positivism in Bengal: A Case Study in the Transmission and Assimilation of Ideology,* Calcutta, 1975. For the development of militant nationalism, see Amales Tripathi, *The Extremist Challenge,* Calcutta, 1967.

4

Love in a Colonial Climate: Marriage, Sex and Romance in Nineteenth-century Bengal*

Studies concerned with the intimate areas of human experience suggest that the institutions and social mores structured around the instinctive drives of mankind—such as sex, love and fear, are not meant to serve the same purpose in every culture.[1] Belief systems, world views and culturally determined expectations from life determine the texture, causation and expression of even our very basic emotions. Nature's purpose for the sexual impulse may be the propogation of the species, but in controlling and harnessing this drive for the ends of social cohesion, different cultures have had very different objectives in view and used very different means. The emotive affects associated with its expression have also varied accordingly.

The present paper is an attempt to explore the implications of an 'external' factor, namely colonial rule and the wide-ranging developments associated with it, for an intimate area of experience in the life of a social group in nineteenth-century India—the Bengali Hindu *bhadralok*. It focuses on a sphere of cultural change where 'private' concerns were profoundly altered through interaction with developments in the 'public' sphere. I have used the quotation marks to suggest that the distinction, as is now often recognized, has limited validity beyond a point. There is a large volume of literature now on women in modern Bengal, especially the changes that occurred in their condition and status in course of the nineteenth century.[2] Such studies necessarily cover some of the themes discussed in this paper. However, its central concern—the affects associated with the relationship between men and women in its sexual context—the elements of change and continuity in this area of experience, has attracted

*A version of this essay is to appear in *Modern Asian Studies.*

relatively little attention.[3] To locate this study in its appropriate context, this paper will perforce have to refer to some data well-known to students of Bengali society.

I

A set of beliefs and values were structured into the institutions and practices concerning marriage and sexuality in *bhadralok* society. The institution of marriage in the Brahminical culture is meant to achieve one specific purpose above all else: *'putrarthe kriyate bharya'*—a man takes a wife in order to beget sons. In an agrarian society where one needs able-bodied men to carry on the essential task of agriculture, there may be perceived economic reasons for this prescription, or the obiter may simply encapsulate a patriarchal preference structured into the system of dominant values. The scriptures, however, link it to a very different, and according to Hindu religious belief, a more fundamental necessity: only sons can offer sustenance acceptable to the manes, and when the time comes, to one's own departed soul. Sons are hence essential for the spiritual salvation of believing Hindus.

The belief was evidently a source of anxious concern to all caste Hindus in Bengal, and, very probably to all Hindus. When his only son gave up the ancestral faith, the poet Michael Madhusudan Datta's father remarried so that he could have a son who would ensure the salvation of his soul.[4] The nationalist leader Bipin Pal's father also declared his intention to act in the same way when his only son became a Brahmo. The elder Pal explained in a deeply moving letter that the son he was about to cast out from his life was dearer to him than life itself because his own salvation and that of all his ancestors depended on him. As a Hindu he had no choice but to try and have another son so that he could repay the *pitririna*, a man's debt to his forefathers and ensure the salvation of his own soul.[5] Confirmation of this well-known concern comes from less elevated levels of society as well. We learn from the memoirs of a Brahmo lady that a prospective mother-in-law, a Hindu, confessed her fears of damnation if her son married outside the Hindu fold and thereby lost his right to offer water to her thirsty soul after her death.[6] The status of a wife in her husband's family as well as the larger kinship group depended crucially on her success in giving birth to sons. To the husband, the mother of his sons was a valued person, worthy of special respect. While polygamy was not very widely practiced, taking a second wife if the first had failed to give the husband a son surely had the approval of society. There are instances of such approval even in the most westernized sections of Bengali society.[7]

As the extended rather than the elementary family was modally the basic unit of social organization, values which helped sustain it dominated all social mores. Resonances of these values are to be found in the most sophisticated literary products of the period. Bankim's ideal heroine, Debi Chaudhurani, trained to live in the light of *Bhagavadgita*, returns to her polygamous husband and dastardly father-in-law after a career in patriotic banditry to work out her *karma* as a Hindu wife.[8] Tagore in one of his most sensitive literary essays describes Uma's initial failure to win the love of Siva when she appeared as an enchantress because such pleasure-oriented love was not conducive to the welfare of all (*sakaler mangal*).[9] A young girl was given in marriage to a family rather than an individual. Felicity for the large family unit rather than the individuals who got married was evidently the primary purpose of the institution. The ideal bride was one who earned the praise of her husband's extended family, the in-laws in particular. The husband is almost peripheral to the daily life of the young bride, as described in the nineteenth-century Bengali memoirs.[10]

If the wife had to accept her husband's family as her own and learn to subject her will to that of others, the relevant process of socialization had to begin early. Child marriage, with the bride no older than eight to ten, and under no circumstances after she had attained puberty, was a necessary concommittant of such a system. Marriage for girls at the age of one to four was not unknown. The brides in the earliest instances of widow remarriage, sponsored by modernizing reformers, were aged six to twelve.[11]

Fear of feminine sexuality and anxiety to control it were of course conscious motives behind the institution of child marriage. The cruder arguments in the debate on widow remarriage evoked the age-old belief in the greater lust of women—allegedly eight times as intense as that of men.[12] The belief system informed by patriarchal values emphasized the occult implications of uncontrolled female sexuality. An unchaste wife was supposed to be a source of endless misfortunes to her husband's family.[13] Child marriage was evidently meant to ensure that this highly disruptive force was contained within the bounds of legitimate conjugal relationship as soon as a young girl became aware of her sexual urge.

Male domination, an unquestioning surrender on part of the wife to her husband's authority, whatever his worth as a human being, is a clearly stated principle in *Manusmriti*, the most authoritative text on right conduct for Brahminical Hindus. Our nineteenth-century sources frequently project the norms of conjugal life as based on uninhibited patriarchy. The husband is a god on earth, the lord and master to whom the wife must offer unquestioning *bhakti*. These values, emphasized in the much revered *Manusmriti*, were supposed to be the bulwark of the Hindu family system down the ages. Such norms are, however, not conspicuous in the literature of mediaeval Bengal. A husband taking a second wife is shown to be anxious to mollify the first. A set passage in every *panchali* portrays the frustration of dissatisfied wives. A husband who is not good in bed is described with some scorn.[14] In the uninhibited love scenes in *Bidyasundar*, the most famous literary work from the eighteenth century, the heroine has better things to do than washing her husband's feet. The Sakta tradition with its emphasis on the worship of the mother goddess enjoined special respect for women. Rajnarayan Basu, generally critical of the received tradition, suggests that these norms had considerable impact on the followers of the cult. The folk tradition as reflected in the *bratas*, special rites performed by women, do underline the ideals of unquestioning devotion to the husband and patient submissiveness. These are however counterbalanced by feminine rituals meant to reduce the husband, through occult means, to the position of a bleating sheep meekly obeying the wife.

But when critics, indigenous or foreign, challenged established practice, nineteenth-century apologists of Hindu ways in Bengal projected patriarchy as the only acceptable principle in no uncertain terms: 'Women must be subject to the authority of men', wrote one author. Others stated the same sentiment in more guarded language.[15]

Maintenance and enhancement of ritual status through marriage was an aspiration somewhat peculiar to the Bengali Hindu tradition. The upper castes in Bengal were segmented horizontally into exogamous gotras or 'clans' descended from the same putative ancestor. There was also a hierarchy of ritual status determined according to the purity of one's lineage. Purity meant a record of correct ritual observance over generations. The most important criterion was the history of a family's marital exchanges. One's ritual status depended very heavily on the record of ritual purity of the families into which one's ancestors had married. Each of the three upper castes—Brahmins, Baidyas and Kayasthas—had their Kulins, families accorded the highest ritual status and hence much sought after in the marriage market. Among Brahmins, Kulinism produced an extreme form of hypergamy as marriage of their daughters to Kulin bridegrooms was an object of aspiration to all Brahmins.[16] It is not clear exactly when Kulin polygyny assumed its exaggerated form, but it was a fact of Bengali social life by the early years of the nineteenth century. For the poorer Kulins, marriage became a profession: the wives lived in their parental homes and the husbands visited their in-laws for a few days each year, if that, to collect their stipend. Kulinism was originally based on nine-fold criteria which included secular components like wealth, righteous conduct and scholarship as well. But a Kulin's status in the nineteenth century depended exclusively on his family's record of ritual purity. Since a Kulin girl could not marry a non-Kulin, they were often given in marriage to much younger or much older bridegrooms and often had to remain spinsters. Again, as marriage was an essential rite for a woman's salvation, even a nominal marriage to a dying man was preferable to spinsterhood. The anxiety to ensure that their daughters did not remain unmarried led to the custom of infant betrothal among a section of Brahmins.[17]

The social consequences of the beliefs and values enshrined in the institutions concerning marriage can be summed up as follows. Child marriage was universally practiced, except in the case of the Kulin women who might have to wait till very late in life until a groom with suitable ritual status had been found. Polygamy, widespread among the Kulins who constituted a small segment of caste Hindu society, does not appear to have been much in vogue among non-Kulins. Enforced widowhood, as is well-known, was mandatory for Bengali caste Hindus. The anxious concern of the reformers regarding the condition of the widows suggests not merely the sharpening of certain sensibilities, but the possibility that they accounted for a very large proportion of women of 'marriageable age'. One can only speculate if this was always so or a development of the eighteenth and nineteenth centuries. The reformist tracts refer to the impact of the law prohibiting *sati*, but the widows burnt on the funeral pyre do not appear to have been numerous enough at any time to affect the total number. The demographic factors responsible for this situation, if it did exist, have to be sought elsewhere. To conclude, the emotive affects of man-woman relationship were largely determined by the institutions I have described—child marriage, extended family households, enforced widowhood, Kulin polygamy and the associated phenomenon of enforced spinsterhood.

The flip side of the efforts to rigidly control feminine sexuality was extensive exploitation of women and surreptitious subversion of the norms on which the extended family was based. The contemporary sources are quite explicit on this point.[18]

The state and the church have played a central role in regulating marriage and sexual conduct in the west. The Indian experience is very different in this respect. Codes of social conduct were embodied in the *smriti* texts, and more crucially in *desachara*, i.e., traditional practice, known to and accepted by all concerned. They were enforced infrequently by caste councils or the village elders. But sanctions operated in less structured ways most of the time. The elders within the extended family, men as well as women, were the guardians of sexual morality and proper conjugal conduct. And watching over all one's actions was the eagle-eyed kinship group, the *jnatis* whose wrath could 'sever the wings of the god-bird Garuda himself'.[19] Sanctions could be harsh and involve loss of caste. These were inevitably harsher in the case of women who literally became homeless when punished for any real or supposed delinquency. As neither the husband's family nor the parents dared accept such unfortunates, prostitution or suicide were often the only alternatives open to them.[20]

II

Perhaps the most important institutional determinant of the emotional affects in matrimony was the age of the bride at marriage. The miseries of the child-bride are a recurrent theme in Bengali folklore. Most accounts of pre-puberty marriage written by women, however, open with tales of childish pleasure at the pomp and grandeur of the wedding ceremony. The gifts of costly jewellery and expensive sarees, the feast, music and illumination enchanted the child-brides who knew that all these pageantry were for their benefit, though the pleasure was mixed with vague apprehensions. Rassundari writes: 'Then I felt quite pleased; there will be the wedding, musicians will come, everybody will join in the joyous ululation. But I can not enumerate all the anxious thoughts which also crowded my mind. . . . I felt very scared and spent my days weeping all the time. . . . Everyone tried to comfort me, but no way would the misery in my heart go away.'[21] The real trauma came at the moment of departure from the parental home. Rassundari compares the state of her mind at the time to that of the sacrificial goat quaking with fear just before slaughter. Haimavati writes how the realization that she would indeed have to leave the parental home dawned on her and how she sought to avoid the calamity in desperate fear. Her ultimate hope that her father would help her out of her mortal danger proved to be futile. The memory of that excruciating misery remained with most women the rest of their lives. Rassundari despairing of any help from human beings asked her mother if God almighty would accompany her and was assured that he certainly would.[22]

Deep anxiety and a sense of helpless misery darkened the first experience of life in the in-law's home. Rassundari thus recalls her first few months in her husband's home more than half a century later: 'People keep birds in cages for their own amusement. I felt my predicament to be similar. I became a prisoner in that cage for the rest of my life; there was no hope of escape so long as I lived. . . . There was so much festivity, so many people . . . but I did not know any of them, so I began to cry. My heart was breaking.'[23]

Bengali nursery rhymes are full of references to the cruelty the brides suffered at the hands of the mother-in-law and sisters-in-law. Popular images of the child bride's life confirm that image of suffering. Exceptions to this pattern are, however, numerous in our sources. The people in Rassundari's new home were far from cruel. They assured her that this was indeed her own home, and the people her own people, but this did not stop her tears. Her mother-in-law took her in her lap. She felt she had found a new mother. She was treated with more kindness than she had known at home. But still for three months she wept all the time. Then, to quote her words, 'the bark of a tree from a far away place grew into the body of another plant. How strange, how mysterious, are the ways (of God).'[24]

This description is not untypical. Haimabati, married to an unmitigated scoundrel, found some solace in her mother-in-law's kindness. Prasannamayi, the daughter of a westernized zaminder and civilian, was gently protected from the unwelcome curiosity of the villagers who found her ways strangely alien. Kindness to a child-bride could assume spectacular forms. Poet Tagore's mother received from her princely father-in-law, Dwarkanath, toys studded with rubies and diamonds worth one hundred thousand rupees. Keshab Sen's mother, in describing her father-in-law's great affection for the child-bride also remembered his gifts of sweets and freshly minted coins.[25]

The institution of child marriage precluded sex before puberty in pre-modern times, at least in theory. The young couple went through a 'second wedding' after the wife had menstruated for the first time. The latter occasion had its appropriate ritual, '*pushpotsav*', the festival of flower, an occasion for saturnalian scenes out of bounds to men.[26] The rite of second wedding had apparently become relatively rare in the nineteenth century, though most child brides spent a year or more in the parental home before moving into the husband's home on a permanent basis. But there is nothing to suggest that sex before puberty did not occur or that it was in fact even frowned upon. A child bride, married at nine or even earlier, would often return to her husband's home before she had attained puberty.[27] By contrast, such restrictions appear to have been observed much more rigidly in Maharashtra though precocious boys did their best to get round them.[28] Haimabati Sen, in her account of her experiences as a medical practitioner, mentions one incident in which a bride aged eleven bled to death as a result of rape by her husband.

The data on the sexual side of conjugal relations within the traditional system of marriage as experienced and perceived by women are expectedly limited. We have, however, a graphic account in the memoirs of Haimabai Sen which were not meant for publication. She was not yet ten and her husband was forty-five. Her experiences were probably not atypical except that the age difference in her case was well above average though by no means exceptional. She writes: 'My elder sister-in-law used to take me to my husband's room. Whenever I fell asleep, somebody used to remove my clothes. I would feel scared on waking up and again wrap the clothes around my body.' On another occasion she screamed when her husband tried to pull her towards him and felt a great contempt for the man when he lied to his mother to cover up his misdemeanour. Later, a neighbour's mistress interceded on behalf of the husband. Haimabati, however, persisted in her uncomprehending refusal. Incomprehension, shame, fear and disgust rather than arousal marked her response to these first lessons in sex.

It is often stated that the child brides knew all about sex thanks to the obscene conversation in which women habitually indulged. The nineteenth-century Bengali memoirs provide little evidence in support of such statements.[29] To my knowledge, Haimabati's memoirs are the only account written by a Bengali woman which refers explicitly to matters sexual. She mentions that she once woke up and found her lecherous husband having sex with a prostitute. The incomprehensible scene sent her into a state of shock and she took months to recover from it. Rassundari's account of her childhood projects an image of total innocence verging on stupidity. If sex was a part of the child bride's marital experience before puberty, in all likelihood she learnt the relevant lessons from nature or a precocious husband. If she derived any pleasure from sex, we have no evidence for the fact. Rassundari in her memoir, however, recalls with joy and wonder how her body flowered and bore fruits through God's miraculous ways. It is not clear if this statement is *inter alia* a reference to a happy sex life.[30] Girish Bidyaratna's joyous account of sex in boyhood, referred to below—he was twelve and she eleven—implies that his partner shared his ecstasy. The fact that their difference in age was only one year suggests that the child bride may indeed have joined in the game with some enthusiasm.[31]

The husband, as already noted, is almost a peripheral figure in the memoirs written by Bengali women other than those whose life-style was changed considerably by new conditions of employment and who broke away from the extended family households. Prasan-namayi, who is known to have had a very unhappy marriage, hardly mentions her husband. Rassundri is conscious of the fact that she had been virtually silent about her husband in her memoir and makes up for it in a page-long encomium on his character and happy references to the occasions when he appreciated her life skills. Haimabati does write at length about her middle-aged first husband, but only with resentment and aversion. As is well-known, in an extended family household wives were not to talk to their husbands during day-time, especially in the presence of others. A modest wife drew her veil to cover her face when the husband or any of his older relations were around. Rassundari went to the illogical extreme: she shyly withdrew behind a door when her husband's horse walked into the courtyard.[32]

The polygamous home, by all accounts, was the abode of misery. A co-wife in feminine vocabulary was a thorn in one's side (*satin kanta*). The critics of polygamy underline the fact that the *bratas* performed by women had as one of their prime objectives deliverance from the danger of marriage to a polygamous husband. A famous satire describes the 'partition' of a husband's body, each of the man's two wives claiming a side as her sphere of influence. The misery of the Kulin wife who hardly ever saw her husband is a constant theme in the reformist literature.[33]

There is little by way of evidence regarding the experience of polygamy coming from women who had to endure it. One remarkable exception is the memoir or rather the reminiscences of Nistarini Debi, an aunt of the famous revolutionary, Upadhyaay Brahmabandhab. It throws an unusual light on the emotive affects of Kulin polygamy as experienced by women. She refers with contempt to her Kulin grandfather who had fifty-four wives, but describes her grandmother's first encounter with the man as follows: 'So long as her husband was there, she walked about near him, her veil properly drawn. It was as if she was trying to imprint the image of this handsome man on her mind the way one meditates on the image of one's deity.' The handsome man demanded his rightful stipend as a Kulin husband. The wife was delighted to give him her last ornaments, deeply obliged to have been of some use to her lord and master. Such spirit of selflessness is rarely encountered, Nistarini comments, among novel-reading modern girls. She also wrote approvingly of her father who agreed to marry a second time to satisfy his father's lust for money. 'Our husband is our God, he is all we have,' she concludes. When her husband, whom she had known only for a short while, died, she felt she had lost everything: one of her co-wives broke down totally when she was informed of the tragedy. This lady had not met her husband even once after the wedding.[34]

Tradition however did not prescribe only abject surrender to the husband's will. Dwarkanath Tagore's wife sought the opinion of pundits on her duty as a Brahmin when she learnt that her husband had broken the taboos regarding comensality by dining with Englishmen. Advised that she should not touch him but continue to perform her other duties as a wife, she lived accordingly the rest of her life.[35]

In a domestic world where there were strict rules of avoidance in relation to the male sex (there were important exceptions to this rule in practice, as noted below) the child wife's daily life was spent most of the time with other women in the family. Her happiness at this stage depended more on her relation with her husband's mother, sisters, female cousins, aunts etc., rather than with her husband. Such relationships could be marked by mutual tensions as well as affection. Haimabati recalled in her old age the kindness of her husband's cousins and nieces, as well as the constant nagging of his sister. She describes how one little girl who was not ill-disposed towards her, embarrassed her by broadcasting details of her gaucheries. Praphullamayi, a daughter-in-law of Debendranath Tagore, talks of the bonds of deep mutual affection among the women in the Tagore family. But she also records the history of tensions in her father's family—how her grandmother, pushed beyond endurance by her daughter-in-law, had induced Praphulla's father to take another wife and how one of Praphulla's sisters was driven to death by the cruelty she suffered in her husband's home. Dewan Kartikeya described how in an extended family wives constantly quarrelled if one of the brothers had a high income and the others were dependent on him.[36]

In a system under which a girl married into a family rather than simply another young person, her conjugal experience was indistinguishable from her experience of family life. In that context, her life passed through clearly marked stages, each with its specific duties, expectations and distinctive emotional colouring. The first few years after marriage were spent in the role of a new bride. As the first children were born and passed through their years of childhood, she matured into the role of a young wife eventually inheriting the role and status of the mistress of the family from the mother-in-law, if she happened to be married to the eldest son. With her sons grown up and married she gradually retired into the role of mother. Widowhood altered her status and condition of life. Rassundari writes of her widowhood, 'I had a golden crown on my head. That crown has fallen from my head.' As mentioned above, Nistarini, the wife of a polygamous Kulin who had lived with her husband only for a short period, records a similar feeling of desolation at the news of her husband's death. She only thanks her stars that she got the news in time so that she did not unwittingly violate the ritual taboos binding on widows. For Rassundari, however, the new situation which she compared to the life of a *sannyasin*, an ascetic, had its compensations. 'Now my name is mother', she commented. Her considered judgement on her life is very positive: 'I have spent my life happily and in great joy surrounded by husband, sons, daughters-in-law, other members of the family and neighbours.'[37] Arguably, her assessment of her life as a wife and a householder was not atypical, given a modicum of affluence. One remarkable feature of her self-assessment is that she considered her otherwise happy life as having been spent in bondage to others. The other memoirs written by nineteenth-century Bengali women are less articulate in their awareness of bondage.

Rassundari's happy assessment of her life as a wife and a householder has to be read with her description of back-breaking drudgery which was a central feature of that life. The rules of ritual purity imposed a heavy burden of domestic duty on the women in traditional families. Even the wives of very rich zamindars had to cook for the members of the extended family as well as the never-ending stream of house-guests. Saradasundari's mother-in-law, whom she describes as kind though short-tempered, insisted that the child-bride should polish the floors. Rassundari had twenty to twenty-five servants, but she had to cook for her husband, twelve children and the servants as well. She often fell asleep without any meal, having worked hard from early morning till late at night. She recalls these experiences in her old age with a measure of amusement rather than any resentment. She tells us how once she sat down to her first meal of the day long after midnight when the child on her lap pissed into her plate. She treats the episode as a playful dispensation of a somewhat naughty Divinity. Yet her only complaint against her fate was that in her days of youth women had no freedom, especially that they were excluded from education.[38]

References to the marital experiences in the memoirs written by men are much more frequent and often quite explicit. In general, they project an image of marital happiness. At times, the language evokes memories of great felicity. Nineteenth-century Bengali literature is replete with tales of childhood love. Girls grew up expecting to be married off by the age of twelve at the very latest. Medical evidence suggests that they reached puberty relatively early. The husband was usually an adolescent aged fourteen to eighteen. If we are to believe the record of men's memoirs, strong mutual attachment was not uncommon in these circumstances and the feelings described in some of the autobiographies are not very different from modern notions of romantic love. Sub-teenage love has become a familiar feature of the American social scene. One need not treat the Bengali experience in an earlier age with incredulity. Dewan Kartikeya writes convincingly of the intense emotional attachment which the wives felt for their husbands and the deep happiness the men of his generation derived from their marriage in childhood. In his opinion, their emotional security gave this system of marriage a distinct advantage over the uncertainties of courtship, English style. Pandit Girish Bidyaratna, who married at eleven a ten year old girl to whom he had been engaged since the age of one, wrote appreciatively of the fact that his wife had acquired an adequate amount of flesh by the time of marriage. He fell in love with this short-haired girl while returning home after the wedding. As they had to share a room with others during the first year of their marriage, opportunities for cohabitation were limited, though not altogether absent. Still, when he had to return to Calcutta after his weekend visits to the village home, he wept for days on end, so sharp were the pangs of separation. A couple of years later they had a room to themselves and made up for lost time. 'I have no words to describe the joy in which we spent our nights', he wrote, adding somewhat sadly, 'now at the age of seventy, . . . my life is bereft of all pleasure.' Girish Bidyaratna's uninhibited recollection of sexual pleasure has resonances of a very ancient Indian tradition—a delight in the pleasures of the body without any sense of shame. Victorian critics of Indian society saw this attitude as degenerate lechery.[39] That description, like other pejoratives used by Macaulay and friends, were accepted as valid by most Western educated Bengalis. The fact had interesting consequences for their psyche which I shall discuss later.

It needs to be noted that all men did not share Girish or Kartikeya's romantic and passionate view of matrimony. Prasannamayi mentions the advice given by an uncle to his doctor nephew devastated by the death of his wife: 'Why all this lamentation? A wife is no more than a pair of slippers. You have lost one pair; I shall get you an even better one.'

It is difficult to reconstruct the history of deviations from the approved norms of sexual behaviour in any society, because such activities are necessarily clandestine. The 'traditional' norms in Bengali Hindu society permitted a degree of tolerance, at least so far as men were concerned. Hypocrisy, our sources point out, was not a characteristic vice of the traditional society. People did not think too badly of extra-marital sexual indulgence, though Brahminical ideals put a high premium on the control of one's instinctive drives. Men who lived by such ideals were also not uncommon.[40]

At the same time Tantricism and certain other religious cults had mystical rites based on sexual practices as essential parts of their mystical regimes. *Bhairavi chakras*, in which Tantric practitioners participated with their female partners was common enough in some parts of Bengal. New sects like the *Kartabhajas* had emerged in the late-eighteenth or early-nineteenth century. Some of these flourished as classless freemasonries and their practices had strong sexual overtones. Vaishnav gurus, it is alleged, at times emulated Lord Krishna in their dealings with their female disciples.[41]

More secular deviations from the approved norms of sexual conduct were of course not unknown. The wealthy had in their service professional dancers and singers who would sometimes perform in transparent attire and even very sober men would not hesitate to join them on the dancing floor.[42]

Immorality had more surreptitious outlets as well. The Bengali counterparts of penny dreadfuls rejoiced in accounts of illicit relationships within the extended family. Haimabati Sen's unpublished memoir provides a number of actual instances of such deviant behaviour. The great Vidyasagar himself in his campaign for the legalization of widow remarriage cited the exploitation of hapless widows by male members of the family as one of his arguments. The *Tatvabodhini Patrika* wrote: 'Even married women were attracted towards devious ways by the example of widows who had been corrupted. . . . In truth, as a household contains very large number of people—brothers, nephews etc. and generations of women are cooped up in the zenana, horrendously immoral acts, worse than prostitution, do occur. The combination of circumstances cited are no doubt strong influences contributing to adultery between persons belonging to prohibited degrees.' Kulin women who remained spinsters or had only nominal marriages were similarly exploited. Children were born fairly frequently to wives of polygamous husbands who never visited their wives. Abortion was cited as a widespread social evil by reformers who wanted to legalize widow remarriage and abolish polygamy. Women who strayed from the straight and narrow often ended up in the brothels of Calcutta or Benares.[43]

But the evidence suggests that connivance must have been at least as common as punishment, partly because the extended family feared that scandal would affect their ritual status as well as secular standing. Vidyasagar mentions almost institutionalized arrangements to legitimize conception when a Kulin wife had no contact with her polygamous husband.[44] Haimabati records one incident in which the mother-in-law intervened to stop the public humiliation of her daughter-in-law caught *in flagrante* with her lover. The informality of the mechanisms for imposing social sanctions permitted a measure of laxity. Sanctions usually operated in an insidious way. Women had to watch their steps very carefully in the in-laws' home or risk a great deal of niggling mental cruelty. It was more often inflicted by other women in the family than by the men. More extreme sanctions appear to have been relatively rare, because the internalized values were the most effective means of control and, for reasons stated above, the enforcers had good reasons for condoning delinquency. It is also necessary to emphasize that deviation in all probability was precisely what the term implies and not modal behaviour in any sense.

One form of sexual activity was considered unmentionable in Bengali culture. Our sources are conspicuously silent on the theme of homosexuality. Explicit references to the practice are however not entirely absent. Radhakanta Dev's famous letter which led to Derozio's dismissal from Hindu College accused some teachers of the college of connivance at various misdeeds including sodomy. A manuscript diary, written by Kaminikumar Datta, the younger brother of Aswini Kumar Datta, refers explicitly to a homosexual affair. Other memoirs talk vaguely of immorality among young people in rural areas. Since their access to the fair sex was limited, the immorality in question very probably subsumed homosexuality.

III

The norms, mores and deviations, I have described so far probably represent long-established patterns of social behaviour, though my account is based on nineteenth-century evidence. Very probably, such social behaviour and associated affects were also modal in the nineteenth century though the impressionistic evidence available is not adequate for any sort of quantification. Changes traceable to various facets of the colonial encounter began to modify the attitudes, conduct, and the emotive affects associated with man–woman relationships first among small groups of people. The modalities, so far as one can judge, changed very slowly though sharp and sudden discontinuity marked the lives of a handful of men and women.

Expectedly, the first indications of basic change in attitudes affecting even the most intimate concerns are to be found in the life history of the students of the Hindu College. Or perhaps one should go a bit further back in time. Bishop Heber has recorded the responses of Raja Radhakanta Deb, the highly conservative leader of Hindu society to the presence of European ladies at the Bishop's reception. While the Raja would not dream of emulating this example, he expressed his appreciation of the way in which such civilized mingling of the sexes enhanced the quality of life. The first generation of Hindu College students boisterously defied all taboos on food and drink during their student days but later only a few deviated in practice from the inherited way of life, though the faith in its worth and validity had been badly shaken by the exposure to the rationalist thought of the enlightenment.

A small number did match their thoughts with appropriate action. K.M. Banerji left the Hindu fold. Dakshinaranjan Mukherji defied social norms to court and marry the widowed maharani of Burdwan, an adventure which nearly cost him his life. The poet Madhusudan found it impossible to marry the little girl his parents had selected for him. His reaction to the proposal as stated in a letter to his friend, Gourdas Basak reflects the new sensibility: 'It harrows up my blood and makes my hair stand like quills on the fretful porcupine.' His quest for an acceptable partner ended in his two successive marriages to European ladies.[45]

But the vast majority of the newly educated were content to adhere to inherited practices. Even the members of the highly enlightened Tagore family, including the poet, accepted, without fuss the sub-teenage brides selected for them by the elders, often from relatively poor families because their low caste status among Brahmins and unorthodox ways were barriers to suitable marriage alliances. As one member of the family, Satyendranath's daughter, Indira Devi points out, the cultural and social gap did not stand in the way of marital happiness. Nor did the fact that the wives were mere children at the time of marriage. Rabindranath Tagore's poems in memory of his wife, *Smaran* (In Memoriam) bear witness to an intense and passionate love.[46]

Rational scepticism was not the only factor which induced a rejection of tradition. The educated Bengalis' confidence in their own culture was badly shaken by their new rulers' continual criticism of Indian society and religion. The racial stereotypes integral to these ethnocentric assessments pictured the Bengalis as an effiminate and degenerate race. Though such judgements were questioned from time to time, educated Bengalis appear to have accepted them by and large. Even the defenders of the Hindu tradition wrote of a glorious past and a degenerate present while prescribing agendas for recovery. References to the powerful English and weak Bengalis were an integral part of the nationalist discourse. Even an old-fashioned pandit like Girish Bidyaratna tried to explain the alleged physical degeneration of Bengalis. He traced it to the 'immature' semen of adolescent fathers, an unfortunate feature of child marriage. The loss of cultural self-confidence had reached such depths that even a patriot like Rajnarayan Basu was hesitant to admit to an Anglicized host that he missed his habitual supply of mustard oil lest his friend should consider him an unreformed Bengali.[47]

A belief in the superiority of English ways was the other side of this lack of confidence. That the said ways were superior was not to be questioned because the English themselves said that they were. Such simple faith eventually produced a backlash, but it was long in vogue and some never lost it. It was projected in sober terms by sophisticated trend-setters like Satyen Tagore. Keshab Sen preached it in his grand rhetorical style for he was 'overwhelmed by the charms of English family life'. Even a passionate patriot like Bankim Chattopadhyay proclaimed that the Bengalis' salvation lay in the imitation of all that is good in English culture, because the less civilized had always progressed by imitating those who were more advanced.[48]

The agenda for social reform in nineteenth-century Bengal derived partly from a mood of introspection informed by new sensibilities, the end product of complex interaction with western culture as well as a profound sense of inferiority, itself a product of that interaction. Rammohan's plea for abolition of *sati* or Vidyasagar's campaign in favour of widow remarriage were not simply attempts to emulate western mores. The encounter had triggered off processes, especially a serious if at times anguished mood of introspection, which induced a basic reorientation of attitudes. These attitudes were no mere clones of their western counterparts. A mixture of rational considerations, a genuine concern not to overstep scriptural prescriptions and an intense emotionalism—which reminds one of the sixteenth-century Vaishnava anxiety for the salvation of all human beings—informs the discourse on social reform in nineteenth-century Bengal. An awareness of inequities in one's immediate social environment was integral to this new orientation, though it was mostly confined to matters affecting one's own class. The sense of inadequacy generated by colonial rule and sensitiveness to western criticism aggravated the resulting anxieties. The preoccupation with issues like widow remarriage, polygamy, child marriage and women's education, areas of social life which were distressing in terms of the new sensibilities, has to be understood in this context.

It has been suggested that western romantic literature had a major impact not merely on aesthetic sensibilities of the western educated Bengalis, but on their expectations from life, especially in the area of relationship between men and women. Bankim wrote that every college student in Bengal knew by heart the balcony scene in Romeo and Juliet. The yearning for romantic love, allegedly the product of such literay studies, apparently could not be satisfied within the institutional framework of child marriage and the extended family.[49]

I have cited evidence which indicate that child marriage did not preclude romantic attachment and the taboos inhibiting free communication between husband and wife could stimulate rather than stifle the yearning for love. New job opportunities in the colonial bureaucracy away from home induced young men to get their wives to join them, and there was a dramatic change in the ambience of family life. Conjugal relations, informed by new sensibilities and at last free from the taboos which had to be observed under the authority of the elders, assumed an altogether new character. The wife of a young Deputy Magistrate described the happiness of her peer group as follows: 'Besides they were very much in love with us, willing to lay down their lives if we so wished. . . . How could women who had such husbands at their feet be unhappy?'[50] This lady's husband accused her of cruelty if she failed to write to him regularly. He habitually addressed her as 'my dear' and she writes how she waited eagerly for his return when he went on tours.

The Brahmo enthusiasts and preachers introduced a new dimension in their marriages. The wife was expected to be their true companions in faith and support them in times of trial.[51] The wives often lived up to such expectations. The educated husband now frequently appeared in the role of a teacher. Manuals were written to help husbands with the task of educating their wives. In one of the more popular manuals, written in the form of dialogues, the husband expresses the hope that the wife will surpass him in learning.[52] The oft-repeated argument that women had to be educated so that they could be fit companions of their educated husbands was evidently not the only conscious motive behind the male initiative to educate their wives. There was a prolonged debate on what was appropriate education for women. While the centrist position on this emphasized education which would help women perform their duties efficiently as wife and mother plus an elementary knowledge of the world to broaden their minds and cure superstition, a more egalitarian approach was not unknown. Ramesh Dutt in his comments on the condition of women in England observed that the only way women could be truly free and equal of men was to open all careers to them.[53] Kailasbasini, whose pride in her husband's love for her has been cited above, showed a will of her own in refusing to give up the traditional Hindu practices, for while she had accepted her husband's spiritual beliefs, she would not do anything to risk her connections with their network of relations.[54]

Purdah also became a major issue. A change in social mores in this regard had profound implications for relationship between men and women. Satyen Tagore created a sensation by taking his wife out in an open carriage. When the other ladies of the Tagore household followed this example, Calcutta society treated the matter as a great scandal. But before long other Brahmos also defied the seclusion taboos. The often transparent sarees they wore at home was considered indecorous by their men and there were curious experiments with hybrid semi-western styles until the Parsee style saree introduced by Mrs Satyen Tagore set the fashion. The issue of women appearing in public caused great controversy. Even the reformer Keshab was not willing to see them at his meetings sitting outside the screen provided for them. More radical Brahmos finally broke the taboo. There was a prolonged debate in the pages of the periodical *Somprakash* on the question and freedom without liberal education was considered dangerous for the women's morals. A correspondent signing herself as 'a chaste wife' asked if one should first learn to swim before getting into water. Sibnath Sastri's autobiography provides plentiful evidence of free mixing between men and women among the Brahmos. Nabin Sen's memoirs also project similar patterns of social conduct among the government functionaries in the district and subdivisional towns of Bengal. Dewan Kartikeya records how this new freedom of social intercourse transformed the quality of life for the men and women of his generation.[55]

One logical consequence of the altered expectations from conjugal relationship was the quest for consensual marriage. The Brahmos led the way in this matter as in many other areas of social life. Consent however had little meaning so long as the custom of child marriage persisted. The custom had come under attack even from people who did not believe in consensual marriage. Western critics described it as barbaric and the criticism appears to have struck home. Besides, many features of the system, especially motherhood at a very early age, were seen to be cruel and socially dysfunctional. The agenda for national reconstruction rejected child marriage on the ground that the system produced unhealthy children, destroyed all buoyancy by burdening men with the responsibilities of family too early in life and generally contributed to national degeneration.[56] We do not have the statistics on the upward trend, if any, in the average age of marriage in Bengal. But change in this respect appears to have been very slow except among the Brahmos and, very probably, the average age at marriage for girls was under twelve as late as the 1920s.

Changes in attitudes as well as economic conditions gradually undermined the ideological basis of the extended family. Here too western criticisms and the general sense of inadequacy which prompted continual comparisons with English ways induced a belief that the system undermined initiative and was hence a factor in the alleged social degeneration of Bengalis.[57] An offshoot of this critical attitude was the notion that a man should not marry before he was economically independent. Those who married widows, under the authority of the new law and very rarely with parental consent, usually had to live up to this new norm.[58] But a general movement in this direction depended of course on the average age at marriage. As the modernizers were also opposed to great difference in age between husband and wife, economically independent husbands were a rarity so long as the bride was a girl of twelve to fourteen.

The Brahmos, as already noted, were the first to introduce a form of consensual marriage. Here too the initiative was taken by the elders and there was little courtship with or without chaperones. Only, the would-be husband was introduced to the girl and after the two had talked for a while the elders asked both parties if they were willing to go ahead with the marriage. The engaged couple had opportunities of meeting after this and there were instances both in fiction and real life where the girls exercised their freedom to break off the engagement. As modernizing families ceased to observe strict segregation of women, the parties to consensual marriage sometimes knew each other before marriage was actually suggested.[59] But consensual marriage was by no means universal in any section of Bengali society. As already noted, even in the trend-setting Tagore family parents continued to choose spouses for their children who had little say in such matters. The emphasis on consent had unusual expressions among the ideologues of the Brahmo Samaj. Sibnath Sastri, forced into a bigamous marriage by his father, later tried to induce his second wife to divorce and remarry. She firmly refused. Durgamohan

Das arranged a remarriage for his widowed step-mother aged four-teen.[60]

Romantic love is a pervasive theme in Bengali literature from the early eighteen-sixties onwards. The Calcutta stage projected it to enthusiastic audiences and Bankim wrote of it in a way which made it credible in the context of contemporary experience. This was not to the liking of the more conservation elements who accused him of corrupting the youth with his tales of love and war.[61] Brahmo ethos with its strong overtones of Victorian puritanism, as also the tradi-tional emphasis on the elders' right to choose spouses for the young confirmed such attitudes. Even the enthusiastic readers of Bankim treated love in real life either as an irrelevant joke or a form of deviant behaviour.

The biographical literature does provide a few instances of romance leading to marriage. Some of the early rebels against establ-ished social mores like Michael, Dakshinaranjan and Gyanendra-mohan Tagore courted the ladies whom they eventually married. The poet Nabin Sen, who was in the habit of falling in love repeatedly from a very early age, did manage by a cleverly planted suicide threat to get his father to secure for him the bride he wanted. But this ro-mantic alliance was so unusual that the city of Dacca where the bride lived was filled with hair-raising tales of the couple's death-defying love for each other.[62] Incidentally, the heroine was aged ten at the time of marriage and the choice was his rather than hers. The younger generation of the Tagore family had some experience of courting. Indira Devi writing in her old age recalled that she did re-ceive romantic attention. One forelorn lover would come and stand under a tree in front of her house every day hoping to catch a glimpse of the fair lady. This devotion inspired one of Tagore's better known songs—*pratidina hai* etc (everyday he comes and leaves in vain). Indira had a prolonged correspondence with her future husband.[63] Her cousin, Sarala Debi, had enough admirers to inspire her to write a satire, *Premik Sabha* (The Association of Lovers).[64] We also have glimpses of romantic love in humbler levels of society. A Brahmo missionary wrote that when he decided to get married he could only think of the melancholy face of his friend's widowed sister, the girl he eventually married.[65] But courtship or romantic love preceding marriage was very much the exception to the modal pattern of behaviour.

Romantic love appears to have flourished more after marriage than as a pre-maritial emotional experience leading to happy union. There is plentiful evidence to prove that a new intensity of emotion in conjugal relationship for which there is little precedent in the pre-modern past was now a part of the *bhadralok's* life experience. The greater intimacy made possible by the hosuehold set-up of the bureaucrats and professionals in urban and suburban areas, new sensibilities generated by a complex set of circumstances and the expectations informed by exposure to romantic literature, western and Indian, all contributed to an ambience of romance in marriage. Kailasbasini's not very literate diary, Jnanendranath Das's epistles to his dead wife interspersed with the letters they had actually exchanged, the strange tale of B.C. Roy's parents' painful aspiration towards spiritual love unpolluted by physical desire (of which more later), Bankim's descriptions of playful to intense attachment and his confession of his immense debt to his wife are all parts of a vast body of available documentation bearing on a new feeling for one's partner in marriage.[66]

Yet the age of the bride at marriage was seldom above twelve. The fact does not appear to have been a serious barrier to romantic feeling in men. The civilian and historian R.C. Dutt who deplored the limitations to women's freedom in England and was in favour of all careers being opened to women, saw nothing incongruous in projecting a girl of thirteen or twelve as the beautiful heroine of a novel based on contemporary life. The Brahmo leader,[67] Bijaykrishna Goswami recalled his conjugal life with his five year old wife who would lie down on his book to stop him from reading so that she might have his full attention. The adjustment of emotions and expectations to the realities of inherited social practice against which few revolted gave an unusual colouring to the affects of marital life.

Beyond reasonable doubt, the new sensibilities sharpened by romantic literature stimulated a yearning for romantic love, especially in young men. It seems unlikely that such expectations were always matched by the experience of conjugal life. The poet Nabin Sen writes very openly of his frustrations, though as a modern young man he had insisted successfully on having a say in the choice of his bride. The discourse on women's education underlines the cultural gap between the college educated husbands and their often illiterate wives. The failure of communication often led, we are told, young men to seek the company of prostitutes.[68] The argument seems somewhat specious because the prostitutes were not culturally or educationally superior to the housewives. The impetus behind the male initiative for women's education came largely from their desire for better communication with their wives. The frustrated lover, in and out of marriage, is a central figure in Bengali fiction of the late-nineteenth and early-twentieth centuries. Their portraits are understandably more convincing than those of the successful hero.

The biographical literature contains hints of extra-marital love and at times hard data. As access to women unrelated to one other than courtesans was strictly limited, romantic attachments as much as illicit relationships did develop within the extended family. Dewan Kartikeya writes of his platonic love for a lady who was evidently a married relation. He also records his sense of revulsion when the object of love sought a full-fledged affair. Nabin Sen, a narcissistic braggart, mentions several extramarital affairs in his autobiography. He also describes one grand passion and how he asked his eldest son to place his beloved's farewell letter on his funeral pyre. The new sensibility is evident in all references to such relationships. Kartikeya writes with deep sympathy of the love of a young prostitute which he did not reciprocate. 'Her life may be polluted but her love was not'. The famous actress Binodini speaks very openly of her life as a kept woman but also asks in a spirit of bitter defiance if society was not responsible for the life she had been forced to choose.[69]

A depressing feature of the new sensibility was a mood of morbid introspection focussed on sexuality. There is nothing in the tradition which suggests that sexuality itself was ever considered an evil or that people spent a great deal of time brooding over the sinfulness of their sexual fantasies. Brahmos, influenced by the Christian doctrine of sin, appear to have been obsessed with notions of purity in such matters. Keeping diaries in which young people confessed their sinful thoughts became a popular habit.[70] A thirteen year old boy wrote in his diary, 'This wretched person is a slave to his passions'.[71] Ramkrishna's famous disciple Ramchandra Datta described how his sinful mind phantasized on sex with the women he met. The poet Krishnachandra Majumdar confessed that such obsessive thoughts which he tried to fight by thinking of his mother eventually stimulated sexual fantasies about his mother herself.[72]

Colonial rule had created centres of administration where the functionaries often had to live as single men. Prostitution flourished in the small towns and of course Calcutta, a boom city in the earlier half of the nineteenth century, when men, we are told, met socially in brothels. The hetaeira tradition of northern India found a new market in Calcutta.[73] The reformers' effort at purifying such evils partly explains the repressive attitudes.

Not illogically, the new puritans drew upon old ascetic ideals. Haimbati's husband declared to his newly married wife that he had taken a vow of celibacy for six months. He eventually fathered six children. Dr B.C. Roy's parents did adopt successfully the vow of celibacy after they had produced several children. Prakash Ray mentions in their 'joint memoir' how they transformed a practical necessity, contraception, into a spiritual quest for platonic love. They kissed one last time, uttering Satyam, Truth with a capital T, and vowed not to touch each other again below the neck. The decision nearly broke the wife's heart. Eventually when she went to Lucknow for higher education, the two tested their love by stopping all mutual communication. When spiritual love finally triumphed, they celebrated a spiritual wedding, the wife bedecked as a Buddhist nun, her head duly shaven. The assembled Brahmo brothers and sisters applauded this supreme triumph in ecstatic joy.[74] I have suggested above that the new Indian sensibilities were no clone of their western counterparts and had no precedents in the Indian tradition. The evidence just cited, though somewhat extreme, perhaps proves my point.

Politics does not often influence the love life of mankind in general, but the colonial context produced curious interactions. Bankim in his *Anandamath* had conjured up a story of patriots living as ascetics to liberate the motherland. One of the protagonists, a married man, was joined by his wife in male attire but the vow of celibacy was not to be broken until the motherland had been liberated. In fact both achieved martyrdom on the field of glory. This fictional account provided role for the early revolutionaries like Brahmabandhab. As Nirad Chaudhuri points out, even men of his generation perceived a conflict between the demands of love and service to one's country.[75] Vivekananda called upon young men and women to serve the nation as a band of ascetics. He was partly influenced no doubt by the Christian missionary example, but a belief in the irreconcilability of patriotic dedication and happy family life was a factor in his preference presumably because the demands of the family would be a serious distraction.

But something more than practical necessity was at stake in these prescriptions. He and his fellow mystics were all initiated into celibacy by their master, Ramakrishna who perceived sex and spiritual regimes as mutually irreconcilable, even though the tradition saw no necessary conflict between the two. Celibacy, *brahmacharya*, as one possible precondition for the mystical quest is no doubt a part of the Hindu tradition. But the nineteenth-century Bengali discourse on national reconstruction based on the reconstructed individual, standing strong and pure, ready like a sharpened sword to serve the nation, emphasized celibacy as a value in itself and as a means towards achievement of spiritual, moral and physical strength. The story of Vivekananda's early life reflects this concern.[76] It was a concern which appears to have been widely shared by the idealistic young in the latter years of the nineteenth century. An old prescription meant for those seeking *brahmopalavdhi*, realization of Brahman, now served mostly secular purposes. It was now expected to bolster up the insecure ego of colonial youth convinced of their degeneration and weakness of body and mind.

Emotions considered appropriate in a given context are not necessarily a part of people's actual experience. However, to educated Bengalis the notion that they rose above the humiliations of political subjection in the serene and transcendent experience of their love life became a part of their articulated ideology. The family as haven acquired a new meaning in the colonial context. The idea was expressed very powerfully in the introductory part of Tagore's famous *Premer Abhishek* (Love's Anointing).[77] Given below is a very free and inept translation of some of the relevant lines:

Why talk, my beloved, of all the insults, the misery of life in the world outside?
A small man am I, my master, a foreigner, an Englishman
Barks out his harsh commands from on high.
He does not know my language,
To him, my misery means nothing
But listen my master,
Here, sheltered in my private heaven,
I am the king.
Oh my love, I am blessed,
Blessed that my soul is filled with your love.
You have made me king.
On my head you have placed the crown of glory.

Were such sentiments a part of middle class Bengali consciousness? Nirad Chaudhuri, born in 1897, and an uncompromising admirer of British rule in India, assures us that they were.[78]

NOTES

1. For a discussion of the relevant historiographical ideas, see Lawrence Stone, *The Past and the Present Revisited*, Routledge and Kegan Paul (London and New York, 1987), chs 18 and 19.

2. See Ghulam Murshid, *Reluctant Debutante: Response of Bengali Women to Modernization, 1849–1905*, Sahitya Samsad, Rajshahi University (Rajshahi, 2nd impression, 1983); Meredith Borthwick, *The Changing Role of Women in Bengal 1849–1905*, Princeton University Press (Princeton, 1984); Dipesh Chakraborty, 'The Difference–Deferral of Colonial Modernity: Public Debates on Domesticity in British Bengal'; Tanika Sarkar, 'A Book of Her Own: Autobiography of a Nineteenth-century Woman', *History Workshop Journal*, 36, 1993.

3. A major exception is Nirad Chaudhuri's brilliant literary study, *Bangali jibane ramani* (Women in Bengali Life) (Mitra o Ghosh, Calcutta, 3rd impression, Bengali year 1378 [1971]).

4. See Jogindranath Basu, *Michael Madhusudan Datter Jibancharit*, Sukhamay Mukhopadhyay (ed.) (Ashok Pustakalay, Calcutta, 1978), 6–7.

5. Bipin Pal, *Sattar Batsar* (Calcutta, Bengali year 1362 [1957]), 226–30.

6. This informations as well as a number of others cited in this paper occur in a manuscript memoir written by one Haimabati Sen. Born around 1866, married at the age of nine and widowed the following year, Haimabati or Hem later remarried and trained herself to practice as a medical licentiate. This remarkable memoir is unique in its detailed account of domestic life in nineteenth-century Bengal. The manuscript was discovered by Geraldine Forbes. Professor Forbes and I have prepared an annotated English translation of this memoir which is now in press.

7. Prasannamayi Debi, daughter and sister of civilians and educated at home by an English governess records with approval the action of a zamindar's daughter who prevailed on her father to take a second wife because her own mother had failed to produce a son and heir. See Prasannamayi Devi, *Purba Katha* (Reminiscence) (Subarnarekha, Calcutta, 1982).

8. See Bankimchandra Chattopadhyay, *Debi Chaudhurani*, concluding chapter.

9. Rabindranath Tagore, *Prachin Sahitya, Rabindra-rachanabali*, 5 (Calcutta, Bengali year 1392 [1985]), 514–15.

10. A remarkable instance of such marginalization is found in the earliest memoir written by a Bengali lady, Rassundari Debi, discussed in several contexts below. See Rassundari Debi, *Amar Jiban* (My Life), in Nareshchandra Jana *et al.* (eds), *Atmakatha* (Autobiographies), vol. 1 (Ananya Prakashan, Calcutta 1981).

11. See Binay Ghosh, editor, *Samayikpatre Banglar Samajchitra* (Picture of

Bengali Society in Periodicals), vol. 4, *Tatvabodhini Patrika* (Theological Journal), 201, 206–7.

12. Ibid., 160.

13. For a detailed discussion of these beliefs in mediaeval Bengal, see T. Raychaudhuri, *Bengal under Akbar and Jahangir: An Introductory Study in Social History* (2nd edition, Munshiram Manoharlal, Delhi, 1969), Introduction.

14. See Raychaudhuri, *Bengal under Akbar and Jahangir*, Introduction.

15. Satyacharan Mitra who declared himself to be a propagator of Hinduism quoted an anonymous author on the frontispiece of his highly popular tract, *Strir Prati Swamir Upadesh* (Advice from a husband to his wife): 'be handsome or ugly, energetic or lacking in spirit, a husband is entitled to the unquestioning devotion of a chaste wife. This is the true meaning of chastity for a chaste wife.' Further down on the same page he quotes the reformer Keshab Sen: 'The flowers which God has created for men are not for you; again, the flowers which have blossomed for you in heaven are not for men.'

16. There is a large body of literature on Kulin polygamy produced by the reformist critics of the system in the nineteenth century. Ramnarayan Tarkaratna's satirical play, *Kulin Kulasarbasva Natak* (Calcutta, 1854) is perhaps the best known literary work on the subject. Also see Iswarchandra Vidyasagar's tract on polygamy, *Bahubibaha*, in his collected works, Tirthapati Datta (ed.), *Vidyasagar Rachanavali*, Tulikalam (Calcutta, 1987), 873–1088.

17. See Girishchandra Bidyaratna, *Balyajiban* (Swayam Likhita) (Boyhood Days, Written by Himself), 8, in Nareshchandra Jana *et al.* (eds), *Atmakatha*, vol. 1.

18. See for instance, Vidyasagar, *Bidhababibaha Bishayak Prastab*, in *Rachanabali*, 706.

19. See Raychaudhuri, *Bengal under Akbar and Jahangir*, Introduction.

20. See Ghosh, *Samayikpatre Banglar Samajchitra*, vol. 4, 178. The once popular 'penny dreadful', Bhubanchandra Mukhopadhyay, *Haridaser Guptakatha* (first published 1897) (Bishwabani Prakashani, Calcutta, 1987) contains numerous incidents in which women are forced to leave their homes. The doyen of Bengali literary studies, late Sukumar Sen, believed that this novel provided the most authentic description of nineteenth-century Bengali society.

21. Rassundari, 15.

22. Haimavati, married at the age of nine, recalled her trauma when she wrote her memoirs in her seventies. Also Rassundri, 15–16.

23. Rassundari, 17.

24. Ibid., 18.

25. Prasannamayi describes her predicament owing to her 'education' (the fact that she could read) and western-style clothes which earned her

the title of *'mem bau'* (European bride) and how her mother-in-law defended her against such calumny. See her *Purbakatha,* 44. Also See Debi Saradasundari, *Atmakatha,* 8, 9 in N. Jana *et al.* (eds), *Atmakatha,* vol. 1 and Praphullamayi Debi, *Amader Katha* (Our Story), in Somendranath Basu (ed.), *Smritikatha,* Baitanik Prakashani (Calcutta, 1986), 26.

26. One text refers quite casually to the practice of dancing in the nude during this ritual. See Satyacharan Mitra, *Strir prati swamir upadesh,* 5.

27. See for instance, Saradasundari, *Atmakatha,* 8.

28. See Harinarayan Apte's famous Marathi novel, *Pan Lakshyant Kon Gheto,* Bengali translation by S. Kamtanurkar, *Kintu Ke Khabar Rakhe* (New Delhi, 1971), 243f, 249f.

29. Dr Tanika Sarkar, who has recently interviewed a number of Bengali ladies to collect data concerning their life experience, was told by one octogenerian that the first time she saw her husband without clothes she thought that the unfortunate youth was endowed with a tail.

30. Rassundari, 44.

31. Girishchandra Bidyaratna, *Balyajiban,* 16.

32. Rassundari, 33, 57–9. Nistarini Debi, *Sekele Katha,* 27 in N. Jana *et al.* (eds), *Atmakatha,* vol. 2.

33. See Vidyasagar, *Bahubibaha,* in *Rachanabali,* 866; Dinabandhu Mitra, *Sadhabar Ekadasi* (Calcutta, 1866).

34. Nistarini Debi, 8, 11, 19, 21, 29.

35. Kshitindranath Thakur, *Dwarakanath Thakurer Jibani* (Calcutta, Bengali year 1376 [1969]), 74–5.

36. Praphullamayi Debi, *Amader Katha,* in Somendranath Basu (ed.), *Smritikatha,* 26–8. Kartikeyachandra Ray, *Atmajibancharit,* 24–5 in N. Jana *et al.* (eds), *Atmakatha,* vol. 1.

37. Rassundari, 34, 35. Nistarini Debi, 29.

38. See Prasannamayi Debi, 7, 30; Rassundari, 24–6; Saradasundari, 8.

39. Kartikeyachandra Ray, *Atma-jibancharit,* 47, in *Atmakatha,* vol. 1; Girishchandra Bidyaratna, *Balyajiban,* 12, 14, 16.

40. See Bankimchandra Chattopadhyay, *Kabibar Iswarchandra Gupter Jibani o Kabitwa* (The life and poetical genius of the poet Iswarchandra Gupta); Iswarchandra Vidyasagar describes in his autobiographical sketch the high Brahminical ideals by which his forefathers lived. See his *Vidyasagar Charit,* in *Vidyasagar Rachanavali,* 408.

41. See Kartikeyachandra Ray, 73, 74; Mahendranath Datta, *Srimad Vivekananda Swamir Jibaner Ghatanabali;* Akshaykumar Datta, *Bharatiya Upasak Sampraday* (first published 1870, 1883; new edn., Calcutta, Bengali year 1394 [1987]), 220–8.

42. Kartikeyachandra Ray, 83.

43. See Vidyasagar, *Bahubibaha,* in *Rachanabali,* 866–7; Binay Ghosh (ed.), *Samayik Patre Banglar Samajchitra,* vol. 4, 160–1; Bhubanchandra Mukhopadhyay, *Haridaser Guptakatha,* 143.

44. Vidyasagar, *Bahubibaha, Rachanabali,* 866–7.
45. See *Samayik Patre Banglar Samajchitra,* vol. 4, 209; Jogindranath Basu, *Michael Madhusudan Datter Jibancharit,* 92–7; Manmathanath Ghosh, *Raja Dakshinaranjan Mukhopadhyayer Jibancharit* (first published, 1917, new edn., Calcutta, 1982), 37–44.
46. Indira Debi, *Jiban-katha,* in *Ekshan,* 19 and 20 (Bengali years 1399, 1400); Rabindranath Tagore, *Smaran,* in *Rabindra-Rachanabali,* 8, 7th Reprint (Calcutta, 1977), 59–63; also see Prabhatkumar Mukhopadhyay, *Rabindra-jibani o Rabindra-sahitya-prabeshak,* ii (Calcutta, 1977), 59–63.
47. See Vidyasagar's views on the civilizing influence of contact with the English, *Bahubibaha,* in *Rachanabali,* 881. For Girish Bidyaratna's views on 'immature semen', see his *Balyajiban,* 15. The *Tatvabodhini Patrika* commented: 'The sort of labour which the English, a strong people living in a cold clime, can undertake and endure is sure to undermine the health of the weak-bodied people of this country.' See *Samayik Patre Banglar Samajchitra,* vol. 4, 190. Also see Rajnarayan Basu's autobiography, *Atmacharit,* 47 (Calcutta, 1961, 4th edition), 43–4.
48. Keshab Sen, 'Impressions of England', in *Diary, Sermons, Addresses and Epistles,* 3rd edn. (Calcutta, 1938), 487f; Bankimchandra Chattopadhyay, 'Jatibaira' (Racial animosity) in *Bibidha Prabandha,* Bangiya Sahitya Parishad edn. (Calcutta, 1941), 341–6; also 'Anukaran' (Imitation); S. Tagore, *Amart Balya Katha* (Story of My Childhood), first published 1915, reprinted as Rabindraprasanga Granthamala (4), 2nd edn. (Calcutta, 1967), 4–6.
49. For a moving literary statement of this thesis, see Niradchandra Chaudhuri, *Bangali Jibane Ramani;* for Bankim's reference to the students' familiarity with the balcony scene, see 'Sakuntala, Miranda o Desdemona', *Bibidha Prabandha,* 83.
50. Kailasbasini Debi, *Atmakatha,* 16 in *Atmakatha,* vol. 2.
51. See for example the autobiography of the Brahmo preacher Bangachandra Ray, *Amar Kshudra Jibanalekhya* (A Portrait of my Insignificant Life), 38 in *Atmakatha,* vol. 4. Other Brahmo stalwarts like Keshabchandra Sen, Prakash Ray etc. were also courageously supported by their wives in times of their trial.
52. Satyacharan Mitra, *Strir Prati Swamir Upadesh,* 5.
53. R.C. Dutt, *Three Years in Europe, Being Extracts from Letters Sent from Europe by a Hindu* (Calcutta and London, 1873), 87f, 91.
54. Kailasbasini Debi, 25.
55. For the debate on women's education, see Meredith Borthwick, op. cit., ch. 3; for Kartikeya's comment on the joys of free mixing, see Kartikeyachandra Ray, op. cit., 28; also see Nabinchandra Sen, *Amar Jiban,* in Shantikumar Dasgupta and Haribandhu Mukhati (eds), *Nabinchandra Rachanabali,* Dattachaudhuri and Sons (Calcutta, 1974), part I, 277–86.

56. See Iswarchandra Vidyasagar, *Balyabibaher Dosh* (The Evils of Child Marriage), in *Rachanabali*, 679–85.

57. See *Samayik Patre Banglar Samajchitra*, vol. 4, 247.

58. See Gurucharan Mahalanabish, *Atmakatha*, 29f, in *Atmakatha*, vol. 4.

59. Haimabati describes two incidents in which she was introduced to prospective bridegrooms and her consent to marriage was sought by the guardians. The first of these two young men visited her for quite some time until she decided to break off the engagement because of his mother's objections. She accepted and married the second young man. The heroine in Tagore's *Gora*, Sucharita broke off her engagement to Panu Babu. See Rabindranath Tagore, *Gora*, in *Rabindra Rachanabali* vol. 6 (Calcutta, 1976).

60. Sibnath Sastri, *Atmacharit*, 87f in *Atmakatha*, vol. 5. Sudhiranjan Das, *Ja Dekhechhi Ja Peyechi* (What I have Heard and what I Have Received) (Calcutta, 1969), I, 33.

61. See Prabhat Mukhopadhyay, 'Nishiddha Phal' (Forbidden Fruit), in *Galpa Samagra* (Omnibus Collection of Short Stories), part II (Calcutta, 1987), 271.

62. Nabin Sen, *Amar Jiban*, in *Nabinchandra Rachanabali*, vol. 1, 160ff.

63. Indira Debi's Memoirs, in *Ekshan*, vols 19 and 20, Bengali years 1399 (1992) and 1400 (1993).

64. Sarala Debi Chaudhuri, *Jibaner Jhara Pata* (Life's Fallen Leaves), 2nd edn. (Calcutta, 1982), 100–1.

65. Srinath Chanda, *Brahmo Samaje Challish Bachhar* (Forty Years in Brahmo Samaj), 2nd edn. (Calcutta, Bengali year 1375 [1968]), 129–30.

66. Kailasbasini Debi, 16, 19, 29ff; Jnanendranath Das, *Mahashanti o Nidra* (Eternal Peace and Sleep) (Calcutta, 1919); Prakashchandra Ray, *Aghor-Prakash* (Calcutta, 1921); Bankimchandra Chattopadhyay, *Bishbriksha* (The Poison Tree), *Bankim Rachanabali* (Patra's Publication, Calcutta, 1983), vol. 1, 204–8.

67. Rameshchandra Datta, *Samsar-katha*, in Jogeshchandrachandra Bagal (ed.), *Ramesh Rachanabali*, *Samagra Upanyas*, 391. Amritalal Sengupta, *Jogamaya Thakurani* (Madaripur, 1916).

68. See Ghulam Murshid, *Reluctant Debutante*, ch. 3.

69. Kartikeyachandra Ray, *Atmajibancharit*, 34–5, 37, 83–7; Nabin Sen, *Amar Jiban*, I, 147–53, II, 150ff, 166ff, 194ff; Binodini Dasi, *Amar Katha o Anyanya Rachana* (My Story and Other Writings) (First published Bengali year 1319 [1912], revised edn., Calcutta, 1394 [1987]), 62.

70. See Bangachandra Ray, *Amar Kshudra Jibanalakhya*, 33 in *Atmakatha*, vol. 4; Pratapchandra Majumdar, *Ashish* (Blessings), 65, 67 in *Atmakatha*, 4.

71. Kaminikumar Datta's Diary (Manuscript). I was allowed to consult the manuscript by Mr Datta's granddaughter, Ms Krishna Dutt.

72. Krishnachandra Majumdar, *Ra Ser Itibratta* (History of Ra Se), 17–19.

73. Kartikeyachandra Ray, *Atmajibancharit,* 31–2; Somnath Chakrabarti, *Kolkatar Baijibilas* (The Courtesans of Calcutta) (Calcutta, 1991).
74. Prakashchandra Ray, *Aghor-Prakash,* chs 9, 10, 17, 25, 26, 31.
75. Niradchandra Chaudhuri, *Bangali Jibane Ramani,* ch. 6.
76. Mahendranath Datta, *Srimad Vivekananda Swamir Jibaner Ghatanabali,* 3 vols, 4th edn. (Calcutta, 1977), vol. I.
77. Rabindranath Tagore, *'Premer Abhishek'* in *Sadhana,* Phalgun, 1300 (Bengali year); also *Rabindra Rachanabali,* vol. 4, 544–7. This introductory part of the poem was left out in later editions because the poet's Anglophile friend, Loken Palit had objected to it.
78. Niradchandra Chaudhuri, *Bangali Jibane Ramani,* 210–11.

5

Transformation of
Religious Sensibilities
in Nineteenth-century Bengal*

Whatever the validity of the now discarded concept, 'the nineteenth-century renaissance in Bengal', there is very little doubt that there were significant changes in the mental world of the middle-class Bengali Hindus in course of that century. The story of those changes may not be earth-shaking in importance in the context of world history, but they were of profound human interest. For one thing, it is often a very unlikely story. A sixteen year old boy sets out on a career path aiming at surpassing Homer. Another youth, at eighteen, is driven by a desire to encounter Godhead. A grandson of Brahmin pundits, himself a considerable scholar, decides that Samkhya and Vedanta are false philosophies. A young man of the world writes in five languages to tell the world what he considers true religion and acquires three more to have a better understanding of the matter. These stray examples from the life stories of famous men had their counterparts and resonances in the lives of less striking individuals. And that fact makes an exploration of nineteenth-century Bengali sensibilities a worthwhile project in human terms, even though they were probably not unique in any sense. The exercise holds for us the same sort of promise as we expect from literature. The debate as to whether the literary and intellectual efflorescence of the time, the advent of extraordinary individuals, constituted a renaissance or not becomes irrelevant in this context.

It is well known that religion, or to be more precise, exploration of religious truth, became one central concern of nineteenth-century Bengali Hindus. Much has been written on the reforms and innovations of the period as also the attempts to shore up the values and

*Surendra Paul Memorial Lecture delivered at the Ramakrishna Mission Institute of Culture, Calcutta.

prescriptions of orthodoxy and regenerate a pride in the Hindu identity. This lecture is concerned less with the ideas and activities focussed on reform and counter-reform and their causal roots and more with the emotional affects, the state of feelings associated with man's perpetual quest for something beyond his mundane existence or a reality which confers value and meaning on that very existence. To anticipate my argument, I shall suggest that in this crucial area of human concern our forefathers experienced a profound change, albeit that change was not uniformly distributed over the entire social space. Further, our sensibilities to-day among believers and non-believers alike, have little affinity with their counterparts in the preceding century. Perhaps one critical example will illustrate my point. We learn from the nineteenth-century autobiographies that school children in Bengal habitually debated the nature of Godhead, whether he had any form or was formless. The protagonists of formlessness had one clinching argument in their armoury. If God had a material form and was also omnipresent, how was it that we did not dash into him at every turn? It is unlikely that students debating earth-shaking issues in Calcutta coffee houses to-day will be much excited by such irrefutable logic.

The study of sensibilities, of how people feel about or react to things, is a difficult, if not almost impossible pursuit, especially when it concerns man's most intimate areas of experience. You have to guess at what really went on in people's mind on the basis of written words. When people write about their feelings on such matters—and very few people actually record their inner thoughts—they invariably impose an artificial structure on their spontaneous responses. This implies a distortion. Since one writes mostly with readers in view and rarely in a confessional mood, the distortion may be often intended, consciously or otherwise. One supplements such direct, if not entirely dependable evidence, by other people's observations. An empathic observer's account of a mystical celebration may tell us more about what went on in the minds of the celebrants than any personal statement from a participant. A great artist can get at the truth in such matters with a surer touch than any autobiography. What better record of the mind of neo-Hindu orthodoxy than Rabindranath's *Gora*? But yet truth remains elusive. We can at best guess at the reality of feelings. But one increasingly appreciates that such uncertainty is true of all historical statements. The task is only a little harder when one tries to explore the world of human feelings.

It is best to start with the pre-nineteenth century background so as to appreciate the extent and nature of the changes which followed. Of course, there were significant changes over time in the centuries preceding the nineteenth. Yet perhaps it is possible to identify certain dominant traits in Bengal religious sensibilities as bench marks against which one can assess the later developments.

The evidence of the pre-nineteenth century Bengali literature— the *panchalis* or *mangal kavyas*, Vaishnava lyrics and biographies, Ramprasad's *shyama-sangeet* and the like—project two distinct levels of religious sensibility. One, perhaps the dominant note, is that of domesticated religiosity—a pervasive sense of belief in and adoration of multiple deities as well as other superntural beings, not all very benign, inspired by an ardent hope that faithful worship and observance of ritual duties would ensure the well-being, *mangal* of all one cared for. The worshipper is humble in spirit, accepting his lowly place in an often threatening universe, careful to please all the supra-human powers that be as much as the more tangible lords of the earth. The worship and the ritual observances have a contractual side to them. The gods are expected to respect their side of the tacit agreement in return for adoration and more material offerings. Perhaps it would not be wrong to say that the element of continuity in Bengali religious sensibility, the one which pervades the conscious-ness of the majority, both the masses and the more privileged, is characterized by this sense of domesticated piety. I use that term to mean a state of feeling contained within the limits of domestic concerns and not transcending those concerns to reach out to more intense or wider consciousness indifferent to one's worldly needs. This description is, of course, a half truth: for underlying or co-existing with moderate and modest piety, there was often a strain of deep spiritual faith manifest in the frequent invocation of the Supreme Being, the ultimate saviour, the one who alone could grant salvation or save humans in times of great danger. It is this faith which consti-tuted a bridge between day to day piety and the ecstatic devotion of the Chaitanya movement as well as Ramprasad's songs, the second most prominent element in the tradition of Bengali religious sensibility. The mysticism of the folk cults like the *Bauls* and *Sahajiyas* was similarly informed by 'god-madness', an other-worldly indif-ference to material concerns. Finally, in so far as it is possible to classify the components of so elusive an area of human conscious-ness, the ascetic–esoteric traditions of *tantra* and *yoga* in their various manifestations were marked by the mystical quest for ultimate realization as well as a lust for miraculous powers. The religious consciousness of an individual could simultaneously contain one or more of these traits ranging from simple-hearted piety to ambitious striving after supreme knowledge.

The structure of religious consciousness and the emotional affects which went with it did not change overnight in nineteenth-century Bengal. As I shall note later in this lecture, there were marked continuities between 'modern' and 'pre-modern' times in this particular area of Bengali life, though even the continuities had subtle nuances absent from the earlier manifestations of similar phenomena.

One commonplace of the received wisdom on our social and cultural history in modern times is that all changes were the result of western impact—assimilation and adoption of ideas and cultural artifacts originating in the west, culminating in some sort of an imperfect and incomplete synthesis. The new emphasis on the hegemony of the dominant culture—the notion that the imperial power had an agenda for cultural domination to which the indigenous intelligentsia surrendered virtually without resistance (even the defiant gestures of self-assertion were patterns of acquiescence in a veiled form)—is essentially a variant of the older thesis. I have argued elsewhere that for our culture the contact with the west and the colonial experience itself were catalysts. Like a chemical process, they initiated changes which acquired a measure of autonomy. The end result was no simple synthesis, perfect or imperfect, of two different traditions nor an uncomplicated triumph of one culture over another. It was a new product essentially different from both the indigenous inheritance and the elements of western civilization which impinged on it. Bengali religious sensibilities in modern times are striking end products of this catalytic process.

Let me try and illustrate my point first with reference to the movement generally recognized as the first attempt in modern times to 'reform' Hindu society and religion, I mean the Brahmo Samaj. In terms of sensibilities, the origins of this movement has some very unusual features which have not been adequately emphasized in the relevant literature.

The founder of the movement, Raja Rammohan, wrote his first tract attacking the worship of idols long before he had had any encounter with western culture. His uncompromising monotheism, which later rejected Christian Trinitarianism as much as Hindu polytheism, has identifiable resonances of the belief fundamental to Islam, the notion that it is the ultimate sin to attribute to the creator multiplicity in any form. No doubt the Raja's exposure to Perso-Arabic education which he shared with many others of his class sowed the first seeds of this hard and clear faith. One wonders, however, if there were others who felt comparable doubts about the practices of popular Hinduism. Down to the middle years of the nineteenth century, Persian, if not Arabic, was a part of an educated Bengali's cultural equipment. We read of Hindu gentlemen learned in the language and deeply versed in Persian literature in remote parts of eastern Bengal. Did their delight in Hafiz ever go with any doubts about the practice of image worship, or did they, like Rammohan himself see in the latter only a symbolism consistent with the belief in one God, but unlike him felt no need to reject the popular practice? We do not have any answer to the question. The uncle in Rabindranath's *Chaturanga* is an atheist in the tradition of *nyaya*. But were there individuals in real life who shared Rammohan's misgivings about popular Hindu belief and practice under Islamic or *naiyaika* influence? Sibnath Sastri's *naiyaika* father did preach atheism to his young son, but he too insisted on adherence to orthodoxy in practice. Many of the great *naiyaikas* were also scholars of *smriti* and happily earned their living by prescribing ritually appropriate action in accordance with the latter tradition. If their intellectual training altered their beliefs and the associated affects, we have little evidence to go by.

To return to the main point in my argument, the central tenet of the first reform movement in Bengal began with a maverick invocation of a familiar doctrine, acceptable to Hindus and Muslims alike, but which the founder of the movement felt very strongly to be inconsistent with popular Hindu practice. His pronouncements on the matter remind one almost of the more aggressive stances of the Islamic faith. Yet his compromises with the received tradition reveal a fascinating pattern of sensibility. Even idol worship and polytheistic belief were acceptable, but only for the ignorant who needed such props to conceive the reality of a supreme being. The universal truth of one and only God, invisible and without any physical form, to be worshipped by all without distinction of race of creed was not, according to Rammohan, accessible to the ignorant. He self-consciously projected a system of belief and worship meant for the enlightened, that is an intellectual elite. It was no religion for the masses. No wonder it made only limited headway. This intellectual doctrine was however enunciated within the Hindu tradition. The selection of scriptural and philosophical texts, including a Tantric work, to proclaim the true ancient faith was very much within the orbit of Hindu reform. Only the militant emphasis on a single godhead ascribed a meaning to the Upanishadic texts which were probably never interpreted in quite this way in the past.

If I am not entirely mistaken, Rammohan made no distinction between brahman and Iswara and in his dualistic interpretation of what he described as the ancient and true faith of India as well as the universal truth underlying all religions, he *prescribed* the worship of a personal God, not any quest for the knowledge of ultimate reality manifest in the universe. There is an area of his *vita religiosa* about which little is known. He was initiated into the Tantric way, but we do not know what he actually practised or what he sought in terms of spiritual realization from the esoteric practices of Tantra. His writings suggest a virtuous man of the world with a liberal intellectual understanding of 'rational' faith, rather than a man of strong mystical propensities. And at no point did he discard tradition as he understood it. He even invoked the *saiva* tradition to justify the practice of taking a Muslim mistress.

The well-known facts of Rammohan's religious beliefs I have just narrated show little sign of any western impact, catalytic or otherwise. Yet he greatly admired the civilization of Europe and had a profound reverence for the ethical doctrine embodied in the New Testament. His encounter with western thought generated ideas, agenda and preferences which have few antecedents in the culture in which he was brought up. I could argue that here too he selected and rejected cultural traits in ways which gave his thought an autonomous character in the formation of which the west had been a catalytic influence, but this is not the appropriate occasion for that discussion. I should only like to underline here the vehemence of missionary response to his admiring tracts on the precepts of Jesus. Evidently, he read in them something very different from the traditional Christian interpretation, a meaning acceptable only to such marginal elements as the Unitarians. And talking of sensibilities, his gentle rebuke to his Christian critics for rubbishing the faith of a vanquished race who were in no position to hit back and his refusal to hit back in kind indicate a level of refinement which must have been rare in his time anywhere in the world. In matters of religion, one can only say that his strong rationalist inclination was accentuated by his encounter

with western thought. It led him to underline one particular interpretation of his country's inheritance of faith in a universalist spirit.
His rationalist approach to religion and his tolerance were by no
means the dominant mode in western religiosity at the time. His
religious sensibility did not privilege faith over reason. Only he saw
no conflict between the two. True faith had to be consistent with reason. The rest was either allegory or the concoction of deceitful schem-
ers out to exploit people.

To sum up, the religious sensibilities of India's pioneer in modernization was marked by a respectful acceptance of the inherited tradition, a strong feeling, probably enhanced, if not generated by an
Islamic education, that only the monotheistic element in it was the
authentic tradition, a deep admiration for the ethical teachings of
Christ along with a total rejection of Christian dogma and adoption
of rationality as the one criterion by which religious faith like all
other human concerns was to be judged. The end product was a universalist non-denominational monotheism, intellectually accessible
to the elites, which had resonances of an Upanishadic and mediaeval
Indian doctrine. It was no part of contemporary European thought,
though arguably Rammohan's formulations were informed by his
encounter with the west. His exclusive emphasis on reason as the
ultimate crucible for testing the validity of faith was something unique
in his days. We have here an example of catalytic impact rather
than any simple borrowing or synthesis of two cultures. This concern
for rationality in an area of human feelings generally conceded to
faith became one powerful strand in the religious sensibilities of the
educated Bengali.

In the Brahmo reformist tradition, the rationalist preference is
powerfully manifest in the writings of Akshay Datta. He justified his
belief in a creator in terms of teleological arguments, described
nature and hence science as the book of God, rejected all dogma
and legends of incarnation as allegory and passionately regretted
the inadequacies of the scientific, empirical tradition in India. His
close friend and associate, Iswarchandra Vidyasagar, a member of
the Tatvabodhini Sabha, probably shared his beliefs and sentiments
as is suggested by his one cryptic statement on the subject of Divinity
'Iswar chaitanyamay', 'The creator has his/her being in consciousness.' Bankimchandra in his earlier writings similarly underlined a
rationalist faith in his passionate rejection of irrational beliefs which,

he once thought, was the Brahmins' strategy for safeguarding their privileges and power.

It is significant that in the mid-nineteenth century, Akshay Datta's *Bahya Bastur Sahit Manaber Sambandha Bichar* was highly popular reading among the educated in Bengal. Dr Alexander Duff informs us that the rationalist and radical writings of Tom Paine sold at four times the original price in Calcutta. By all accounts, rationalist thought which questioned all received tradition, indigenous or foreign and critically assessed or justified in terms of reason even wnat was accepted, had become central to the Bengali intellectual discourse.

Religious sensibility was profoundly influenced by this need to seek rational validation for belief and action. Eventually, the majority of Hindus might reject the Brahmo credo which had its origin in such rational assessment of tradition, but over time they took on board much of the questioning of traditional practice. These practices were not abandoned, but the belief system on which they were based was seriously undermined. The reformed Hindu, so-called, did not give up ancestral rituals but his faith in their meaning and efficacy had withered away. To take one critical example, not only had the practice of *Ganga-yatra* virtually disappeared by the turn of the century, the educated Hindu with continued faith in the redeeming quality of the holy water at the moment of death must have been very rare by that time. This was a measure of total discontinuity in one significant area of religious sentiment. D.H. Lawrence commented that one striking transformation in human emotions in modern times was linked to the loss of faith in an after-life. It altered the totality of one's world-view and required new validation for one's notions of good and evil as well as one's codes of ethics. The educated Bengali who had accepted reason as the criteria for judgements had similarly undergone a quiet revolution in his mental life. No longer secure in the uncomplicated beliefs of his fore-fathers, his religious sensibilities were now rooted in uncertainties, replete with questions to which there were no answers. Akshay Sarkar, writing at the turn of the century presented a very negative picture of the mental world of the Bengali *bhadralok*. Questions had replaced faith and a shaky agnosticism had become in effect the real religion for many.

The process by which this end result was reached is a critical example of the catalytic impact central to my argument. Western philosophical thought and less enlightened missionary criticism had shaken the certainty of faith among the educated Hindu. Had these ideas and criticisms been simply the product of another culture with which the indigenous population had no equations of power, they would have probably had very little impact. But these were the pronouncements of the master race, of a civilization recognized overtly or covertly as superior. Their pronouncements were taken very seriously at different levels of understanding. The moderately educated person, not equipped to take on the westerners' criticism at a level of adequate argumentation, and aware that the rulers and the chaplains on their ships considered his faith superstitious or even barbarous, resented such rubbishing and responded with enthusiasm to propagandists who projected, often with very crude arguments, the superiority of Hinduism and justified a whole range of irrational practices. Others, at various levels of sophistication, spoke of the 'true faith' of the Hindus, arguing either that it was not very different from the monotheistic beliefs of Christianity or that it was a subtler faith, nobler in its tolerance. But one change was almost universal. Persons exposed to the new type of education no longer took their ancestral faith for granted. The doubts generated by the contact with the west induced some soul-searching. In an unexpected way the contact with the west led to a preoccupation with religion probably to an unprecedented degree. The emotional ambience of this concern could range from a consoling belief in the Hindus' spiritual superiority to a resort to rationality sorting out the acceptable from the unacceptable in the received tradition.

The anxieties I have just described appear to have been much less pronounced among one section of the educated Bengalis— namely, their women. The faithful wives of Brahmo converts might reject worship of images. One convert to Christianity was willing to suffer for her convictions. Kishori Mitra's wife, tutored by her husband to lose faith in ritual practices, stuck to them because she did not want to be cut off from her society. But the small number of autobiographical statements by women which have survived from the nineteenth century rarely reveal any angst or doubts about traditional beliefs and practices. On the contrary, we have Rassundari's deeply moving account of how, following her mother's advice, she called upon Dayamay, 'the merciful one' in her moment of deepest anguish, certain that He and He alone would come to her help. The cultural and emotional divide between the *bhadralok* and their ladies had

many dimensions. The power of affects associated with the traditional faith in the case of women was one of the most significant
facets of that divide.

Continued attachment to traditional belief and practice or reason-
based reassessments of all faith culminating in virtual agnosticism
were not the only two patterns of response to questions of religion
among the nineteenth-century *bhadralok*. The catalytic impact of the
west induced other patterns of religious affects as well. Some of
these came very close to actual imitation or adaptation of western,
specifically Christian, ways though here too there were significant
elements of selection, rejection and modification. Keshab's initial
redefinition of the Brahmo creed and later the Sadharan Brahmo
Samaj come closest to this description. Keshab's pronouncements
are full of Christian resonances. His sermons read almost like those
of the Anglican church. He even accepted Christ as the Son. But the
Divinity of Christ was firmly rejected as was Christian dogma in all
its forms. Besides, his religiosity both before and after he founded
the *Nababidhan* was marked by intense emotions, a quality of passionate devotionalism which he found lacking in western Christianity
when he visited England. Both he and the Sadharan Brahmo Samaj
adopted some of the organizational forms of Protestant Christianity,
but clericalism never struck roots in the emotional ambience of the
Samaj. The Brahmo *acharya* or *pracharak*, frequently a layman with
other occupations, never became the counterpart of a Christian
priest. As a cultural symbol, arguably, the *samaj bhavan* never had
the same associations as a church.

It is the secular aspects of Protestantism, especially non-conform-
ism, which profoundly influenced the followers of the Sadharan
Brahmo Samaj, and indirectly the 'reformed Hindus'. Certain worldly
virtues, like discipline, self-restraint, parsimony along with moral
rectitude, especially truthfulness and rejection of illicit pleasures
became parts of the Brahmo religious persona. No doubt, this redefinition of religiosity was partly produced by an admiration of Victorian
virtues, especially the alleged charms of the English family life. But
partly it was a reaction to the *dolce vita* of colonial Calcutta as also
the dissolute drunkenness of the westernized Bengali, especially the
'England-returned'. The catalytic nature of all this impact is illustrated by one peculiar feature of Brahmo religiosity: the excessive
pre-occupation with one's sinfulness and the inclination to shed

profuse tears both for love of God and in contemplation of one's sins. This tendency was a relatively late importation, thanks probably to Keshab, because neither Rammohan nor Devendranath were given to unrestrained weeping. Barada Babu in *Alaler Gharer Dulal*, held up as an ideal for all good and true men to imitate, was an expert in that art. But some Brahmos at least had doubts about the validity of this concern with sinfulness. Durgamohan Das told Sibnath Sastri that there was no reason for him to consider himself sinful since he was, by all accounts, a very decent and honest person. He added that those who shed profuse tears at Brahmo prayer meetings were probably scoundrels in secret. Arguably, the apotheosis of tearful repentance and describing oneself as a poor sinner owed at least as much to Vaishnava sensibilities as to Christian ones. The much admired Victorian Englishman was not generally given to weeping in public or, for that matter, dancing for non-secular reasons, again a practice which some Brahmos had inherited almost certainly from the Vaishnavas. Thus, even in direct adoption of Christian ways specific elements of traditional responses came into play and determined how particular cultural artifacts were transformed.

In a rough enumeration of religious affects in traditional Bengali culture at the beginning of this lecture, I have pointed out that ecstatic devotionalism and a mystical longing for union with the Godhead were among their components at least since the advent of Sri Chaitanya. These strands complemented and also informed the simple piety of popular Bengali Hinduism. At the level of the masses, cults such as Baul and Sahajiya embodied similar affects. Transcendental dimensions of religiosity, often projected in very personal and individualistic terms, were powerful features of the nineteenth-century scene. In the Brahmo movement Debendranath's mystical yearnings and Keshab's ecstatic surrender to the Divine will, often expressed in chanting and dance, were two very different expressions of this tendency. Devendranath, unlike Rammohan, departed from the established tradition of Hindu reform in selecting from and even editing the Upaniṣadic texts according to his personal preference which excluded non-dualism. His *Brahma-dharma*, it has been correctly pointed out, had strong resonances of Christianity. Yet this statement is in some ways a half-truth. It does not take account of his strong nationalistic resentment against the denationalizing effects of hob-nobbing with the Europeans as well as Christian proselytization. It also underplays the implications of his deep immersion in

Hafiz and the Upanishads, texts which project sensibilities very different from Christian mysticism. Mysticism is always rooted in the experience and longing of an individual. But its cultural determinants and social context link it to the experience of others and give it a specific location in history. In these terms, Devendranath's individualistic interpretation of the theistic tradition reflect an unselfconscious assertion of autonomy probably traceable to the ambience of rationalism which encouraged such freedom. Yet the content of his religious affects, permeated by Hafiz and the Upanishads, hark back to India's ancient and mediaeval tradition. The impact of the west led him unconsciously to find solace in one particular area of the syncretist heritage where denominations become irrelevant. Yet he did not transcend his resentment against the Christian missionary intrusion. His rationalist protégé, Akshay Datta, also shared that resentment. In such instances, as in many others, the catalytic impact induced soul-searching and an eventual solution of one's religious angst in highly individualistic interpretations read into particular elements of the received traditions.

The most maverick example of such individualistic response is to be found in the *vita religiosa* of Keshab and his followers, especially in the Nababidhan phase. Keshab's universalism and syncretism used the language of Christianity and evoked the emotionally charged devotionalism of the Vaishnava tradition, complete with *kirtana*, ecstatic dancing and floods of tears. It subsumed elements of the guru cult: on one occasion, the devotees fell at the feet of the leaders beseeching them to put in a word to the Lord in favour of the poor sinners: *prabhu, amar hoye iswarke duto katha bolben*. Even more striking was Keshab's private prayer on his death bed, overheard by Mr Farquhar: *Buddher ma, sakyer ma, nirvan*. There is no precedent for this extraordinary amalgam of the cult of the Virgin, Buddhism and theistic piety in any known religious tradition. It is worth emphasizing that this prayer came from a man in extreme pain and had no audience in view.

Religious angst which had multiple expressions became a marked feature of nineteenth-century Bengali life. It has no counterpart in the following century and probably had none in the preceding, Ramprasad Sen being the one known exception. In the later decades of the nineteenth century, a large number of young people became deeply concerned with questions of faith, and, more significantly, with a quest for the ultimate religious experience. The numbers who came to hear Keshab's lectures were not merely interested in his oratory. Guru cults flourished, probably to an unprecedented degree.

This new anxiety has been traced by some to the growing frustration and disillusionment of the young educated Bengalis. The high hopes once entertained of the civilized British leading their Bengali acolytes into a millennium of prosperity and high culture had evaporated. The number of school leavers and graduates far exceeded the job opportunities. Racism and obtuse missionary criticism of Hindu belief and practice had on the one hand undermined the earlier enthusiasm for British rule and, on the other, generated the obscurantist responses of Pandit Sasadhar and the preacher, Krishnaprasanna Sen. The popularity of these two and the often ridiculed new tendency among the young to return to ritually pure ways underline the deep psychological need for cultural self-assertion. All modern science was to be found in the Hindu scriptures and every popular superstition had profound spiritual or scientific meaning. Such inanity did not however beguile the more sensible. The definition of cultural self-identity had focussed heavily on religious belief and practice from the early years of the century. This pre-occupation over a period of some fifty years or more had led in some to a quest for what is central to the religious experience, especially in the Indian tradition.

The advent of Ramakrishna, while it certainly was located in a specific historical context, belongs to a tradition which is not necessarily linked to the colonial experience. Saints, venerated by the people and emerging from among them with a syncretistic message based on personal experience, was very much a feature of the Indian middle ages. There is a timeless element in the advent of mystics who have appeared in every culture in all ages and spoken in remarkably similar language. Yet the mediaeval Indian antecedents of Sri Ramakrishna are indeed pronounced. It is in explaining his appeal that one has to consider the colonial experience of the Bengali middle class. For the believer, he offered in his own life an answer for their spiritual angst, accentuated by the bleak material prospects of the late nineteenth-century India. He offered a prospect of spiritual peace which did not require any false assertion of superiority. Another powerful movement of that period, one which invoked the tradition of ecstatic devotionalism, was the neo-Vaishnavism of Sisir Ghosh. But in an odd way, this very Bengali movement had overt Christian resonances as manifest in the title of Ghosh's biography of Sri Chaitanya, *Lord Chaitanya*. Except for his overt acknowledgment of the Christian presence and the contemporary references in his *Kathamrita*, Ramakrishna's sensibilities and utterances reflect only the universalist element in Indian, especially the mediaeval Indian tradition. And he spoke in the language of the people virtually untouched by the colonial experience.

The complex religiosity of Swami Vivekananda, a theme I have discussed elsewhere, drew upon the mystical experience and teaching of his Master. He conceded its existential truth despite his fierce rationality. His deep empathy with the sufferings of the masses, his egalitarian preferences, his ardent nationalism drew him to a programme of service which, its name onwards, was very Christian in style. The content was however original, especially in his emphasis on educating the masses. Bankim had conceived his agenda of national reconstruction in a religious idiom. Vivekananda, with his known admiration for *Anandamath*, gave that agenda a practical shape. In the process he made service to humanity and a self-denying dedication to the national cause, an element in the religious affects of his fellow Bengalis. Here perhaps we have a direct adoption from the Christian, especially missionary, agenda. But the strong patriotic motives which inspired Vivekananda informed this new pattern of religiosity with political content, a fact which became evident when revolutionaries at the turn of the century turned to Swamiji's writings in quest of an impassioned ideology. Further, the invocation of Ramakrishna and the impact of Vivekananda's firebrand personality altered profoundly the Christian elements of the relevant affects. The renouncer serving man in the Divine cause and to regenerate India was no replica of the meek preacher of Christ's words.

To appreciate the nature of religious affects in nineteenth-century Bengal, an impressionistic look at their contemporary counterparts might be interesting. It is worth noting, that less than a century ago, political consciousness of radical Bengalis was coloured deeply by a passionate religious faith. Anything similar is unthinkable to-day. Even the defenders of Rama's birth-place invoke a secular idiom and, arguably, are concerned more with political gain than devotional urges. Religious controversies, questions of correct ritual conduct, though they are still observed by the more orthodox, are not even a marginal feature of the current social discourse. Pujas, especially those of the Mother Goddess, continue to flourish to the accompaniment of shrill and raucous music and exotic dancing. But probably, devotionalism is not the dominant affect in such festivities. Guru cults and cults of Godmen have had a great revival in Bengal as well as other parts of India. Fashionable club-going ladies observe fasts in honour of Santoshi Mata and other new entrants into the Hindu pantheon. But arguably, unlike the western acolytes who seek spiritual peace from their Indian gurus, the affluent Indian devotees of multiple Babas are more interested in securing miraculous guarantees for their material welfare—help in forging contractual arrangements with the supra-natural. It makes eminent sense in uncertain times, windfall profits and expansion of job opportunities in the corporate sector. Does old-fashioned devotionalism survive in the modest Bengali home? Perhaps, but it has moved certainly to the periphery of one's emotional life.

A famous historian once remarked that the past was never like the present. This cursory exploration of one area of our consciousness in the last century illustrates the truth of that statement.

6

Swami Vivekananda's
Construction of Hinduism*

Swami Vivekananda represents the high noon of a Hindu revival, both in popular perception and serious historical literature. Expectedly, in the VHP's 1993 celebration of the centenary of the Chicago Congress of Religions where Vivekananda made his debut they claimed the Patriot-Prophet as one of their own. Amiya P. Sen's study of the Hindu revival published in the same year,[1] a work of scholarly and analytical excellence, confirms this received perception, even if it recognizes the complexity and nuances of Swamiji's mission. I draw upon the same material as has been used in Sen's work and arrive at a very different conclusion, that the Hindu revival, a phenomenon I would prefer to describe as the Hindu reaction, was at best peripheral and for the most part antagonistic to Vivekananda's concerns. His role and his personality were misinterpreted in his own time for identifiable reasons. The persistence of that misreading is, however, less justified.

There are three distinct, though necessarily interrelated features in Swamiji's religious concerns. First, his personal quest was defined early in life as a quest for ultimate realization. He sought its fulfilment as a disciple of the saint, Ramakrishna. The Ramakrishna order of monks which he set up shared his faith in the guru. But Vivekananda refused to propagate their very special perception as to who Ramakrishna was and the reasons for his advent. I argue, however, that he too had full faith in that perception, a fact which set a limit to any sense of identity with the prevailing modes of Hindu reaction. Ramakrishna himself has been identified as one major source of Hindu revivalism, a thesis which needs to be scrutinized very carefully.

*First published in W. Radice, ed., *Swami Vivekananda and the Modernization of Hinduism* Delhi, 1998.

The second component of his religious concern was articulated during his first visit to the USA and Europe. It consisted in an exposition of what he considered to be not only the highest spiritual truths attained in the Indian religious tradition, but the ultimate truth underlying all religious beliefs—Aldous Huxley's highest common factor. He also did his best to counter the mischievous propaganda which had long presented Hindu faith and practice as forms of extreme barbarism. The rapturous reception he received in India as a hero of militant Hinduism derives primarily from this two-fold agenda for his actions abroad. But the way his role abroad was interpreted in India had more to do with the cultural insecurity of middle-class Hindus in his day than with what he actually sought to achieve. And the stereotyping of Vivekananda as a militant Hindu has persisted for less obvious reasons.

His agenda for national revival in which the Ramakrishna Order of monks and nuns were to play a central role is the third component of his religious concern. The monistic doctrine of Vedanta was to be the inspiration of this activity; but the virtues he preached for the benefit of Indians was not particularly Hindu, and in fact not particularly religious in any accepted sense of the term. There is, however, a self-consciously Hindu orientation in this agenda but only up to a point. More important, he rejected with contempt the central planks in the propaganda of Hindu reaction. The fact that he had an equal lack of regard for the Babu-sponsored reforms has obscured that act of rejection. His agenda for national regeneration was unique for his time and that explains much of the contemporary as well as later misinterpretations of his objectives.

His personal faith, a belief in Advaita, non-duality without any qualification, is summed up in a letter to one of his American devotees:

He who is eternal, without limits, omnipresent and all-knowing is not an individual person, but only a consciousness. You, I and everyone else are but manifestations of that consciousness. Finally everyone must become his image in full . . . and then in reality everything will become one. Religion is nothing but this. The obsolete and lifeless rituals and notions regarding godhood are but ancient superstitions. [BR 7:293]

He also accepted without qualification the doctrine of *māyā*. 'This world which you behold', he told his disciple Sarat Chakravarti, 'also does not exist. Everything is an act of imagination.' [SSS:67]

Advaita, or non-duality as projected in Vedanta, is certainly a central theme in the Brahminical tradition. But in the perceptions of Vivekananda and his guru it transcended the limits of any particular religious or cultural tradition. They certainly did not see it as a part of any denominational creed. Ramakrishna stated his faith in the basic unity of all religions in a folksy epigram, *jato mat tato path* ('there are as many ways as there are creeds'). Vivekananda developed this simple notion, the truth of which Ramakrishna is said to have realized through his own mystical experiences, into a systematic philosophical statement. The Vedas, in his view, were eternal in the sense that they contained timeless truth. Further, all religious and metaphysical notions were inherent in Vedanta. The doctrines of duality, qualified monism and monism were but three successive stages in man's spiritual progress. Hinduism was the form which Vedanta had assumed as the end product of Indian beliefs and practices. Dualism was its first stage. Christianity and Islam were also dualistic faiths and as such expressions of the Vedantic truth shaped by particular cultures in historic times. Buddhism on the other hand was an embodiment of non-duality or yogic consciousness. [BR 7:157] In these terms, all religions had to be accepted as true and not simply tolerated. All divisiveness was traceable to ignorance. The distinction between castes, religions and races ceased to have any meaning for the enlightened. [SSS: 35] The plea is not for syncretism *à la* Keshab Sen but a recognition of the fundamental unity of all religions. Its cultural antecedents were the doctrines of the medieval saints and the Upanishadic dictum, *ekam sad, viprāh bahudhā vadanti* ('the truth is one, only the sages state it in many different ways'). Vivekananda summed up his personal faith in one simple statement: 'Truth alone is my God; the entire world is my country.' [Letter to Alasinga, BR 7:193] What could be further from the preoccupations of Hindu chauvinists either in our time or in the nineteenth century?

There is an aspect of Vivekananda's personal faith which certainly belongs to the Hindu tradition, but which he firmly refused to project beyond the immediate circle of his fellow believers. I refer to the belief of Ramakrishna's disciples that their guru was an incarnation of the Deity. Vivekananda was under some pressure to declare this faith as the foundation of the Order's credo, the central plank of all their religious propaganda. There is little reason to doubt that he more than shared this faith. It was he who composed the mantra for the worship of Ramakrishna in the monastery: *sthāpakāya cha dharm-asya sarvadharma-svarūpiṇe, avatāravariṣṭhāya rāmakṛṣṇāya te namaḥ* ('We bow to Ramakrishna, the greatest of all incarnations, the founder of *dharma*, he who was the embodiment of all religions'). [SSS: 70] The rules he laid down for the members of the order contained the following instruction:

. . . Teach them that one may bow to all other deities, but we worship only Ramakrishna . . . The other deities have become old and obsolete. We have a new India now, a new Deity, a new faith, a new Veda.

He wrote to his fellow disciple, Sivananda, in his characteristic irreverent slang, 'I do not have the least doubt that Ramakrishna is the father of God himself . . . We do not know if Krishna was ever born or not, Buddha and Chaitanya now appear to be hackneyed. Ramakrishna Paramahansa is the latest and most perfect . . . Can anyone else be compared to him?' But he was averse to forcing this belief down people's throats partly because he did not want to establish another sect. [BR 7:75] Besides, he explained, 'I understood him very little. I consider him so great that I am afraid to say anything about him, lest I . . . demean him by painting him in my own light.' [SSS: 146] In the Indian tradition, every incarnation has a particular purpose. The reason for the advent of Ramakrishna according to Vivekananda was to end sectarianism in all its forms and hence the disciple could not risk founding one more sect in the name of the master. [SSS: 26] The belief in incarnations combined with the faith that Ramakrishna was born to end all sectarianism locates Vivekananda in a curious relationship to the Hindu tradition. The very acceptance of a notion peculiar to that tradition is mobilized to transcend all allegiance to any particular creed.

Yet there was an element of ambivalence here. Vivekananda celebrated the ritual worship of Durga, Kali and Lakshmi in the monastery he set up, and would have sacrificed animals but for Sarada Devi's refusal to allow it. And all this was done in accordance with the prescriptions of Raghunandana. The orthodox pundits who came to the monastery went back satisfied that the monks of the order were true Hindus. These rituals were of course unacceptable not only to non-Hindus, but to Hindu sects like the Vaishnavas. [SSS: 225ff.]

To repeat, Swami Vivekananda's image as the champion of militant Hinduism derives above all from his mission in the USA and Europe. But one needs to emphasize here that he certainly did not go to the USA primarily with the object of propagating Hinduism. The purpose of his visit is stated quite explicitly in a letter to Mary Hale: 'In fact I came here with the object of quietly raising some funds; but I have been caught in a trap, and now I shall not be left in peace.' [BR 7:25] Shortly before his death he again told his disciple Sarat Chakravarti that one major object of his Western mission was to find some way of providing for the poor in India. [SSS: 235] It is not quite clear how he proposed to set about achieving this end. We have somewhat imprecise references to his two-fold expectation— that he might help secure Western technology for India's industrial development and that the Americans would help with funds to set up a monastery in India which would be the centre of a programme for ameliorating the condition of the masses. The available record how- ever suggests that his plan of action in the West emerged gradually and was partly determined by changing circumstances.

Arguably, that plan had very little to do with the propagation of Hinduism in any accepted sense of the term, despite the fact that he stood forth as the representative of the Hindu religion at the Chi- cago Congress. What he actually said in different sessions of that Congress needs to be analysed carefully. His famous speech at the inaugural session emphasized his pride in belonging to a religious tradition which taught people to accept all religious opinions as true: 'We do not merely tolerate all religions, but accept them all to be true.' He quoted the *Śivamahimna stotra: rucīnāṃ vaicitryād ṛjukuṭila- nānāpathajuṣām, nṛṇām eko gamyas tvam asi payasām arṇava iva* ('You alone are the object of all human quest, the way all rivers merge into the ocean. They follow straight or winding paths because their tastes happen to vary'). And the concluding paragraph ended with the ex- pression of a robust faith that sectarian conflicts which had drenched this earth with human blood would now come to an end. The speech on 19 November was ostensibly an exposition of Hinduism. It ad- dressed the metaphysical and philosophical foundations of Hindu practice—the concepts of Brahman, *karma*, duality and non-duality. But its central emphasis was on a spiritual or rather mystical ideal: 'Hinduism does not consist in any effort to believe in any creed or dogma; its prime object is the realization of the transcendent, to merge in the ideal . . .' He concluded by congratulating the Americans for their initiative in declaring that one encountered God in every religion. As leaders of human civilization it was their preordained task to carry forward the flag of universalism.

The Hinduism he preached in the West during the years which followed was also primarily an exposition of Vedantic metaphysics. Besides, he also lectured and wrote on the fourfold path to realization: *karma*, action without attachment, *bhakti*, the path of devotion, *jñāna*, knowledge and *rāja-yoga*, the techniques of a mystical regime expounded in Patanjali's *Yogasūtra*. The Vedic and Puranic *Karmakāṇḍa*, ritualistic duties so central to Hindu practice and beliefs, is totally absent from these exposition.

In a letter written to a fellow disciple in December 1895, he explained the nature of his mission in the West:

I am not writing any book on Hinduism at the moment . . . Every religion is an expression, a language to express the same truth, and we must speak to each in his own language . . . We will see about Hinduism at some point later. Our main concern is his (i.e. Ramakrishna's) religion. Let the Hindus call it Hindu religion—and let others similarly name it (what they like) . . . Does our master belong only to India? India's degeneration is the result of such narrow attitudes. Any beneficial outcome is impossible unless these are destroyed. [BR 7:246–7]

There is no scope for misreading this statement. He was in the West to preach the universal spiritual truth embodied in the life of his guru. The Hindus might call it Hinduism and others by other names, but his concern was to break down all such barriers. The same idea is made even more explicit in a letter to Mrs Bull:

My master used to tell us that Hindu, Christian etc. are but different names (of the same truth). They are barriers to fraternal feelings between human beings. We must first try to break these down . . . Even the best among us behave like monsters under their evil influence. Now we have to work hard to break these down and we will surely succeed. [BR 7:127]

In his farewell speech at the Congress of Religions he stated unequivocally what he did not want:

Much has been said here about the common ground for unity among religions . . . But if anyone here hopes that such unity will be achieved by the triumph of one of the many religions now current and the destruction of others, I tell him, 'Brother, yours is a false hope.' Do I wish that the Christians should become Hindus? God forbid. Do I wish that any Hindu or Buddhist should become Christian? God forbid. [BR 1:33]

The purpose of his Western mission appears to have unfolded over time. This evolution was related on the one hand to the development of his perception of the West and on the other to the growing clarity of his plans for India. The former is marked by an increasing admiration for the West, not so much for its material achievement as for the immense energy which informed it. He conceptualized it in terms of *rajas* or 'this-worldly' virtues one associated with the Kshatriyas, and saw in it a moral quality of great merit. He also perceived a fundamental difference between the dominant value systems of India and Europe. Celibacy and purity, he concluded, meant very different things in the two cultures. The Western equivalents of these terms were virtue and courage. The ultimate human aspiration in India was *mokṣa*, liberation; in the West, it was a virtuous life on earth. [BR 7:271] The West, inspired by the quality of *rajas*, had reached the ultimate limits of worldly enjoyment and was now hungry for something else. Science having undermined their faith, Christianity could no longer satisfy that hunger. India, which had nothing else left to compare with the West, still had an immense spiritual heritage. The way to attract the homage of the immensely powerful West was to expound that inheritance to them. In this, India still had an immense advantage and could forever be a teacher to the West. This would be like a repetition of an old history. Greece conquering Rome. [BR 7:247] In return, India could learn from Europe and America the worldly knowledge she needed so badly. A brotherhood of man would emerge on the basis of this fair exchange. [SSS: 7] Vivekananda developed an even larger aspiration in the West. The mighty West, he felt, was now ready for yoga, the path to the ultimate realization of the divine in man which was not accessible to the weak. The great power which had created *their* material civilization could now be harnessed to inaugurate a spiritual millennium for mankind.

Such transcendental and non-denominational aspirations were counterbalancd by a cultural propaganda which had nationalistic over-tones. The vocabulary and concerns of that propaganda had a clearly Hindu orientation, the sort of thing which might even warm the cockles of RSS-VHP hearts. However, one needs to consider this propaganda in its proper context, even though one must be careful not to rationalize away what the Swami actually said. It is necessary to remember his mercurial temper and his tendency to lash out against whatever he considered unacceptable. This traits in his personality undermined much of his popularity in India and also alienated quite a few friends and devotees in the West, including some persons very close to him. Besides, he went to the USA equipped with a fair experience of rather ignorant missionary propaganda against Hindu belief and practice. He encountered the same in its most blatant form in America, a fact documented in detail in Marie Louise Burke's multi-volume compilation. Besides, while some of his best friends were indeed Christian missionaries, his love for their vocation was somewhat limited. He had to deal with questions in the USA as to whether Hindu mothers actually threw their babies to crocodiles, as described in missionary tracts on India. He replied that this was indeed so, but he personally had been rejected by discriminating crocodiles because as an infant he was much too fat. In a more serious vein he combated all statements regarding the condition of Indian women projected by the Ramabai Circle, even though at home he was often a virulent critic of the same practices. The reason for this, as he explained to Sister Nivedita, was that only a fool would wash his dirty linen in public. Incidentally, it should be noted that in a letter to the lady editor of *Bhāratī* he expressed his great admiration for Ramabai and what she had achieved for India in the West. Evidently, his motive in countering her accounts of Indian womanhood in the USA was inspired by nationalism rather than Hindu chauvinism. Otherwise his admiration for a Hindu widow who had converted to Christianity cannot be explained. He was however an uncompromising opponent of all religious conversion and was convinced that nearly all conversions to Christianity in India were based on the exploitation of Indian poverty. And he made no bones about stating this belief of his in particularly strong language. A further element of Hinduness (if that is the correct word) in his propaganda was the belief that Christianity owed its origin to Hindu and Buddhist influences. But here probably the element of nationalism which also had pan-Asian dimensions was more important than any Hindu chauvinism. One has only to recall in this context his proud accounts of Islam's contribution to modern European civilization and his comparison of Christianity's historic record with that of Islam, tilted very much in favour of the latter.

Vivekananda's Indian agenda, more than his personal faith and his mission abroad, does up to a point provide evidence in support of the thesis which projects him as a hero of neo-Hinduism, albeit a reformist one. His chief handiwork back home, the Ramakrishna Mission, did have in practice a strong Hindu orientation, both in its ideological pronouncements and in the sections of the population it actually served. Swamiji's self-conscious and persistent efforts to counterbalance this bias however needs to be emphasized. In a letter dated 1897, he states specifically that from the very beginning the Mission did not discriminate between the different communities of India in their programme of service. [BR 7:446] His plans for national reconstruction gave a priority to the Hindus, but chiefly in a chronological sense. In his view the decline of India was the end result of its culture of discrimination, its long tradition of contempt for others. [SSS: 176] That decline began the day the contemptuous epithet, *mleccha* was invented. [BR 7:29] To reverse that process, it was first necessary to raise the entire Hindu community from its fallen state and then revitalize the whole of mankind. The process of regeneration for the Hindus had to proceed step by step. First, divisions within each caste had to be abolished, then all castes had to be given the sacred thread until every Hindu had attained the status of Brahmins 'because all Hindus were brothers'. [SSS: 78] Despite the revolutionary implication of such a programme as spelt out by Swamiji ('. . . the Brahmin and the Chandal must be placed on an equal footing') it does sound like an agenda for Hindu communal solidarity.

Such an interpretation of his objectives are however countered by other features of the same programme. The Ramakrishna Mission under his leadership dedicated itself to 'the task initiated by Ramakrishna of establishing a close relationship among the followers of all religions in the knowledge that all religious beliefs in this world were but the varied expressions of the same eternal truth'. [SSS: 56–7] He declared that the reason for the advent of Ramakrishna was the destruction of communal barriers, *sampradāy-bihīnatā*. [SSS: 26] In a letter to a fellow disciple written in 1894, he spelled out what the projected organization must avoid at all cost:

Make sure that the universalist attitude is not hampered in any way. Everything must be sacrificed, if necessary, for that one sentiment—universality . . . universality—perfect acceptance, not tolerance only, we preach and perform. [BR 7:56–7]

The monastery, guided by the spirit of Ramakrishna, was to be the centre for the union of all faiths, *sarvadharma-samanvay*. [SSS: 112] The movement's mouthpiece, the *Brahmavadin*, was to contain translations from religious texts in Arabic and Persian as the basis for an enquiry into the fundamental truth underlying all scriptures. He explained his understanding of the advent of Ramakrishna in the following words:

The *satyayuga,* the age of truth, dawned the day he was born. All divisiveness ended from that day . . . He was the one who would resolve all conflicts—all distinctions, between Hindus and Muslims, Christians and Hindus all these disappeared. Those sectarian conflicts belong to another age; in this age of truth everything is submerged in the flood of his love. [BR 7:252]

The point of radical departure in Vivekananda's Indian mission, where he stood apart from all reformers of that era, was his emphasis on the masses, the deprived and the underprivileged people of the country. Service to the poor, in the belief that in serving them one served God, does have antecedents in the Hindu tradition. And other Indian reformers like Ranade had organized volunteer groups to offer help to those most in need. But Vivekananda's understanding of the Indian problem differed from theirs, because he attributed to the underprivileged in India a centrality in the life and history of the country in a way which has no precedents. I have argued elsewhere that in course of his travels in India as a *parivrājaka,* a mendicant, he discovered Indian poverty and developed a passionate empathy with the Indian masses. As he told a fellow disciple, he had not found God in his travels but had learned to love human beings. What is especially remarkable is that there was no element of condescension in his faith that the grand achievements of Indian high culture were insignificant compared to the contribution of the masses. One boasted of one's ancestors who had written a few philosophical texts and constructed a few temples, but remained oblivious of the poor on whose labour the whole structure of civilization was raised. It was his firm belief that the future belonged to the masses and the only worthwhile task before the educated middle classes in India was to make them aware of their power, especially through education. [BR 7:276]

It has been argued that such statements were little but rhetoric and that Vivekananda had no worthwhile plans for the exploited social groups. He certainly was no Mao-Tse Tung and had no plans for a social revolution. He functioned as a pragmatist inspired by a certain idealism and it is in these terms that one must assess his programme of action. He wanted the Mission named after his guru to develop as a band of dedicated ascetics, both men and women, whose primary task would be to attend to the physical needs of the poor and bring to them the benefits of modern education. Education of the masses, eradication of illiteracy, was of primary importance.

He had no faith in any religion that was unconcerned with the physical misery of human beings [BR 7:27] and was contemptuous of *bhadralok* politics which paid no attention to such things as mass illiteracy. A few thousand graduates, he argued, could not be the basis of a nation. [BR 7:36] India had become a land of the dead. Educating the masses was the only way to revive it. [BR 7:241] Once they were aware of the world around them and their own power they would know what to do. People of his own class would have no further function in Indian life. It is difficult to read into this agenda any message for Hindu revival.

Of course the programme he chalked out for the Mission had less mundane concerns as well. The dedicated missionaries were to preach the message of Vedanta and try to realize its ideals in their own lives. Detailed instructions were laid down as to what to avoid—like *lokācāra*, or popular practices, and *bāmācāra*, the extreme form of Tantricism. A knowledge of the Yogas was also to be propagated. In all this the non-denominational spirituality of the doctrines was to be emphasized.

Such an agenda was of course within the Hindu tradition and could well be construed as one form of contribution to Hindu nation-building. Yet, any careful reading of Swamiji's words and writings leaves one with a very firm impression that the centre point of his Indian agenda was an effort to create mass consciousness and the minimum physical conditions required for the purpose. His ultimate aim, to use current and somewhat inappropriate vocabulary, was empowerment. Hindu revivalism was inconsistent with such an objective. The regeneration of the Indian people, with the masses installed in the position of primacy which they had always been denied, rather than the revival of Hindus or Hinduism, was evidently his goal. But he wanted this worldly purpose to be informed by a high spirituality, because in his perception human life, and in fact the entire universe, was an indivisible totality. That spiritual message was derived from the Vedantic tradition as realized in the life of his guru, but projected repeatedly as a universalistic faith. And the message was to be preached by a band of dedicated celibates freed of any worldly attachments.

Interestingly, while he continued to write on philosophical themes, there was no repetition in India of his Vedantic lecture tours. He explained in answer to a question that India, sunk in abject poverty, was a land of *tamas*, the brutish inertia which was the least worthwhile quality in human beings. Spirituality was not for the weak nor possible on a hungry stomach. Indian veins must throb with this-worldly virtues, with *rajas*, before the country could absorb the heroic message of non-duality. His aim, he explained, was a Western-type society in India, with a powerful material civilization, but inspired by Vedanta. Some day he hoped to establish institutions for technical education to improve the agriculture, commerce and industry of India. The export of Indian industrial products would then be promoted abroad and Indians would be encouraged to consume home products only. [BR 7:376, 445].

Elsewhere he stated that he wanted the future Indians to have strong Muslim bodies and Vedantic souls. Incidentally, he was among the earliest nationalist thinkers to claim the Indo-Islamic past as part of the Indian heritage. His disciple, Sister Nivedita, records his intense pride in the artistic inheritance of the Mughal era and his admiration for the Mughal policy of taking Hindu brides so that the rulers of India had Muslim fathers and Hindu mothers. No Hindu revivalist of his day could have shared this particular enthusiasm.

His tensions with the different strands in the Hindu reaction of his days needs to be spelled out. It is important to remember that Hindu orthodoxy found him and his ways unacceptable. They questioned this non-Brahmin youth's right to be an ordained monk. They considered his journey across the black waters a violation of taboo and they suspected that he had not observed ritual taboos about food and comensality when he was abroad and of course they were right. His answer to such criticism was unequivocal:

When was I an orthodox Puranic Hindu? [BR 7:211] I have read carefully into our scriptures and find that spirituality and religion are not for the Sudras. Even if he observes the taboos about food etc. and journeys abroad, he does not acquire any merit. It is all wasted effort. I am a Sudra and a *mleccha*—why should I bother about all that? [BR 7:392]

He described the Hindu orthodoxy of his days as a religion of 'don't touchism' where virtue had finally found a shelter in the purity of cooking pots. The florid adjectives he used to describe the educated Hindus leave Macaulay's description of Bengalis cold at the doorstep: 'crushed by the wheels of caste divisions, superstitious, without an iota of charity, hypocritical, atheistic cowards'.

His contempt for certain specific manifestations of Hindu reaction in the last quarter of the nineteenth century is recorded in picturesque detail in his Bengali work, *Bhābbār kathā* ('Matters to think about'). It is impossible to do justice in translation to his racy style, but it seems worthwhile to give some extracts, for they establish beyond reasonable doubt that the man who wrote these could not be a Hindu revivalist. I quote one famous passage on the then familiar efforts to prove that all Hindu superstitions had a scientific explanation:

Gurgure Krishnabyal Bhattacharya is a great scholar. All knowledge concerning the entire universe is at his finger tips . . . There is nothing that he does not know and especially knowledgeable is he regarding the movement of electricity and magnetic forces from the tip of one's pigtail to all the nine orifices in the human body. And by virtue of this knowledge he is peerless in his ability to explain scientifically such matters as the [scientific necessity for] impregnating ten year old girls . . . As to evidence or reasoning, he has made things so simple that even little children can follow his arguments. You see, there is no religion outside India; within India none but the Brahmins have the right to understand it; among the Brahmins too everybody except the Krishnabyals is utterly worthless, and among the Krishnabyals Gurgure alone counts. Therefore whatever Gurgure says is self-evident truth. There is a lot of education around, people are getting somewhat restive, they want to understand everything, taste everything; therefore Mr Krishnabyal assures everyone, 'Have no fears; I shall explain away whatever doubts may bother you and do so in a scientific manner. Stay just as you were. Put some mustard oil in your nostrils and enjoy very sound sleep. Only, do not forget my fees.' And the people said, 'We are saved. What danger were we in! To actually get up from our beds, in fact move about! What botheration! They shouted, 'Long live Krishnabyal', turned over and went to sleep again.

He castigated what he described as the mindless imbecilities of popular Hinduism in equally strong language:

Today there are bells [for the worship], to-morrow there will be trumpets in addition and the following day yak tails will be waved . . . and people are regaled with 2000 absurd tales; the wheel, the mace, the lotus and conch shell; the conch shell, the mace, the lotus and the wheel etc. etc. This is what is described in English as imbecility . . . Whether the bell should be rung on the right side or the left, whether the sandal paste mark should be placed on the forehead or some other part of the anatomy; people who spend their days and nights in such thoughts are truly wretched. And we are the wretched of the earth and are kicked around because our intelligence goes no further.

The lines which follow have a peculiar relevance to the contemporary strategies of Hindu chauvinism:

Ten million rupees are spent to open and close the temple doors at Kashi and Brindaban. Now the Deity is changing his attire, now he is having his meal, or maybe he is providing *piṇḍa* for all the ancestors of the stupid bastards [the priceless expression he used in Bengali is *aṭkuṛīr beṭā,* i.e. sons of barren mothers] and all the time the living god perishes for the want of food, for want of education. The banias of Bombay set up hospitals for the bed bugs. No matter if the human beings die [for want of care] . . . A mortal sickness is abroad in our land. The entire country is one vast lunatic asylum. [BR 7:8–9]

His prescription for the country's material and spiritual well-being in this context was simple and direct: 'Throw away the bells and the rest of the rubbish into the river Ganges, and worship the incarnate God in man, worship all that are born as human beings.'

Amiya Sen in his monograph on Hindu revivalism has discussed at length the massive campaign against the Age of Consent Bill. He identifies it, correctly to my understanding, as the high watermark of the Hindu reaction. Vivekananda described that agitation as a matter for shame. [SSS: 31] Again I shall quote his words because there is no other way one can convey adequately the vehemence of his feelings on the subject:

. . . I deeply despise the custom of child marriage. . . . Our people are pay-ing for this grievous sin. I shall be an object of contempt to my own self if I support this monstrous practice directly or indirectly. . . . I must kick hard with all my might at the inhuman custom known as child marriage. [BR 7:232; also 107]

Vivekananda's iconoclastic contempt for much in the Hindu tra-dition was not confined to the contemporary scene. His diatribe against the inanities of neo-Hindu scientism to which I have referred concludes with a swipe at the mindless ritualism of the Hindu tradi-tion. What could one expect of a culture, he wrote, in which the best minds have been debating for over two millenia whether to eat with the right hand or the left. He lashed out at those who blamed the Muslims for the Hindus being allegedly forced to adopt the purdah system. He referred his correspondent to the *Gṛhyasūtra*—the pro-vision that a girl child must be given in marriage before she learns to masturbate, *hastād yoniṃ na gūhati.* [BR 7:107] And then there is that famous passage on the *aśvamedha* sacrifice as prescribed in the Black *Yajurveda:*

Tadanantaraṃ mahiṣīm aśvasaṃnidhau pātayet ('Thereafter make the queen lie down beside the horse. . . . And then they all had a drunken orgy.')

Vivekananda wrote, 'The sacrificer, the priests, their assistants, everybody. Heavens, Sita was in exile, Rama celebrated the sacrifice on his own. I was relieved to learn this.'

It is difficult to imagine the protagonists of the Rama temple controversy or their intellectual ancestors, if one can use that expression legitimately, writing that passage. Vivekananda did not spare even the great Vedantin, Sankaracharya for his lack of generosity in denying to non-Brahmins the right to supreme knowledge, and his cruelty in forcing his defeated Buddhist opponents to immolate themselves. I have quoted him at some length to establish that there was an unbridgeable chasm between his sensibilities and those which inspired the Hindu reaction in his time. He was not just a reformer who wanted to rid Hinduism of some of its blemishes. He had a deep feeling of revulsion for many of the fundamentals of the Brahminical tradition. His concern was only with an inheritance of high spirituality which, he believed, was realized in its ultimate perfection in the life of his guru. And he read in that life also a message of universalism. He sought to base a movement on that message, a movement which would revive India and do so by helping the masses achieve their rightful place in the life of the country.

This role which he gradually defined for himself has been transformed in popular perception into one of leadership of a Hindu revival. The Ramakrishna–Vivekananda movement, we are told, stemmed the tide of reform and helped restore people's confidence in the popular Hindu tradition, earlier shaken by Western as well as reformist criticism. In the process, the tide of reform which had swept the educated sections of society was turned back. I question this thesis for a number of reasons.

Vivekananda certainly had little sympathy for what he called Babu-inspired reform. In fact, he had undisguised contempt for the social class from which he came. It derived partly from the fact that he saw them as blood-suckers totally indifferent to the masses. There were many meetings organized by the *bhadralok*, he said, but he had not come across even one for the masses by sucking whose blood the *bhadralok* had become *bhadralok*. [BR 7:374] He was of the belief that criticism without sympathy, which he saw as the hall-mark of *bhadralok* attempts at reform, was of little use. Besides one could not change society by deliberate attempts at change, for social change had its own laws. All that one could hope to do was to create a consciousness through service, example and propaganda and leave it to people to work out their own destiny. [SSS: 22, 20; BR 7:185, 371] He did not oppose reform, but he did not see any particular point in the effort. It had produced very little result, in his opinion.

There is no identifiable link between the movement he sponsored and the decline of interest in reform. As Partha Chatterji has shown in a seminal essay,[2] the *bhadralok* did not abandon their efforts to alter the conditions of women. They had achieved their basic goals in this respect. Besides, notwithstanding the alleged apathy of reformers and Vivekananda's unwillingness to support reforms, the desired changes came about slowly through the operation of impersonal forces. Through women's education, a slow rise in the age of marriage, and a decline in polygamy, the hoped-for objectives of the reformers were eventually achieved. Widow-remarriage never became popular among Hindus, an evidence in support of Vivekananda's belief that social change has a certain autonomy and can be forced only to a limited extent. The religious debates regarding the nature of the Deity, whether He or She had a form or not, and the relevance of idol worship, had long lost their urgency. The majority of Hindus, educated and uneducated, had never given up the worship of images. Even the illiterate villager believed that he worshipped, not an image, but something else that it symbolized; and whatever the merit or demerit of the doctrine, Vivekananda did not preach polytheism. The cult of Ramakrishna, like the Vaishnava movements of the nineteenth century, stimulated an upsurge of *bhakti*, a recurrent and characteristic phenomenon of Bengali social life. Incidentally, this particular tendency had become manifest in the lives of the Brahmos as well. Not only Keshab with his Vaishnava-style *kirtans*, but the non-conformist Brahmos like Sibnath Sastri were imbued with this new spirit, very different from the rationalistic and this-worldly concerns of Rammohan and his immediate followers. The new rationalism of the early nineteenth century had become a part of the *bhadralok* social culture, but it had to co-exist now with a much older tradition of emotional religiosity. That emotionalism was soon to inform a new impulse which had no precedents in Indian life, namely revolutionary fervour. I draw attention to this transition in attitudes only to emphasize that the appeal of Ramkrishna–Vivekananda has to be located in a context which is not coterminous with the Hindu reaction of that time. I have argued at length that Vivekananda found the basic values informing that reaction profoundly repugnant. Yet he has been and continues to be claimed as one of the great leaders of Hindu revival. His cultural vocabulary and style of action were partly responsible for it. But it is also interesting to note how selectively a movement or its devotees can interpret the messages of a leader. The mission he set up, for instance, has been more concerned with social service in general than with educating the masses. Its preoccupation with universalism generally omits references to Swamiji's enthusiasm for Islam and the Indo-Islamic heritage. The psychological insecurity which explains the great enthusiasm for the absurdities of theosophy, a movement which was careful to pay homage to the spiritual superiority of Hinduism, also inspired much of the enthusiasm for Vivekananda who was believed to have achieved great victories for Hinduism abroad. His deep concern for the masses made little or no impact on his middle class followers. At best, they could respond to his call to serve, but his passionate plea for efforts which would restore the masses to their rightful position in Indian society went unheeded. Little was done by anyone for mass education. Vivekananda was right in thinking that social and cultural change has a certain autonomy and individual effort can have but limited impact on their course. His plea for self-sacrificing service soon inspired a pattern of activity which he had considered futile— namely, revolutionary effort to end foreign rule. Vivekananda had a two-fold agenda which he had time to pursue for less than a decade: to preach an universalist spiritual faith based on the life of his master which he saw as the ultimate realization of the Vedantic truth, and secondly, to create a mass consciousness through service and education. The seed fell on very infertile ground. He was hailed in his own time as a hero of Hinduism who had conquered the West. Today understandably the VHP has the audacity to claim him as their own. I have argued that it is difficult to imagine him as the ideological ancestor of people who incite the ignorant to destroy other people's places of worship in a revanchist spirit.

ABBREVIATIONS

BR: Swami Vivekananda, *Bāṇī o racanā* [Collected Bengali Works], 10 vols (Calcutta, 6th edn. 1982).

SSS: Saratchandra Chakrabarti, *Swāmī-śiṣya a sambād* (Calcutta, 5th edn. 1982).

NOTES

1. A.P. Sen, *Hindu Revivalism in Bengal 1872–1905: Some Essays in Interpretation* (Delhi, 1993).
2. See P. Chatterji, 'A Nationalist Resolution of Women's Question', in K. Sangari and S. Vaid (eds), *Recasting Women: Essays in Colonial History* (New Delhi, 1989), pp. 233–53.

7

Muslims and Islam in Swamiji's Vision of India—A Note*

The record of Indian nationalism contains a notorious failure. The emerging Indian nation failed to secure and retain the allegiance of a significant section, perhaps the majority, of politicized Muslims. Whatever the complex explanation for this failure, one relevant factor is often emphasized in the historiography of modern India: early Indian nationalist thought was too exclusively Hindu in its self-perceptions to be acceptable to Muslims. It excluded the Muslim presence and its contributions to the life and civilization of the subcontinent. In fact it had a pronounced tendency to rubbish the Indo-Islamic past and read into the six centuries of Muslim presence in India a history of enslavement and oppression. India's story of political dependence was seen to begin not at Plassey but with Mohammad Ghori's victory over Prithviraj. In fact nationalist thinkers even saw the British paramountcy as a providential decree, a liberation from Muslim tyranny. Despite pronounced ambivalence on the question of attitude to Muslims and the inheritance of Indo-Islamic culture, the relevant perceptions in nationalist ideology were certainly marked by negative attitudes, or at least a massive act of omission.

The past invoked by nationalist thought in nineteenth-century India is almost exclusively a Hindu past. The struggle for liberation as envisaged in the relevant literature refers equally exclusively to the attempts of Hindu chieftains to preserve their autonomy from the onslaught of Afghan and Turkish rulers whose religion happened to be Islam. These medieval struggles were repeatedly portrayed as a Titanic crusade between Islam and Hinduism. This particular vision of history is certainly of late-eighteenth and early-nineteenth century origin. A pundit of Fort William College was probably the first Bengali

*A version of this paper was published in R.K. Dasgupta (ed.), *Swami Vivekananda: A Hundred Years since Chicago.*

writer to refer to the reign of the Bengal Nawabs as tyrannical Muslim rule. Later, in British historical writings on India, from James Mill onwards, the simple dichotomy between Hindus and Muslims is repeatedly projected as the characteristic feature of Indian society over the centuries. Eliot and Dowson in their classic compilation, *History of India, As Told by Her Own Historians,* underlined the alleged fact of continuous Muslim tyranny over Hindu subjects, a perception of Indian history favoured by a section of orthodox Muslim chroniclers who disapproved of the pragmatic policies adopted by the Sultans and the Mughal Emperors. It is this view of history which informed nationalist perceptions of the Indian past and coloured attitudes towards the Muslims, and it is this view which was repeatedly projected on the Calcutta stage and the Parsi theatre of Bombay, as well as the historical romances of the nineteenth century.

As Indian nationalism entered an irridentist phase in the later decades of the nineteenth century, the negative perception of Indo-Islamic history and the role of the Muslims in Indian life acquired a passionate intensity. Around the same time the emotive features of increasingly militant nationalism came to be informed by an assertion of the Hindu identity. That identity was based on an essentialist, objectified construct with many faces. This marriage of romantic nationalism with celebrations of a constructed Hinduism is generally described as the Hindu revival.

Through a peculiarly odd misperception, Swami Vivekananda is seen to be a leader of this revival. I do not deny that the impact of his charismatic role in Indian history did feed into the growing preoccupation with the Hindu identity, but his own perception of nationalism and India's future was far more inclusive. In fact it was so uncompromisingly critical of much that he rejected in the Hindu social reality, both past and present, that to label him a Hindu revivalist is almost certainly an anachronism. His attitude towards the caste system, his concern for the oppressed masses, his view that the upper-caste educated Hindu had no role in future India, his contempt for aberrations like child-marriage and his total rejection of ritualism hardly fit the image of a Hindu revivalist. Nor does his inclusive view of Vedānta, which he saw as informing all religious faiths. The syncretic heritage of his guru is certainly inconsistent with the image of a militant Hindu.

If we are to locate Vivekananda in an appropriate space in the history of Indian nationalism we have to focus on an area very remote from Hindu chauvinism. The purpose of this paper is to highlight an aspect of his thought which fitted in with an emerging feature of Indian nationalism in his days but went way beyond the limits of the perception and feeling on this subject articulated by others.

While literary and polemical writings in the protonationalist phase did virtually exclude positive references to the Indo-Islamic past, political initiatives often had a less exclusive approach to formulations of the Indian identity. As early as 1861 Rajnarayan Basu established a Society for the Promotion of National Feeling among the Educated Natives of Bengal. The Indian Association established in 1876 was inspired by a vision of 'a united India'. Its objectives were no less than 'the unification of the Indian races and peoples upon the basis of common political interests and aspirations' as well as 'the promotion of friendly feeling between Hindus and Muhammadans'. A review of Musharraf Hussain's famous novel contained a cryptic comment that the name of the nation (*jati*) was Bengali, not Hindu or Muslim. A patriotic writer noted with some concern that the repeated references to *jaban (yavana)* tyranny on the Calcutta stage were unlikely to endear the Hindus to their Muslim fellow-countrymen or, for that matter, contribute to national solidarity. Rajnarayan in his final testament, *The Hopes of an Old Hindu*, projected his dream that Hindus and Muslims would cooperate in the Indian National Congress, and thus 'help build a glorious future for their common motherland'. Bhudev, despite his passionate advocacy of orthodox ritual, was among the first to speak of Muslims as foster-brothers having shared the same mother's milk for six centuries. Vivekananda's attitudes towards Muslims and Islam have to be read in the context of this particular strand in Indian nationalism. But, to repeat, his pronouncements on the subject as on everything else were original and informed by intense emotions.

It is in fact this intensity of emotion which distinguishes his perceptions of the Indo-Islamic past from that of his contemporaries. The new ambience of nationalism, as noted above, did not exclude a degree of ambivalent regard for the Indo-Islamic past. Indian nationalism inevitably contained a large measure of cultural self-assertion. The cultural past which was projected as an object of pride, the point of reference for claims to superiority in relation to the West, was almost entirely Hindu. Almost, but not entirely. The Bengali protagonists of the new nationalism did frequently find Islam superior to Christianity and 'Muslim rule' in some ways a source of greater happiness than its British counterpart. Bhudev found Islam in his scale of values superior to Christianity as a religion. He based his assessment on the ground that while Christianity with its ascetic founder provided no role model for the man of the world, the prophet of Islam was the perfect man, *Insan-i-Kamil*, who excelled as a man of God as well as a householder and leader of men. He claimed that he had met in Upper India, Muslim savants who were comparable in every way to the sages of ancient India. He had heard them proclaim '*yeh wohi hai*' (All this is but He), which he equated with the *Upanisadic* doctrine that the Universe and Brahman were the same.

He further argued that compared to the Mughals, the British rule had failed in one crucial respect. While the people of India were loyal to the Empire from a rational calculation of self-interest, the British had failed to win the love of their Indian subjects, an area where the Mughals had succeeded brilliantly. Bankim who, I have argued elsewhere, had negative gut reactions *vis-à-vis* the Muslim presence in India, did at the same time state unequivocally that the British rule was the only alien rule in the history of India, adding that alien rule was not necessarily evil. Even in his relative assessment of different cultures, he found the *sharia* superior to Hindu as well as English legal systems in so far as women's right to property was concerned. But he, like most of his contemporary writers, was quite explicit in describing the long rule of Muslim dynasts as a period of tyranny, though he admitted exceptions to this general rule.

To repeat, Swamiji's attitude towards Islam and the Indo-Islamic inheritance was distinguished by his great pride in and veneration for this particular component of our heritage. Sister Nivedita records his intense emotions at the sight of the Mughal monuments and how his voice choked as he described the glories of Mughal architecture. The marriage between Mughal emperors and Rajput princesses acquired ideological dimensions in his view of the Indian past. He saw in the fact that a succession of imperial rulers were born of Muslim fathers and Hindu mothers the peculiar genius of Indian civilization. The eclecticism he had learned at the feet of his guru acquired a political–cultural aspect in this context. It is worth emphasizing that no Hindu revivalist ever looked with favour on this particular feature of Mughal history. Swamiji's admiration for the Islamic component of Indian life did not stop with this particular projection of the past. In his vision of the future too, the ideal Indian would have a Muslim body and a Vedāntic soul.

This joy in the Islamic heritage is perhaps traceable not simply to his nationalist ideology, nor to the all-embracing mystical eclecticism of his guru, but to the environment of his home and childhood as well. His brother Bhupendranath describes the eclectic ambience of the Datta family with particular reference to its component of Indo-Islamic culture. His father Biswanath, a polyglot, knew Arabic, Persian and Urdu, and the last two were his favourite languages. The *Diwan-i-Hafiz* was his favourite reading. The father was also a virtuoso in classical Indian music, perhaps the least denominational and most syncretic element in Indian culture. Muslim *pirs* were venerated in the Datta home and the father's close friends included Muslims. Swamiji's affection for the Islamic past was partly rooted in his direct experience of Indo-Islamic culture—especially its music and cuisine. The Dattas were *bon viveurs* who delighted in Mughal food and Swamiji's own skill in producing these delicacies are well known. His training in music also helped enhance his pleasure in the Mughal heritage.

Besides his joy and pride in the Islamic inheritance his pride in that heritage had a pan-Asian dimension. He wrote and preached at a time when the Orientalist projection of the East–West dichotomy had acquired a positive content in Indian perceptions. Late nineteenth-century Bengali writings underline the allegedly higher moral and spiritual inclinations of Asian societies. The progress of Japanese industrial enterprise had become a subject of comment and reflected glory in the writings of the period. Vivekananda contributed to this conception of a glorified Asia in ways which have gone virtually unnoticed. To him Islam represented a faith and culture superior to that of the West and Western Christianity. In this context he first emphasized the contribution of the Arabs to modern European civilization. He spoke with admiration of the way in which Islamic civilization had promoted a scientific culture and encouraged an enquiry into all aspects of nature without inhibition. He contrasted this with the record of medieval Christianity, its persecution of Galileo and all rational knowledge which might go against Christian dogma as embodied in the Old Testament. The Koran, he pointed out, contained numerous passages which sanctioned and encouraged scientific enquiry. The fact that in the history of Islam both in and outside India there is no record of persecution of intellectual enquiry was a matter of great personal pride to him.

Islam appealed to him also at a very different level, close to his intimate and most personal aspiration—the mystical longings of his soul. His disciples and biographers have often noted that his patriotic zeal and social concern induced an act of self-sacrifice. His intense personal quest for direct and uninterrupted realization of the Infinite had to be relegated to a second place in relation to his role as a world teacher and passionate patriot. He told one of his disciples with a note of regret that these activities had forced on him a relative neglect of the mystical regime. Sister Nivedita records his fits of impatience with this 'worldly role' which kept him away from the Mother. Occasionally in relation to faiths other than the one in which he was born we find him rejoicing in images and attitudes which revealed to him perhaps unfamiliar faces of the Infinite. We find him thus kneeling spontaneously in veneration in a Catholic Church and translating the *Imitation of Christ* into his mother tongue. From the perspective of this spiritual quest Islam had a unique appeal. What appealed was the directness and simplicity of the great message which 'deluged the world in the name of the Lord'. His perception of Islam is stated in the language of ecstasy '. . . No music, no paintings, . . . no priest, . . . no bishop', it was a faith which preached the living God without any resort to intermediaries. Here the created being stood face to face with his Maker, the Master of the Universe, in the blinding light of the desert sun. Here inevitably all men were equal, not merely in theory but in the daily experience of life. Here the Sultan of Turkey could sit and dine with the humblest of his fellow believers while the ideal of equality remained only a copybook moral in the other religion which preached the same doctrine, Christianity.

This adoration of Islam in Vivekananda's written and spoken words does not refer to this-worldly concerns like patriotism or cultural self-assertion. Here its appeal was to an area of experience and anguished search which transcended all national and cultural boundaries. Here Vivekananda reveals himself in his closest affinity to his guru, the realization of the same ultimate truth underlying all religious beliefs. But his language suggests that he discovered in Islam a directness and simplicity of faith not to be found in any other message vouchsafed to man.

To conclude, Vivekananda's message in the way it shaped Indian nationalist consciousness has an unexpected history. The urge for political independence was implicit in much of his preachings but in

no sense was it central to his efforts at nation-building. Yet a generation of revolutionaries was inspired to violent and self-sacrificing
effort through the meaning they read into his words. At a later date
activists and historians have projected him as a proclaimer of Hindu
glory abroad and hence inevitably as a leader of the Hindu revival.
This particular appropriation of his role and message has somehow
ignored his central concern. Yet any careful student of his writings
is aware that his agenda for national regeneration ascribed only one
role to the modern intelligentsia—to help the down-trodden masses
to realize their power so that they could inherit the earth. And the
other message, which is almost completely forgotten, embodied a
vision of future India. It is a vision rejoicing in our multiple inheritance.
In Vivekananda's perception the Indo-Islamic past is central to that
inheritance and the future India of his dreams had a Hindu soul and
a Muslim body. Furthermore Islam with its simple and direct message appealed to his mystical soul in a way that was unique.

BIBLIOGRAPHICAL NOTES

For his strongly favourable comments on the Indo-Islamic heritage, see
Sister Nivedita, *Notes of Some Wonderings with the Swami Vivekananda*, 4th
edn. (Calcutta, 1957), 4, 76. Also her *The Master as I Saw Him*, 11th edn.
(Calcutta, 1972), 204. For his comment on the essentially Indian character
of Indian Muslims, see *The Life of Swami Vivekananda* by His Eastern and
Western Disciples, 2 vols, 5th edn. (Calcutta, 1979), I, 357. For the egalitarian virtues of Islam, see Swami Vivekananda, *The Complete Works of Swami
Vivekananda*, 8 vols, 15th edn. (Calcutta, 1977), II, 371. For his admiration
of the Prophet of Islam, ibid., I, 481–4. For Islam's record of tolerance as
compared to Christianity, see Marie Louise Burke, *Swami Vivekananda in
the West: New Discoveries*, 4 vols, 3rd edn. (1983), I, 249. Vivekananda was
not entirely consistent in all his statements on Islam and on a couple of
occasions he harked back to the popular perception of 'Muslim tyranny' in
India. For a discussion of these, see Javeed Alam, 'Tradition in India under
Interpretive Stress: Interrogating Its Claims', in *Thesis Eleven*, 1994, Number 39.

8

Had He Been Alive Today*

Saints, prophets and all culture heroes often appear to later generations in a light very different from the one in which their contemporaries perceived them. A culture hero to later generations has an aura of universal acceptance. They are often seen as universally accepted figures above all controversies even in their own time. The very nature of greatness precludes such universal acceptance. The truly great are not candidates in popularity contests. More often than not, they take on the daunting and highly unpopular task of changing the world as they see it and of fighting evil regardless of consequences. Vested interests, guardians of received wisdom as well as the merely stupid who are incensed by anyone questioning their habitual ways have united again and again to persecute such extraordinary men and women. Jesus Christ succeeded in uniting against him virtually every one in authority in the society in which he was born. The hatred against the father of our nation eventually crystallized in a fanatic's bullet. Swami Vivekananda was no exception to this pattern of familiar responses: for he was no gentle lamb and attacked with leonine courage all that he perceived to be false and pernicious in Indian society, especially its Hindu component, both past and present. Many sections of contemporary opinion returned his criticism with rare viciousness. That record of venom is there for all to see in Shankariprasad Basu's multi-volume compilation.

Our society to-day is torn by conflict. An aggressive creed of intolerance and hatred, built on a false construction of our past, has been raised by some to the level of patriotic duty. Over the last few months I have read repeatedly into Swamiji's words to discover what his message would have been in a crisis such as ours. I have done so especially since people with whom one would be ashamed to associate have had the audacity to claim him for their own. And I have

*Lecture delivered in Calcutta at the centenary celebrations of Swami Vivekananda's speech at the Congress of Religions, Chicago 1893.

discovered to my joy that his ringing words of fire have an especial relevance to our times. There is a saying in Bengali that one worships the holy river Ganges with water from that very stream. In the same spirit, I shall merely present a series of extracts from Swamiji's speeches and writings to underline what his message would have been in a situation such as the one we face to-day.

One hears a great deal about revivalism to-day and in the view of some we are happy witnesses of a massive revival of Hinduness challenging the godless secularism of yester year. There was a comparable revival in the nineteenth century which, contrary to popular impressions, was often the butt of Swamiji's mordant wit. Among the claims of our nineteenth-century revivalists was the assertion that much that the ignorant secularists of the day saw as ignorant superstition could be explained in terms of higher scientific theories. Here is what Swamiji had to say about this proud claim:

Gurgure Krishnabyal Bhattacharya is a great scholar. All the knowledge concerning the entire universe is at the tip of his fingers. His body is rather skin and bones; his friends say that this is due to the severity of his penances, the enemies ascribe it to malnutrition. The wicked say that such are the end results of producing a score and half children each year. However that may be, there is nothing that Mr Krishnabyal does not know; especially knowledgeable is he regarding the movement of electricity and magnetic forces from the tip of one's pigtail to all the nine orifices in the human body. And by virtue of this secret knowledge he is without peer in his ability to explain scientifically such matters as the [necessity for] impregnating ten year old virgins, the need for collecting clay from the courtesans' door as an essential prerequisite of Durga Worship. As to evidence or reasoning, he has made things so simple that even little children can follow his arguments. You see, there is no religion outside India, within India none but the Brahmins have the right to understand it; among the Brahmins too, everyone excepting the Krishnabyal family is utterly worthless, and among the Krishnabyals, Gurgure alone counts. Therefore whatever Gurgure says is self-evident truth. There is a lot of education around, the people are getting a little restive, people want to understand everything, taste everything; therefore Mr Krishnabyal assures everyone, 'Fear not, I shall explain away whatever doubts you may feel and all in a scientific manner. Stay as you were. Put mustard oil in your nostrils and sleep very soundly. However, do not forget my fees.' And the people said, 'We are saved. What danger were we in. To get up, to actually move about, what botheration.' They said, 'Long live Krishnabyal', turned over and went to sleep again.

The punch line in this uninhibited diatribe links the contemporary syndrome of mindless conformity to the grand tradition: 'After all we are talking of habits that are thousands of years old. How can the human body tolerate changing these? Is it possible to cut the knots which have shackled our minds for thousands of years?'[1] He castigated the received tradition in unqualified terms with the courage and conviction of one who identified with what he saw as worthwhile in the same, 'Oh God! A country where the most powerful intellects have been weighing for two thousand years whether to eat with one's right hand or the left will of course sink into degeneracy. To-day we have bells, to-morrow we have the flute on top of it, day after to-morrow there will be fanning with yak tails . . . On top of all these there are two thousand absurd tales to beguile the people—the disc, the mace, the lotus and the conch shell, the conch shell, the mace, the lotus and the disc etc. etc. etc. This is what is described as imbecility in the English language. . . . We are wretched and kicked around because our intelligence goes no further.'[2] The lines which follow have a resonant relevance to contemporary India: 'If you aspire after anything that may be good for your future, I say throw away the bells and the rest of the rubbish into the Ganges and worship the incarnate God in man, worship all that are born as men. . . . A crore of rupees is spent [each day] to open and close the temple doors at Kashi and Brindaban. Now the deity is changing his clothes, now he is having his meal, now he is offering *pinda* to the ancestors of the stupid bastards. [The original Bengali has the priceless phrase, *antkurer byata*, i.e., children of men incapable of begetting children.] And all the while the living God perishes for want of food, for want of education.'[3]

The ringing 'pseudo-secularism' of this passage is elaborated in his comments on a fictive Brahmin, a veiled reference to some real persons, 'Bimala, having studied the scriptures, has realised that the entirety of mankind is polluted, and such is their nature that they are congenitally incapable of religiosity. A handful of Brahmins in India are the sole exceptions. The ultimate realization attained through meditation and penance is that I am pure and everyone else is impure. This is the religion of devils, of demons, a hellish religion.'[4]

It is true that in the West, Swamiji tried to explain away Hindu practices he otherwise rejected out of hand. The object of such explanations and avowals was nationalistic. Only a fool, he once explained to Sister Nivedita, would wash one's dirty linen in public.[5] His emphasis on the deep religiosity of the Indian people, so prominent in his pronouncements abroad, is less evident in his fiery exhortations to this worldly efforts intended for his compatriots.

For a proper appreciation of Swamiji's views on religion, one has to recall the very well-known yet virtually ignored facts of his *vita religiosa*. It is necessary to remember that he began his career as a passionate sceptic in search of God, the ultimate realization promised to the inspired seeker in the Indian tradition. And he found a Guru who showed him the way. If Paramahansa's life and words were used to stoke the fires of Hindu revival, there is not an iota of evidence to suggest that this was an object he ever had in mind. He belonged, if anything, to the grand tradition of mystical syncretism which India developed in the middle ages in response to the encounter of multiple cultures. His entire religious ideology was summed up in one simple statement, 'There are as many ways as there are opinions.' Ramakrishna's life, in the words of his famous disciple, was itself a Congress of Religions.[6] His Mother was the the Mother of the Universe on whom Hindus or Indians had no special claim.

When the Guru passed away, young Narendra went forth as a *parivrajaka*, a wandering ascetic in quest of supreme realization. The style of the quest was distinctively Indian, the object was not particularly so. In unfolding his spiritual message in the West, he emphasized its universalist dimension. His only claim was that the universal truth underlying all religions had been revealed in its quintessential perfection in the Vedantic doctrine.[7]

He repeatedly emphasized one distinction—between religion and what he described as creeds, i.e., institutionalized doctrinal faiths. These too in his view were revealed by the Deity through his holy men and were meant to suit particular ages and cultures and were hence necessarily different one from the other. But Religion, the underlying truth, was uniform. There was no scope for quarrels there. Quarrels arose over what selfish and cynical men had made of creeds in history to suit their own purposes. Every institutionalized religion was marked by crimes against humanity. Hinduism was no exception, especially since in its popular form it had replaced the higher truths of the faith with monstrous *lokachar*, mindless popular custom. Curiously enough, the creed about which he was the least critical, despite his references to the historical record of aggressive proselytization, was Islam. His famous statement that the future Indian would have a Muslim body and a Vedantic soul is well-known. Less familiar is his veneration of Islam as the one religion which placed the created being in direct relationship to God without the use of any intermediaries or external aid—no pictures, no music, no images.[8] In the spirit of a new–found pride in pan-Asianism, he underlined the Muslim contribution to Europe's civilization.[9]

Swamiji's grand vision of man's spiritual future was summed up brilliantly in his famous speech at Chicago:

Sectarianism, bigotry, and its horrible descendant, fanaticism, have long obsessed this beautiful earth. They have filled the earth with violence, drenched it often and often with human blood, destroyed civilization and sent whole nations to despair. Had it not been for those horrible demons, human society would be far more advanced than it is now. But their time is come; and I fervently hope that the bell that tolled this morning in honour of this convention may be the death-knell of all fanaticism, of all persecutions with the sword or with the pen, and of all uncharitable feelings between persons winding their way to the same goal.[10]

We all know that these hopes have been belied. The time has not come for the 'horrible demons' he so loathed. They flourish in his beloved land as never before. But we will live in the hope that their time will come before long. To recall and broadcast what Swami Vivekananda really said could be one important way of contributing to that desired end.

NOTES

1. Swami Vivekananda, *Bhabbar Katha, Swamijir Bani o Rachana*, VI.
2. Shankariprasad Basu, *Vivekananda o Samakalin Bharatvarsha*, III, 125.
3. Ibid., 125–6.
4. Ibid.
5. Sister Nivedita, *The Master as I Saw Him.*
6. Swami Vivekananda, Speech at the Congress of Religions (Chicago, 1893), *Collected Works*, I.
7, 8, 9 and 10 See footnote 6.

9

Gandhi and Tagore: Where the Twain Met

The differences in opinion and attitude between Tagore and Gandhi are familiar to the students of modern Indian history. Tagore's famous letter to the Mahatma at the inception of the Non-cooperation Movement, condemning it as asceticism and 'orgy of frightfulness' which found 'a disinterested delight in any unmeaning devastation,' 'a struggle to alienate our heart and mind from those of the West', 'an attempt at spiritual suicide' has been quoted often enough as clinching evidence of their very basic disagreement regarding the road to a better future for India.[1]

The poet was also sceptical concerning other features central to Gandhi's agenda, like the latter's prescription that everyone should spin as a part of their daily routine. Tagore failed to see what would be gained by people better suited for other work struggling to become clumsy spinners. Besides the two most eminent personalities of modern India projected two very different self-images. There was little obviously in common between the ascetic in loin cloth and the divinely handsome poet in his flowing robes. One's primary concern was the creation of a moral utopia while the other was a celebrant of life's many splendours.

Yet such genuine differences in opinion and world-view have deflected attention from the vast areas of agreement between the two. This is to be explained partly with reference to the fact that the poet, shrouded in an unfamiliar language and, until recently, very inadequate translations is virtually unknown to modern scholarship outside Bengal. Recent comments in the British literary journals, remarkable for their ignorant arrogance, are a measure of that unfamiliarity. To those who do not read Bengali, Tagore is exclusively a literary person or a mystic of sorts. The fact that some two-thirds of his writings are serious essays, mostly on political and socio-economic problems of India and the crisis of civilization has been more or less ignored in Tagore scholarship. No wonder then that two very dramatic epistles cited above have received greater attention than a great deal of analytical writing which shows the continuity of thought and concern between two most striking individuals of recent times.

An obvious fact which one must emphasize in exploring these affinities is that their individuality notwithstanding, Tagore and Gandhi were both in many was typical products of nineteenth-century India. Central to the intellectual and moral concerns of that time was the attempt to grapple with the colonial experience. Self-conscious emotional and intellectual exercises to work out a *modus vivendi* in a situation perceived to be humiliating generated other related efforts: evaluating the west, introspection into the strength and weaknesses of the Indian tradition and its true character and agenda for reconstructing Indian society. The end results were of course not uniform, but there are identifiable regularities in the thought patterns of modern India's founding fathers. In the spectrum of ideas which constitute the Indian discourse in the nineteenth and early twentieth century, those traceable to Gandhi and Tagore are remarkably similar in many ways. Tagore's thinking on the themes mentioned above can be located squarely within the tradition of nineteenth-century Bengali thought from Rammohan to the poet's contemporary, Vivekananda. The modern Indian antecedents of Gandhi's ideas remain unexplored. His discipleship of Gokhale is known, but little has been written on his relationship to the debate between the *sudharaks*, reformers and the traditionalists in western India. But even a superficial reading into the relevant literature would show that his concerns were not all that different from other social thinkers of his age. In short, the affinities between Tagore and Gandhi can be traced to a large extent to the shared concerns of the nineteenth-century Indian intelligentsia trying to work out world-views and agenda in the context of their colonial experience.

The purpose of this paper is, however, not to trace the sources of their thought. It is only a preliminary exercise aimed at identifying the similarities.

Gandhi's first elaborate comment on the Indian problem, his *Hind Swaraj*,[2] identified one basic evil, modern civilization. It was a threat to all that was worthwhile in human values, not only in India but the world over. The British, as victims of this pandemic, were to be pitied, not hated. It was not any race or nation but modern civilization itself and the Indian infatuation with it that oppressed India. At the heart of that evil civilization was the perception of man as a creature of desires and capitalism had a vested interest in whetting these desires. Multiplication of wants hence become the *sine qua non* of the entire system which dehumanized man, legitimized violence against nature and deprived life of all meaning and purpose beyond the endless fulfilment of desires. The end results of such soul-destroying pursuits were loss of all autonomy, mutual suspicion and violence and the exploitation of man by man. Man, both as worker and consumer, had become slave to machines. Imperialism and racism were integral to such a civilization. Even its apparent benefits were of a highly dubious nature. Modern medicine produced patterns of dependence which were highly unnatural and modern transport, far from making life easier, actually helped spread disease. Wisdom had been reduced to knowledge in quest of power and morality, equated with enlightened self-interest, had become a form of prudence. The much-vaunted dynamism of the West was little more than mindless activism. Only on two points was Gandhi willing to concede some moral merit to modern civilization. He admired its spirit of scientific enquiry for he saw in it a genuine quest for truth. He also found much to learn in the organizational aspect of western life: the civil virtues were informed by the moral qualities of discipline and co-operation.[3]

Tagore, despite his great admiration for many features of western life, was quintessentially in agreement with Gandhi's judgement. Gandhi had described Indian infatuation with the west as *moha*, the high road to cultural suicide. The poet compared the western impact with disease. He did add by way of apology and explanation: 'Everything is for the good in its own place; but even what is good becomes dangerous rubbish in an inappropriate setting.'[4] He was, however, far from certain that everything was for the good in western civilization. His multi-faceted critique of the west focussed on certain basic themes which recur again and again in his writings. Gandhi wrote that money was their God. Tagore states the same idea in a more elaborate language: Every feature of western civilization is an item commanding very high price. Everything from pleasure to warfare costs a great deal of money. Money has become a great power as a result and the worship of money now surpasses all other forms of worship. Everything is therefore difficult to achieve or attain, everything is shrouded in complexity. This is the greatest weakness of western civilization.[5] He linked this apotheosis of money to another central feature of western civilization which he found even more disturbing. Gandhi had condemned its mindless activism. He saw in its excessive effort a sign of inherent weakness, an unnecessary over-expenditure of energy for which there was always a price to pay. In Europe there were already signs that nature was calling for repayment.[6] The excess of effort in every sphere of life had created patterns of elaboration and ever increasing excitement which relegated human beings to a position of insignificance.

The cruel pressure of competition reduces the workers to something worse than machinery. The grand show of civilization which we see from outside astounds us. The human sacrifice which goes on day and night under that facade remains hidden. But it is no secret to Providence: social earthquakes bear witness to the consequences from time to time. In Europe, powerful groups crush weak ones, big money starves out small money and at the end swallows it up like a pill.

This excess of activism generates a poison of discontent. 'The monstrous factories' engulfed in black smoke deprive men of their life-protecting cover of solitude—of space, time and opportunity for restful thought. People become unused to their own company. Hence at every opportunity they try desperately to escape from themselves through drink and reckless quest for pleasure. The affluent hedonists are not much better off. They are fagged out by the endless pursuit of fresh excitement.

They whirl themselves around like dry leaves in a storm of parties, horse race, hunting and travel. In the midst of such whirlwind, they fail to see clearly either themselves or the world around them; everything appears obscure and indistinct. If the continuous cycle of pleasure stops for a moment, they find even that momentary encounter with self, the experience of unity with a wider world intolerable in the extreme.[7]

He was unequivocal in his rejection of this material civilization. He did not believe in it, he wrote to Gandhi, just as he did not believe 'in the physical body to be the highest truth in man'.[8]

In his statements on western civilization, Tagore frequently invoked the concept of relativism which was a commonplace in the cultural discourses of nineteenth-century Bengal. A common theme in this discussion is that one can not judge one civilization from the point of view of another because each civilization had its characteristic proneness. Tagore, citing Guizot, noted the uniqueness of western civilization in its multiplicity of drives and the co-existence of often incompatible institutions and tendencies. Yet, in modern Europe, he identified one dominant concern which transcended all others—namely, an apotheosis of the nation state. Everything was permitted in its service and nothing was allowed to thwart its perceived interests. The end result of such obsessive preoccupation with national self-interest was conflict and eventually self-destruction. If Gandhi condemned the totality of modern civilization as evil, to Tagore its supreme evil consisted in nationalism, which separated man from man and led to destructive conflict.[9] Gandhi, the leader of India's militant nationalism, provided in his writings indirect support for such views. He saw Europe's greed for territories as a function of her aggressive nationalism. The nationalism he prescribed for India was one which would not ignore the interest of other nations, nor make even one's own community its primary concern.[10]

The nineteenth-century Indian discourse on the West was rarely, if ever, informed only by intellectual curiosity. It was inspired mainly by an urge to assess the comparative merits of Indian civilization, its differences with the dominant culture of the time and its relative superiority or inferiority. A quest for cultural self-assurance was often the unconscious motive. A more conscious purpose was to assess the impact of the west, increasingly seen as a threat to the Indian way of life with unfortunate implications for the country. Closely linked to such a perception was a recognition that there were things to learn from the west, and at another, less clearly stated level of understanding, the awareness that the clock of western influence could not be turned back altogether. There were consequent attempts to work out strategies of cultural survival. The agenda for the future—the programmes for national regeneration focussed, *inter alia*, on the question as to what one could adopt from the West. But nearly all such exercises started with an enquiry into the nature of Indian civilization and implicit or explicit comparisons with the west.

Gandhi's *Hind Swaraj*, an uncompromising critique of modern western civilization, was based on an equally strong faith in what he believed to be the values of Indian culture. There is no hint here of any need for self-assurance to overcompensate for any perceived inferiority. Some of his data derive no doubt from the Orientalist paradigm of self-sufficient village communities, which he idealized, but in essence he projects an emotional and ideological preference rooted, arguably, in his life experience of a traditional Indian home. I state this as an *obiter* or a hypothesis the validity of which would not

be very difficult to establish. One could show that he shared his preference for the emotional ambience of Indian life conceptualized as
a cultural value with much more westernized Indians, like R.C. Dutt
for example. While the latter were more welcoming to Europe's influence, they too found western life lacking in terms of the quality of
inter-human relationship. Underlying Gandhi's statements on the
superior worth of India's civilization one can detect his attachment
to a pattern of social interaction which did not privilege the individual
or emphasize achievement over other objects of human aspiration.

The Indian civilization of his imagination was essentially rural in
character in contrast to the city-based modern civilization of the
West. Its survival over millenia despite numberless assaults was
evidence of its viability and moral validity. It was spiritual because
the essentially spiritual nature of man was its discovery. Gandhi recognized an age-old culture hidden under 'an encrustment of crudity'
in rural India and that despite what he saw as the apparent brutish-
ness of peasant life. The self-governing, self-sufficient and harmoni-
ous village communities of yore were the institutional bulwark of
this ancient culture. He saw in the caste system a social order which
recognized the basic differences in human temperament: untouchability was an aberration, a fall from grace. Indian society was essentially tolerant perceiving, from the days of the Upanishads onwards,
the truth underlying apparently divergent beliefs. It was also a grand
synthesis of different cultures, with an infinite capacity for
assimilation. Thus in terms of human values it was superior in every
way to the competitive, materialistic and violence-prone civilization
of modern Europe driven by insatiable desire forever seeking satisfaction of new wants. The British, to bolster up their power, rubbished
Indian culture and Indians, infatuated with the West, believed their
propaganda. Curing Indians of their *moha* was one essential element
of Gandhi's agenda for reconstruction.[11]

Tagore's idealization of Indian society and his implied declaration
of faith in its essential superiority was based on an imaginative interpretation of what he had seen and experienced. He too repeatedly
emphasized its essentially rural character. And what Gandhi had
described as the predominantly spiritual proneness of India's civilization, the poet pictured in terms of very concrete images. He
contrasted Europe's endless and frantic pursuit of pleasure with the
Indians' very different style of quest for happiness:

India has diluted the density of her material pleasures by distributing it among friends, relations and neighbours; and she has simplified the complexity of action and distributed it among various groups. As a result, there is always the space to cultivate one's essential humanity in one's pleasures, one's activity and one's meditations. The trader—he too listens attentively to the bards retelling stories from the ancient scriptures and performs his rituals; the craftsman also reads the Ramayana tunefully. To a large extent this expansion of one's leisure helps preserve the purity of one's home, one's mind and the society at large and saves them from the dense vapours of vice. . . . The forest fires of evil instinct set alight by mutual competition and the crowding in on one another are kept in check in India.[12]

He saw an essential balance, an element of unity between the various aspects of their existence in the life of the peasants in rural Bengal:

. . . There is no grandeur, no complexity there. One does not need a great deal of philosophy, science or sociology to live one's life at this far end of the world and satisfy one's few modest wants. One requires only a few ancient rules which govern the family, the village and one's duties as a subject of the king. They blend very easily with people's lives to become a total vibrant reality.[13]

The poet found the illiterate villagers and the insignificant village beautiful because their steady allegiance to a set of feelings, beliefs and attitudes over many generations gave them a sense of dignity and imparted a quality of sweetness to their life. He saw in their faces an impression of compassionate patience, a simple-hearted trustfulness which moved him. He preferred it to the 'tremendous din of high civilization' which reached his ears from London and Paris.[14] Even in the life of urban India of his times he found a quality of contentment and happiness undiminished by the paucity of material goods. He found it more satisfying and worthier in terms of human value than anything he had encountered in Europe. He cited one concrete example in support of his argument. The Indian villager never turned away a guest or supplicant from his door and did not consider any discomfort entailed by his act of hospitality as discomfort. A profound and age-old belief in the sacredness of this duty had become a part of his emotional make-up.[15] Tagore was not unaware of the miseries of rural life and its pervasive sin of pettiness. Many of his short stories, based on his intimate knowledge of rural Bengal, are tales of man's inhumanity to man. But he still saw the

quality of dignified integrity as the central feature of India's traditional civilization, a quality of wholesomeness he missed in Europe.
In his words, the debilitating and denationalizing impact of the West
had not yet banished from Indian life 'the hard strength of poverty,
the stilled emotion of silence, the chilling peace of dedication and
the grand dignity of renunciation.' And if someday a storm raged
one would see the blazing eyes of the ascetic burning bright undiminished by any external fury.[16]

He also came very close to Gandhi's position in his perception of
India's political traditions. While he did not emphasize the notion of
self-sufficient village republics he questioned the value of state power
and, in fact, of nationhood itself for the life of a people. He shared
with other Bengali thinkers of the nineteenth century the notion that
society rather than the state was the central focus of Indian life.
Like Gandhi, he too was extremely suspicious of centralized state
power. Only, he went further to reject the need for nationhood which
raised barriers between man and man and led to vicious conflict.
The fact that the idea was alien to India was for him a plus point.
His agenda for national reconstruction, like Gandhi's, emphasized
the rural unit rather than the grand edifice of the state.[17]

Tagore discussed at great length and repeatedly the assimilative
power of Indian civilization, the belief first projected by Orientalists
that it represented a grand synthesis, a pattern of unity in diversity.
It had not rejected any of the numerous cultures which had come to
its shores. 'The Scythians, the Huns, the Pathans and the Mughals
had all merged into one single body', he declared in one of his most
famous poems.[18]

The main features of Gandhi's agenda for national reconstruction
are well-known.[19] He saw the central problem of Indian life as not
something of external origin, but a flaw in the Indian character—a
pervasive lack of courage and a consequent tendency to blame others
for one's misfortune. The degradation and humiliations India suffered
ultimately derived from this flawed character, for one is inevitably
trampled if one behaves like a worm. India's infatuation with western
civilization was a by-product of the same weakness, a loss of confidence in one's traditions. Independence for him was a necessity
primarily because it was a *sine qua non* for preserving the very worthwhile features of Indian civilization. The centralized state, which
was to him a dehumanizing machine destroying all sense of personal
responsibility, he considered unsuitable for India's essentially rural

civilization. Though he accepted it as necessary after 1930, the self-governing village communities were to be the base of India's future polity. And Indians would need to go through a process of self-purification, *atma-suddhi*, to escape from hybridization. They needed serious introspection to reinterpret the central principles of her civilization, and learn from others, as she had done in the past, in terms of her own self-perception, not those of western assumptions.

The agenda for reconstruction had to start from the bottom and be based, not on any sentimental attachment to an abstract *Bharat-mata*, but an active love of the people. The worker in the cause had to eschew ostentatious living and refuse comforts denied to others. The constructive programme emphasized village industries, health, education, use and development of indigenous languages, fight against untouchability and integration with India's tribal population. The instrument of self-purification would be the practice of *satyagraha*. India would not close her doors and windows to the world outside and allow 'noble winds from all over the world' to blow, but only on her own terms.

The similarity between Gandhi's programme and Tagore's ideas on the reconstruction of Indian society 1890s onwards is indeed striking.[20] He too, as noted above, regarded the centralized state as an institution alien to India. The colonial state had caused the worst degeneration because Indians now looked for its approbation rather than that of their own society in undertaking any act of service. Petitions and complaints to the government, whining when the authorities failed to respond, had become the prime instruments for the solution of the country's problems. Howls of protest were heard when a respectable Indian was insulted, but no one paused to think that such humiliation was rendered possible by the loss of national self-respect. He welcomed the spirit of *swadeshi*, not because it would harrass the English or stimulate Indian industry, but because it might teach us to give up our comforts and make a modest act of self-denial the basis of national unity. And 'the exit from the dark cave of self-interest' for the wider good of the people would give Indians the courage and self-respect they lacked so badly.

The privileged and the educated, if they desired national regeneration, would have to start with a sense of unity with the masses and construct bonds of love with the impoverished villagers through selfless service. He decried the excesses of the boycott movement during the anti-partition agitation because it hurt the interests of the poor for whom the elite had done nothing expecting unconditional support when it suited the latter. Indians must learn to live by their own strength, *atma-shakti*, and the way to do it was constructive effort in rural India in education, health, handicrafts without any dependence on government. His emphasis was not on agitation but building self-confidence and ties of unity between the elite and the masses. He repeatedly uses an expression for which there is no exact equivalent in English, *kalyan*, moral and material well-being. It is an expression with resonances which encompass the body and the spirit, the individual and wider humanity. Tagore's conception of *kalyan* uniting the entire society bear close resemblance too Gandhi's idea of *sarvodaya*. The former's efforts were not limited to prescriptions. He did set up an organization to implement his programmes and his Sri-niketan was something more than a craft school. Its purpose was rural reconstruction through training in productive crafts suitable for rural society. And while Santiniketan embodied the ideal of universal man, with its emphasis on simple living, joyous education and unity with nature, its affinities with Gandhian ideals were not insignificant.

Tagore's political agenda included the concept of a leader whose authority one would accept despite his inevitable human failures. There is no doubt that he recognized Gandhi as that leader. His initial response to the Non-cooperation movement was very different from his subsequent feelings of revulsion:

It is in the fitness of things that Mahatma Gandhi frail in body and devoid of military resources, should call up the immense power of the meek, that has been lying waiting in the heart of the destitute and insulted humanity of India. The destiny of India . . . is to raise the history of man from the muddy level of physical conflict to the higher moral atlitude.

He saw the movement, not as one for national liberation, but as one for the emancipation of man from national egoism.[21] I am not sure if this perception is very different from Gandhi's vision of satyagraha. A few days after he wrote the above passage, Tagore penned his better known denunciation. As in 1905 so in 1921, he was revolted by the destructive acts which inevitably go with all mass agitations. He rejected what he believed to be the negative implications of the movement in terms of his values. These were not very different from what Gandhi stood for. Only the latter did not see Non-cooperation as a threat to his universalist values. He too, like Tagore in his initial response, saw the movement as a step towards the moral liberation of all men.

NOTES

1. Tagore to Gandhi, March 1921, Gandhi, *Collected Works*, XX (Navajivan Trust, Ahmedabad, 1966), 539, 540–1.
2. See *Collected Works*, vol. X.
3. See Bhikhu Parikh, *Gandhi's Political Philosophy* (Notre Dame, Indiana, 1989), 15–26.
4. Rabindranath Tagore, *Atmashakti* (Strength of One's Own), *Rabindra-rachnabali*, vol. 3 (2nd edition, 3rd reprint, Viswa-bharati, Calcutta, 1975), 555.
5. 'University Bill', *Rabindra-rachanabali*, vol. 3, 595–6.
6. Ibid., 596.
7. 'Nababarsha' (New Year) in *Bharatvarsha*, *Rabindra-rachanabali*, vol. 4, 372–3.
8. Tagore to Gandhi, March, 1921, see note 1.
9. 'Prachya o Pratichya' (The East and the West), in *Samaj*, *Rabindra-rachanabali*, vol. 12, 236–60.
10. See Parikh, op. cit., 60.
11. See *Hind Swaraj* and Parikh, op. cit., ch. 2.
12. See note 7.
13. *Panchabhut* (The Five Elements), in *Rabindra-rachanabali*, vol. 2, 571.
14. Ibid., 571, 572.
15. *Panchabhut*, 570; *Samaj*, 240.
16. *Bharatvarsha*, 368–9.
17. *Atmashakti*, 529ff.
18. See his poem, *Bharat-tirtha.*
19. See Parikh, op. cit., 52–62, 111–17; Gandhi, *Constructive Programme Its Meaning and Place* (Navajivan Press, Ahmedabad, 1945).
20. The following discussion is based mainly on *Atmashakti, Panchabhut, Bharatvarsha* cited above as also *Raja Praja* in *Rabindra-rachanabali*, vol. 10.
21. Tagore to Gandhi, March 1921, *Collected Works*, vol. xx, 539.

II
The Raj Considered

10

British Rule in India:
An Assessment*

'Even those poor bloody fools at the club might be better company if we weren't all of us living a lie the whole time: the lie that we're here to uplift our poor black brothers instead of rob them.'

George Orwell, *Burmese Days*

DIFFERING PERCEPTIONS

Most chapters in this volume have been contributed by British historians. One of the three chapters allocated to non-British scholars has been assigned to an Indian. Presumably, he is expected to provide an assessment of Britain's rule in India which will be different from that of the British contributors.

As the editor explains in his introduction, there is no unanimous British view on the imperial past. It would be equally true to say that there is no unanimous Indian perception of the Raj. There are historians and social scientists in all parts of the world who consider imperialism in all its forms as morally unacceptable and a source of misery to the subject population, a historical phenomenon without any redeeming features. British historians with radical views do not disagree with this severely negative judgement. Yet it would be true to say that in Britain the dominant academic and popular perception of the imperial past, the Raj in particular, is far from negative. The articulated opinions of the governing class on the subject has however changed significantly over time. The eighteenth-century founders of the empire like Clive never pretended that they were in India for the benefit of Indians. Much later, *divide et impera* as a description of British policy in Indian came not from the Indian nationalists but conservative British politicians like Lord Salisbury. The viceroy, Lord

---

*An abridged version of this essay was published in P.J. Marshall, ed., *The Cambridge Illustrated History of the British Empire*. Cambridge, 1996.

Curzon claimed that India, won by the sword, would be held by means of the same instrument. Not long before the transfer of power, Penderel Moon, an idealistic young member of the ICS, was informed by the mandarins in the India Office that the British were in India not to teach Indians the art of self-government but to protect massive British investments in the territory.

But already by the later years of the nineteenth century we have a substantial body of literature underlining the benefits conferred by British rule on India, though the monstrous nature of Indian poverty and its causal connection with colonial rule were also analysed by an English publicist. As the Indian nationalist movement gathered momentum, British writings focussed on the opportunism of the nationalists and their unrepresentative character as well as the impossibility of nationhood for India, hopelessly divided by language and religion. Somewhat paradoxically, the rulers' alleged policy of conceding in stages 'responsible government' to that unlikely nation, a good intention frustrated and delayed only by the divisions within Indian society, also came to be emphasized.

Echoes of these older perceptions can be discerned in more recent British writings as well. The focus now is on the factiousness of Indian society, the historical roots of the country's problems stretching way beyond the advent of the British, the peculiarly Indian character of Indian poverty for which it is wrong to blame the colonial rulers and the very positive economic gains which flowed from imperial policies at least in parts of the country. In short, the dominant academic perception of the Raj in Britain sees South Asia's problems of poverty, illiteracy, internecine conflicts and the rest as being indigenous in origin having little to do with the 190 years of British rule. Further, in this view, the empire did more good than the critics of imperialism are willing to recognize.

Such conclusions are reinforced by a disaggregative approach which questions the validity of any generalization regarding imperial rule or its consequences. Besides, the subject populations are now stated to be important players in the game, almost as important as the rulers themselves if not in fact even more so. In such analysis, the conquered are no longer passive victims but active co-operators in the relevant action including the act of conquest itself. The benefits or otherwise of imperial rule are to a large extent traced to what they, and not the rulers, did or did not do.

In course of a heated debate on Japan's war record, a Japanese historian pointed out that nations do not reassess their historical past radically unless they have gone through the experience of social revolution or crushing defeat in war. Since Britain has been spared such experiences, public perceptions of the imperial past appear to be in broad agreement with the establishment view of the phenomenon: the term 'anti-British' applies to all persons and statements critical of the country's colonial record. It is unthinkable that a British monarch should apologize like the Japanese emperor for ancestral misdeeds to an erstwhile subject people. In popular perception—and pro-imperialist historiography—of course there were no misdeeds for which apologies are due.

Memories of the imperial past remains expectedly selective in Britain. Every British school child has heard of the Black Hole of Calcutta, but hardly anyone knows that four years before the transfer of power a famine, caused largely by administrative bungling, killed some three million people in Bengal. Attenborough's film on Gandhi with its scenes of brutality against non-violent protesters came as a shocking surprise to most British viewers. Here too perceptions have changed over time. Popular images of Gandhi in Britain to-day as a saint, tolerated and somehow rendered viable by the British tradition of fair play, is very different from older views which projected him as a crafty humbug fit to be trampled to death by the viceregal elephant, a measure warmly recommended by Winston Churchill.

If it is difficult for the average British citizen to take a negative view of the imperial past, it is almost equally difficult for the citizens of a former dependency which has gone through a prolonged struggle for independence to acknowledge any benefits of colonial rule. Incidentally, many British scholars ridicule the notion of a struggle for independence in India and see it as irrelevant 'high drama' staged by a minuscule and self-serving minority. However, educated Indian opinion concerning the Raj has changed significantly over time. Early Indian nationalists were ardent loyalists and took pride in being subjects of a world-wide empire. Even those who were highly critical of the rulers' racist policies and varied acts of injustice, declared their faith in the ultimate beneficence of British rule. A famous nationalist thinker, Dadabhai Naoroji, traced the roots of India's poverty to the colonial nexus but to him this unhappy connection was essentially 'unBritish' and for its eradication it was only necessary to make the British public aware of the problem. Gandhi himself was an empire loyalist until 1919. The doyen of Indian historians, Sir Jadunath

Sarkar, remained a firm believer in the beneficence of British rule all his life.

But in post-independence India, serious thinkers and historians who see anything good in the imperial record can be counted probably on the fingers of one hand. Besides, even the best known among these persistent admirers of the Raj, Nirad C. Chaudhuri described the late-nineteenth and early-twentieth century Britishers in India as 'the Nazis of their time'. Any assessment of the colonial record needs to take into account and explain this transformation of elite attitudes among the subject populations, for it betokens a major failure on part of the rulers: the alleged beneficiaries of imperial rule fail to see any benefits traceable to that source.

The historiography of India under the Raj has been hag-ridden by the strong emotional affects which often inform ostensibly rational debates. The preoccupation with giving good or bad marks to British rule, which may or may not be obvious in the writing, has overshadowed exercises in serious analysis. It would be futile to pretend that one can be completely free from this not very relevant concern and try to assess what actually happened without any trace of prejudice.

THE END PRODUCT

In 1947, when the British left India, they transferred power to two, and if one counts Burma, three successor states. Of these, one, Pakistan, has since broken up into two states. India, Pakistan and Bangladesh have adopted Westminister style parliamentary systems of government with periods of lapse into military dictatorship in the case of the last two. The administrative system, including the judiciary, created by the British have survived decolonization though it has been extended and modified to cope with the tasks of economic and social development as well as phenomenal increase in population. Parliamentary democracy and rule of law, despite many challenges and violations, may be said to have become integral parts of the political culture in Britain's erstwhile dependencies in South Asia.

This fact encapsulates the triumph of an ideology which is western, especially British, in origin. It is not, however, the end result of smooth or continuous developments sponsored by the Raj. As is now recognized, the imperial power created representative institutions to facilitate co-operation, contain opposition and reduce the cost of government. Except during the last ten years of British rule, when elected governments in the provinces had some real power, subject to the authority of the provincial governors and the viceroy answerable only to Whitehall, the British bureaucracy who ruled the country was not accountable to any representative body in India. The right to vote to elect legislatures with strictly limited powers was granted to only 2 per cent of the population in 1919 and then to 10 to 13 per cent in 1937. The governments of India and Pakistan introduced adult suffrage and accepted the principle of elected governments account-able to elected legislatures. This was a quantum leap, not the logical climax of gradual evolution. The transition was from oligarchic and autocratic government to representative democracy which was no doubt badly flawed in many ways.

The successor states of the Raj were among the poorest countries of the world. It is estimated that in India some 48 to 53 per cent of the rural population were below the poverty line in 1947: in other words nearly half the population could not afford the minimum intake of food required to sustain the human body. Average life expectation was twenty-nine years. Nearly 88 per cent of the population was illi-terate. The rate of illiteracy was even higher among women. A very high proportion of the predominantly agrarian population was either landless or had no secure rights in the land they cultivated. Majority of those who had secure rights were heavily in debt paying interest at usurious rates. In parts of the country, like Tamilnadu in the south and Punjab in the north-west, agriculture was relatively prosperous while in other parts like Bengal, Orissa and Bihar agricultural output had stagnated or actually declined over the decades so that the popu-lation as a whole had considerably less to eat per head in 1950 as compared to 1900. But some of the agriculturists who could afford to cultivate the higher value crops had prospered and were to prosper even more in the newly independent states. They constituted a very small proportion of the rural population as did the big landlords with vast estates who lived off their rental income without contributing to agricultural production in any way. Such landlords, like the Rajas and Maharajas who also were great landowners, remained loyal sup-porters of the Raj to the very end.

By 1947 India had a small industrial sector consisting of planta-tions (mostly British owned), mines and light consumer goods indus-tries. The two world wars had secured forced protection for India's industries and there was some diversification partly as a result of this. A major iron and steel industry, the product of Indian enterprise, had started producing in 1912. India's international trade had also grown, especially since the opening of the Suez canal. Yet in per capita terms India was nearly at the bottom of the international ladder both in commerce and modern industry. Her economy, overwhelmingly agricultural, had been structurally stagnant for decades. It was indeed served by an infrastructure, especially a railway network, which compared well with that of other dependent countries. But the railway network was heavily oriented to the needs of exports and imports. The majority of India's villages lacked even mud roads serviceable round the year. Modern irrigation, impressive in scale, especially in the Punjab and Sindh, benefitted only 6 per cent of the arable.

Perhaps the one point of strength in the economy was that the country had a highly resilient entrepreneurial class, recruited to a large extent from castes and communities with commercial traditions of long standing, who had made the most of the limited opportunities available under colonial rule. Though facilities for technical education had been severely limited and there was hardly any demand for high skills, Indian universities and education abroad had produced a critical mass of professionally trained personnel and technical skills which later proved to be of value to the efforts at development.

The successor states also inherited the administrative organization of the Raj and the traditions which went with it. These were not best suited to the tasks of social and economic development attempted after independence. The inordinately expensive judicial system and a proverbially corrupt police which was often a law unto itself remain heavy burdens for the underprivileged in India.

The Indian Union had at independence an exceptionally able political leadership who had acquired their legitimacy through their role in the struggle for freedom. They headed an organization which had acted as the chief nationalist forum for many decades and now emerged as the party in power. Its subsequent role as a party machine, often ruthless and corrupt, obscures its earlier charisma as the mobilizer of the masses.

THE COST OF CONQUEST

When the English East India Company made a bid for political power in the mid-eighteenth century, first in the eastern and southern parts of India, the Mughal empire which once exercised control over the greater part of the subcontinent had been reduced to a shadow. Several regional powers, some of which still owed formal allegiance to the emperor and even paid revenue, fought for supremacy and the Company entered the fray to secure and enhance their commercial gains.

The Indian empire was acquired, not in a fit of absent-mindedness but, in the words of a British historian, in pursuit of the public and private greed of the Company's servants. The nurse in Chesterton's poem advised the child visiting a zoo that anything else that might get him would be worse. Similar claims have been made for the British imperium in India, probably correctly. But the initial experience of the conquest was horrendous both in Bengal and southern India. Ghulam Hussain, a contemporary historian, who was otherwise full of admiration for the British, especially their courage and military skills, described how his countrymen were groaning under the Company's yoke. The Company's servants indulged in an orgy of loot. This systematic plunder was at least a major cause of the famine of 1770 which is said to have wiped off a third of Bengal's population. The accuracy of such estimates has been questioned, but the ruinous effect of the famine on the region's economy is not in doubt. The wars in the south where Haidar Ali devastated territories under British control produced similar consequences. And revenues from the immiserized provinces and the Company's subordinate 'allies' funded the military machine for the conquest of more territories and the consolidation of empire.

That empire was nearly destroyed by the great rebellion of 1857, described inaccurately as the Mutiny. The result of complex and multiple causes, the rising expressed the accumulated anger of many sections of the population in north and central India—dispossessed princes, disgruntled soldiers and a harrassed peasantry from whom the Company's army was largely recruited. The rebels committed acts of great brutality and were suppressed in equally brutal ways. The Anglo-Indians bayed for even more bloody revenge. The rebellion created a legacy of racial hatred which affected all aspects of the relationship between the ruler and the ruled.

The leaders of the Mutiny feature prominently in the demonology of British imperial history. It is a significant fact that they were and are viewed very differently in India. Leaders like the Rani of Jhansi and Kunwar Singh are revered heroes in folk memory and nationalist myth has elevated the rising to the status of the First War of

Independence. Such total disjuncture in perceptions is a significant comment on the relationship between the rulers and the subject population.

PAX BRITANNICA

When India passed under the direct rule of the Crown-in-parliament in 1858, there was no one left to challenge that authority: the prolonged wars which had disturbed peace in many parts of the subcontinent during the decline of the Mughal empire and the era of conquest, some 160 years in all, were finally at an end. Banditry, a by-product of wars and anarchy, was soon crushed. For the first time in the history of the region, the entire subcontinent was ruled by one centralized government.

Peace, of course, is preferable to war and lawless anarchy, but the benefits of Pax Britannica were not accessible to all concerned in the same way. If one remembers that the rebellion of 1857 occurred some thirty-five years after the main wars of conquest were over, it becomes obvious that many people in India were less than happy with that peace. The peasants and the tribal people who constituted the majority of the population rose repeatedly in rebellion in many parts of the country throughout the eighteenth and nineteenth centuries. Of course, these risings can be disaggregarated to show that they were caused by very different factors but most such factors can be traced to the massive dislocation caused by the process of conquest and consolidation. The people driven to rebellion in sheer desperation included peasants forced to give up cultivation during the period of plunder, tribes deprived of their hereditary rights to the free use of forest resources, tenants rack-rented or expropriated by landlords created under the new tenures, cultivators hopelessly indebted to usurious moneylenders who benefitted from the new laws of contract or forced to cultivate indigo by white planters on totally unacceptable terms and such others.

And whenever they were in action, the forces of law and order were almost invariably deployed in favour of their oppressors. The new legal system was incomprehensible and too expensive to be of any use to the poor. In the past, justice in matters of civil dispute usually took the form of arbitration by village councils. Such arbitration must have favoured the privileged, but the less fortunate were not ruined. The new equality before the law meant that a Brahmin could now be hanged, but such triumphs of justice were of little consolation to the peasant who lost his land to the moneyleneder or the landlord. The intricacies of the tenurial system and the incomprehensible laws enmeshed the agrarian population in ruinous law suits. There is also plenty of evidence to prove that the people lived in mortal fear of the rapacious police. When a village was robbed, often the first concern of the villagers was to hide the fact from the police lest they should descend to ransack the homes of the poor. Folk songs in every part of the subcontinent record memories of such varied misery. There are none rejoicing in the advent of Pax Britannica.

There were others who shared the unhappiness of the underprivileged. The traditional litteratti maintained by grants of rent free land were deprived of their livelihood if they failed to prove that the grants were authentic. Bulk of the court bureaucracies, especially the Muslims, were reduced to penury. Indians were appointed to high offices of state in the early days of the Company's rule. The practice ceased totally from the late 1780s: a new stereotype, that Indians were dishonest and undependable, became an integral part of the official dogma. Nevertheless, the lower ranks of the colonial bureaucracy had to be opened to Indians, a fact which is now cited in support of the argument that the subject population were active players in the task of government and decision making. Memoirs of middle-ranking Indian bureaucrats leave one in little doubt that they had very little effective power and that they resented the severe restrictions on their career opportunities. The fact that the British bureaucrats in India were among the highest paid by international standards and at times affected a lordly style aggravated the resentment.

Of course, sections of the population were delighted with their prospects under British rule, a fact which explains the enthusiasm for the Raj which persisted well into the twentieth century. The Indian princes and the big landlords, secure in their possessions and privileges thanks to the British, never lost that enthusiasm. The new professional classes and those who had the benefit of western-style education also long retained their faith in the beneficence of British rule, but they criticized many features of that rule 1820s onwards. And their criticisms were not directed only to matters which concerned their self-interest. The abject misery of the Indian peasant is a recurrent theme in Indian writings of the nineteenth century.

THE POLITICAL PROCESS

The legacies of the Raj which are likely to prove most enduring include the political systems and the conflicts which emerged out of colonial rule. These were only partly deliberate creations of the Raj. Essentially these arose out of the workings of colonial government and its interactions with indigenous society.

The primary object of British rule was to protect and enhance the interests of Britain in India. This concern provided the one element of continuity in the otherwise *ad hoc* and shifting policies which are often emphasized in support of the theory that no general statements are possible regarding the motives and consequences of imperialism. So long as there was no conflict with the dominant purpose, welfare of Indians was often an important consideration, especially at the level of idealistic decision makers. Besides, a contented subject population was essential for stable government. The record, however, suggests that conflicts between British interests and policies likely to benefit India in the long run were frequent enough. The impact of such conflict was most obvious in the economic sphere.

As the British in India could be counted in thousands and the subject population were several hundred million in number, co-operation and acquiescence on part of Indians were essential for the functioning of colonial rule. Political co-operation had to be bought at a price— some access to resources and power over which the government exercised firm control. Elite groups competed for these shares of resources and power and they did so partly on the basis of groups and alliances structured into indigenous society, and partly on the basis of 'constituencies' defined by the rulers in terms of their perceptions of Indian society.

Social identities acquired a new political importance as new patterns of consciousness emerged through interaction with western thought and the British presence. We do not encounter in the pre-British past either the idea of an Indian nation or any consciousness of a Hindu community spread across the subcontinent. As the idea of nationhood and political rights seeped into elite consciousness, the facts of being an Indian, or a Hindu or Bengali acquired meanings which were entirely new. And when the new rulers distributed seats in local bodies and legislatures or allocated funds for education, treating communities and in some instances castes as the basic units of society, communities and castes became the constituencies for political competition. The British perception that Hindus and Muslims were two mutually antagonistic monoliths, a notion not rooted in facts, became an important basis for distribution of shares in power and resources. Social and doctrinal difference, which had very rarely been the cause of civil conflict, now informed competition and political antagonisms. Hindu–Muslim rivalry and the eventual partition of India was the end result of this development and the British policy makers, when they did not actually add fuel to the conflict, were quite happy to take advantage of it. Muslim leaders who opposed the nationalist claim to speak for all Indians were certainly courted as potential allies, though at the last moment there was desperate anxiety to prevent the partition of India because it was considered a threat to Britain's world-wide strategic interests. In 1857 Hindu and Muslim chiefs, soldiers and peasants had tried to overthrow the English Company's rule and place a Muslim prince on the imperial throne. If ninety years later a similar initiative was unthinkable, the causal relation between that fact and the workings of colonial rule should be obvious.

Indian nationalism, the idea that the very diverse population of the subcontinent constituted a nation, was also of course a product of British rule in India. The rulers did not encourage the idea and their publicists pooh-poohed the notion that a people so diverse could ever be a nation. Yet the emergence of a colonial elite, in many ways homogeneous in terms of their expectations and frustrations and sharing a language of intellectual discourse as well as the administrative unification laid a basis for pan-Indian nationalism.

The overt racism of the Anglo-Indians which affected the institutions of government contributed powerfully to the growth of nationalist sentiment. All Indians, whatever their status, shared the experience of being treated as racial inferiors. Higher levels of appointment were virtually closed to non-whites. The Anglo-Indians reacted violently against proposals which would make them subject to the authority of Indian judges. The Viceroy Lord Curzon commented that the Anglo-Indian got away with murder because no white jury would find a white man guilty of killing a native. As late as 1930 British officers were advised in a secret army memorandum that they should not kick Indians. The life-stories of Indian celebreties are full of episodes of racial insults. The perception of shared bondage gave credibility to the notion of shared nationhood.

But Indian nationalism acquired its cutting edge and political legitimacy through the words and deeds of the movement for independence. It was inspired by the ideals of representative democracy as practised in Britain and denied to India. Aware of the country's great poverty and pervasive social injustice, problems which the colonial government left untouched, the movement also took on board programmes which would ameliorate some of the misery. But since it sought the support of all social classes, where the interests of the poor clashed with that of the privileged, the tendency was to avoid conflict which meant a continuation of the status quo. But not all along the line. The landless and the share-coppers remained where they were, but the rural classes who had some rights in land and had come to constitute a strong base for nationalism were rewarded at independence. Their chief enemy, the big landlords, lost their land as did the Indian princes.

The effort to mobilize support and sustain an organization based on multiple ethnic elements and mutually conflicting interests, created the basis for a unique nation state, more diverse than any other known to history. Unlike the Soviet Union, it was created with the active consent of the constituent elements and has survived with that consent largely in tact for some fifty years. The absorption of the princely states, the two-fifth of Indian territory which was ruled by autocrats under British protection, into democratic polities with popular support also gave the successor states an edge over the record of colonial rule.

DEVELOPMENT
OF UNDERDEVELOPMENT

The information available concerning the record of India's economy under colonial rule is extremely imprecise. Judgements based on such imprecise data often reflect the writer's preferences rather than any historical truth. We know very little about the trends in population, output or life expectancy until the last decades of the nineteenth century.

Certain things are however clear from this limited data. The population increased, if at all, at a very slow rate, never at even 1 per cent per annum until 1921 when reduced mortality through control of epidemic diseases pushed the figure to 1.3 per cent. There is an ongoing debate on the basis of undependable data as to the record of agriculture. In Punjab and parts of southern India, there was some growth in productivity. The record in the rest of the country appears to have been dismal and the aggregate output per capita declined after 1921 according to some statisticians. There was minute increase in the opinion of others. Insecurity of tenures, the heavy cost of borrowing, minimal investment in irrigation were all factors which contributed to this poor record. The development of railways and the market for agricultural crops, both national and international, encouraged specialization in crop production and stimulated the production of cash crops, including the higher value food grains. The consequent gains were often at the cost of lower value food grains, the main source of food for the majority of the population. India, never an importer of foodgrains in the past, became dependent on imports, and per capita availability declined, a trend which was finally reversed only in the 1970s.

When one reads the European accounts of India and other major Asian civilizations from the early modern age, one often has the impression of reading descriptions of a First World, to use a contemporary expression, written by people from less fortunate climes. Even in the mid-eighteenth century Clive compared Murshidabad, a provincial city, in some ways favourably with London.

Of course, there was a great deal of poverty in pre-colonial times as well but it would be a mistake to see India's twentieth-century poverty as a continuation of pre-modern patterns. Modern underdevelopment is the product of a vicious circle: low-income–low-saving–low-investment. At a time when the bulk of the population was dependent on agriculture which had to support a relatively small and very slowly increasing population (in 1600 the subcontinent had an estimated population of about 100 million as compared to some thousand million to-day), poverty did not mean near starvation, Famines had certainly been a part of Indian life since very ancient times. But in the past these calamities were caused by crop failure. In the nineteenth century, on the other hand, one would have expected food grains to move to areas of shortage, helped by a modern system of transport. Yet as late as 1899 famine mortality remained high because vast sections of the population now lacked the purchasing power to buy food even when it was available.

In the pre-industrial world, India's manufactures like textiles were among the staples of international commerce while a flourishing class of merchants plied their trade from East Africa to the Philippines and as far north as Moscow and St. Petersberg. After 1813, and especially after 1833, when the East India Company virtually ceased to be a trading body in India, India lost her export trade in manufactures, became a net importer of manufactured goods and a supplier of agricultural products to Britain for the first time in her history. The consequent limited growth in agriculture did not compensate for the decline in manufactures caused by the loss of export markets, the demand from the traditional courts and the army as well as the competition of machine manufactures from Britain. The limited urban growth was based for the most part on activities which did not generate economic goods. The modern industries were relatively insignificant. All newly industrializing countries have been dependent on favourable state policies virtually in every part of the world. The British manufacturers seeking access to the Indian market on most favourable terms and the doctrine of *laissez faire* which suited their interests ensured that no protection and hardly any encouragement by the state were available for Indian industries until the mid-1920s and then only in response to persistent Indian pressure.

Thus by 1947, the year of transfer of power, South Asia was a typically underdeveloped region, with a vast and growing population, stagnant agricultural output, a small industrial sector and inadequate infrastructure generating very low per capita income, low saving and hence low investment which completed the vicious circle. This end result was not the logical culmination from the buoyant pre-industrial economy of the sixteenth–seventeenth centuries, but of the workings of colonial economic relationship. This is not to say that India was on the verge of an industrial revolution on the eve of the British conquest, a possibility which was frustrated by colonialism. But the nature of economic change induced by the colonial nexus surely precluded the possibilities of industrialization. It also created bottlenecks which proved to be serious handicaps for later efforts at industrialization.

ENCOUNTER WITH THE WEST: INFLUENCE AND INTERACTION

The British encountered in mid-eighteenth century India a varied, complex and highly developed civilization which was very different from that of contemporary Europe, at least at a superficial level. The British administrators in their attempt to understand this complex reality developed paradigms which emphasized the difference rather than the similarities between the two cultures. It is interesting that the conceptualization of India as one of Europe's others, quintessentially different from the west since the beginning of time, belongs to the high noon of empire. By then Britain and western Europe were convinced of their inherent superiority, the result of cultural evolution somehow similar to the evolution of species. Utilitarian philosophy which inspired early-nineteenth century projects of reform and development in India were inspired by the same ideology. One of its progenitors, James Mill, was convinced that Indians were inferior to the nobler animals. The Orientalists who took a much more sympathetic and respectful view of at least the Indian past were also believers in the simple dichotomy of the East and the West. This belief was passed on to the Indians exposed to western style education.

Education was introduced in India initially at the instance of the new colonial elite who wanted a better knowledge of the English language as a key to careers under the new regime. They also sought access to western science and humanities in the belief that these would generate progress. The British policy makers like Lord Macaulay, contemptuous of oriental cultures, wished to create a class of people who would be western in all but appearance. The need for functionaries who spoke the rulers' language was of course a consideration and the missionaries who were among the chief propagators of western style education hoped to Christianize India.

The long term effects of western education were very different from what the pioneers had expected. It acted as a catalyst generating processes of change which went way beyond simple adoptions of western cultural artifacts. India was not Christianized. If anything, the new appeal to reason which shook the Hindus' faith in their own traditions also militated against the acceptance of Christian dogma. While the products of the new centres of higher learning remained enthusiastic for one feature or another of western civilization, liberal, democratic and egalitarian ideals had much greater appeal than that of constitutional monarchy enshrined in Britain's unwritten constitution. So much so, that at one time educational administrators seriously considered the exclusion of British history, with its record of struggle for citizens' rights, from the curricula of Indian schools and colleges. The cultural self-assertion which went with the politicization of ethnic identities at times fed into social reaction and induced obscurantist posturing. One major end product of the cultural encounter was the articulation of a distinctively Indian nationalism which emphasized the shared cultural traditions of India's diverse population and the belief that the Indian civilization had unique powers of assimilation which had created out of diverse and often warring elements a unified culture, the basis of a future Indian nation.

While this message of co-existence and unity was carried, up to a point successfully, to the mass of population mobilized in support of the movement for independence, the new political culture also had strong divisive implications. Basically, it was the culture of the urban classes exposed to western education and the democratic ideals of the west which had little meaning for the Indian masses. Some of those ideals were communicated to the poor and the underprivileged through Gandhi's self-consciously Indian life-style and the charisma which the leadership and cadres acquired by courting persecution. But as a school of historians now point out very effectively, the masses interpreted the message of nationalism in their own terms, very different from the concerns of the middle class. There was an element of naiveté in the modernizing leadership's expectation that deep-rooted attitudes and beliefs could be altered by waving the magic wands of reason, science and technology. Some of the recent debates in Indian politics on the issue of secularism—the question as to whether it is right or politic for the state to remain neutral or indifferent in matters of religion—focus on the viability of policies based on that attitude.

Western education did create a class of people intellectually and in some ways psychologically in tune with developments of modern civilization in Europe and America. Since they provided the leadership and cadres of the nationalist movement, it would be obviously incorrect to describe them as denationalized. The encounter with western thought triggered off outbursts of creativity in literature and the arts which are remarkable by any standard. Much of this creative effort celebrated the new national consciousness. Yet the fact remains that the percentage of population who understand English in India after some one hundred and eighty years of exposure to English education is less than two. It was substantially less in 1947 when there were seventeen universities and two hundred colleges in the subcontinent as against one hundred and forty and two thousand respectively in the Indian Union alone to-day. And nothing has happened to bridge the chasm created by this cultural dichotomy. Macaulay believed that western culture would percolate down to the masses. This has not happened. The elite's language of political and cultural discourse remains incomprehensible to the masses. Probably this fact rather than the much discussed ethnic diversity of India poses a real threat to the solidity of the nation states in south Asia. On the other hand access to a world language remains a great asset for the educated classes in India. The fact that the Indian Union has the second largest group of technology trained personnel in the world has certainly been facilitated by this linguistic inheritance of the Raj.

THE COLONIAL PAST AND THE SUBCONTINENT'S FUTURE

The vestiges of the Raj are very much present in the life of the sub-continent to-day. Despite attempts to shake it off, especially in Bangladesh, English remains the dominant language of intellectual discourse and, in India, effectively the language of administration as well. More important, the beliefs and attitudes which inform elite concerns as well as state policy can be traced back to the catalytic encounter with western thought under imperial auspices. The chasm which divides the masses from the privileged derives in part from this fact of western 'influence'. It is difficult to foresee an end to these legacies of the colonial past in the near future. One totally negative inheritance of that past, antagonism between Hindus and Muslims, converted at the state level into Indo–Pakistani conflict and Indophobia in Bangladesh, also seems destined to persist. On the positive side, the aspirations towards democracy, economic growth and social equity which emerged in the colonial era, not exact-ly with the blessings of the Raj, are now integral to the life of the sub-continent's population. It would be unwise to speculate about their chances of success.

11

Historiography of India, 1858–1937*

The concerns, methods and findings of Indian historiography for the period of direct rule by Crown-in-Parliament have undergone very basic changes since the Second World War, though there are marked continuities in perceptions in some areas of that very varied enterprise. The sixth and final volume of the *Cambridge History of India* (Cambridge, 1932) typifies the older approach. The various chapters describe the evolution of the imperial legislature and superior governments, district administration, governmental policies regarding matters such as famine, education and finance and the Indian government's relations with Central Asia. Sir Richard Burn contributed a brief, and not entirely dismissive, chapter on the Indian National Congress. It contains an illuminating statement on the venomous Anglo-Indian agitation against the Ilbert Bill, 1883 which sought to remove the racially discriminatory privilege enjoyed by the Queen's white subjects in India: in the countryside, they could not be tried by judges of Indian origin. The agitation, Sir Richard commented, was led by the planters who were particularly liable to be the 'subject of groundless or exaggerated charges'. V.A. Smith in his *Oxford History of India* (Oxford, 1919) agreed that the said planters' fears were not without reason. A much more professional work, H. Dodwell's *A Sketch of the History of India from 1858 to 1918* (London, 1925), based on a fair amount of archival research, extended two hundred thirty-two pages on British policy, including the reforms and forty on what he described as 'political sentiment'. The emphasis in all these works was firmly on the history of British rule, its needs and mistakes. For Dodwell the latter included 'the astonishing blunder of

*A version of this essay will be printed in the *Oxford History of the British Empire*, vol. 5.

the Ilbert Bill'. Such surveys included one which was exceptionally liberal in spirit, *The Rise and Fulfilment of British Rule in India* (London, 1934) by E. Thompson and G.T. Garratt. It gave a fair coverage to the nationalist movement and commented critically on 'the behaviour of responsible Englishmen' who evidently believed that Indians 'should be treated as an inferior race'. The comment was certainly not typical of pre-Second World War British historiography of the Raj.

The older tradition, with its emphasis on British policy, remained one of the strands in post-war historiography of the Raj but it acquired a much greater degree of professionalism. Simple narration and impressionistic comments gave place to a more analytical approach, especially enquiries into the decision-making process based on very detailed research into public and private archives. The monographs on viceroys like Minto, Ripon, Curzon and Irwin and surveys covering wider time periods[1] were now much more concerned with the encounter and interchanges between indigenous politics and imperial policy as also the pulls and pressures within the latter at various levels. Policy-making was no longer treated as the end products of Viceregal will, at most modified by the superior authority of Secretaries of State. One massive work of survey, Sir Penderel Moon's posthumously published *The British Conquest and Dominion of India* (London, 1989) does hark back to the practice of narrative and impressionistic comment as also a preoccupation with discovering where the British went wrong. But it is distinctive in its concern for ethically correct judgements—not a feature of either the old or the new historiography of British India.

If British governmental institutions and policy were the central historiographical themes before the War, indigenous, especially nationalist, politics acquired a similar centrality in the post-war literature on Indian history since the 1857 rising. This new preoccupation is first traceable to an initiative of the Indian government who appointed a commission for writing the history of the independence movement. The person originally in charge of the project, an Indologist, R.C. Mazumdar, refused to abide by the new official perception which saw the struggle for independence as a unified and heroic endeavour and all opposition to it as acts of betrayal encouraged by the imperialist ruler. He left the project to produce his own version of the struggle in three volumes, *History of Freedom Movement* (Calcutta, 1962–63). It is a somewhat simplistic narrative with a very overt

Hindu nationalist, especially Bengali, bias which implicitly accepts the theory that the Muslims constituted a separate nation and criticizes the leadership for their pro-Muslim and allegedly anti-Bengali policy. Mazumdar repeated the statement in a somewhat different format in the last two volumes of *The History and Culture of the Indian People*[2] which he edited. At the centre of his argument is the nationalist perception that independence was wrested from a reluctant colonial regime who were forced to surrender power in stages. The one virtue of these volumes is the detailed information they provide which are not easily accessible in any other secondary work. P. Sitaramayya's *History of the National Congress* (2 vols, Bombay, 1946–47), the official history of the organization is an amateurish and unsatisfactory account by comparison. The official project eventually produced a four-volume work, Tarachand's *History of the Freedom Movement* (Delhi, 1961–72). It reflects on the one hand the nationalist perception and on the other undertakes a rudimentary analysis of the class basis of the movement. In its latter aspect it drew heavily on Marxist writings like R.P. Dutt, *India To-day* (London, 1947) and A.R. Desai's *Social Background of Indian Nationalism* (Bombay, 1959), works which traced the origins of Indian nationalism to the aspirations and frustrations of the colonial middle class.

The earliest writings on modern Indian nationalism are however not of Indian origin. Under colonial rule, Indian writers generally avoided the topic and pronouncements on the subject came mostly from people who had an unqualified faith in the permanence of empire. The idea of an Indian nation was an absurdity to writers like Sir John Strachey, Verney Lovett and Valentine Chirol.[3] It was a figment of imagination invented by a small group of self-serving English-educated Indians. A society so divided by language, religion and caste could never aspire to nationhood. Writing three years after the split between Moderates and Extremists in the Indian National Congress, Chirol predicted in 1910 the imminent demise of that seditious organization. There were other variants within the pro-imperialist perception of indigenous politics. Writing in the last decades of the Raj, Coupland did not deny the reality of Indian nationalism, but emphasized the divisiveness in indigenous politics, especially the Hindu–Muslim problem and the unreasonable attitudes of the nationalists as the main factors which frustrated the government's policy of handing down power in graduated doses.[4]

The notion that nationalism was the concern of the unrepresentative few and that consciousness of a wider identity transcending ethnic and parochial boundaries was never achieved remains central to the arguments of an influential section of historians. Judith Brown in her two monographs on Gandhi estimated the minuscule proportion of the population directly involved in the mass movements and concluded that Gandhi's agenda were failure because none of his stated goals were ever achieved.[5] As the title of her monumental biography suggests, Gandhi lived and died a prisoner of unrealized (and unrealizeable) hopes of unity. The support he secured was mediated by 'contractors' and 'sub-contractors' who found him useful for reasons of their own. Those reasons had little to do with either aspirations for political independence or resentment against perceived injustice, especially racism.

Racism as a factor in the colonial nexus has received inadequate attention from historians. One monograph discusses how the official elite in India, mostly drawn from the British middle-class who sought to emulate the aristocracy, considered the preservation of social distance 'essential to the maintenance of structures of power and authority'.[6] Sumit Sarkar has analysed the implications of this policy for the development of nationalist sentiment. Nirad Chaudhuri qualifies his great admiration for the British *imperium* in his discussion of the social apartheid in India and concludes angrily that the British in India in the latter days of the Raj were 'the Nazis of their time'.[7]

As Brown points out in her survey of modern Indian history, recent research has unravelled the complexities of nationalist politics partly by focusing on the provinces which, owing to the constitutional arrangements especially since 1919, were the chief arenas for indigenous political action. Aspiring regional elites formed networks of alliances which could put pressure on the provincial government, the source of power and patronage, for realization of local goals. And the same logic of power politics led to countrywide networks which sought to pressurize the central authorities for achieving provincial goals. The studies of southern India by Washbrook and Baker explore the structure of the networks based on client–patron relationships between 'rural–local magnates' and people further down the socio-economic ladder. If this was the structure of Indian politics, the dynamics derived from governmental initiatives towards constitutional reform, meant to secure support and acquiescence and lower the cost of governance. Each initiative accentuated the competition between rival groups of networks some of whom ended up as the 'haves' and the others as 'have nots' of power. At the prospect of each new initiative the 'have nots' organized agitations to see how far the government could be pushed and to secure legitimacy in the eyes of the constituents. The ruling power made concessions, not to the agitators, but in order to confer credibility on their collaborators until a point was reached where further concession equalled decolonization. And throughout these see-saw movements the overriding concern of the rulers was the long-term interests of Britain in terms of power and resources. The limits to concessions were set by that overriding purpose.

The above summary[8] of a highly sophisticated and gradually evolving interpretation inevitably distorts a complex set of arguments developed through a large number of monographs and articles which do not speak in the same voice. I have tried to identify only what can be described as their common denominator. The latter includes the perception, not explored in any detail, that for Britain the Indian empire was a source of power and profit and policy was geared to the task of securing these in perpetuity. But the British were aided in the task by their Indian collaborators, 'sub-imperialists' who shared their gains as junior partners in the imperial enterprise.

This line of argument has come in for expected criticism. It has been identified, not quite fairly, as a sophisticated restatement of the old colonial perception of Indian nationalism seen to be nothing but theatre and rhetoric covering up a cynical quest for material gain. Since the Indian empire was no doubt based on extensive collaboration on part of the indigenous elite and acquiescence on part of the masses, this approach has certainly enriched one's understanding of the entire historical process. It is, however, difficult to accept the view that genuine opposition was no more than collaboration by other means or that nationalism, a powerful force in many parts of the world since the nineteenth century, was mere make-believe in the Indian case. Such analysis also pays inadequate attention to non-rational factors like frustration, a pervasive feeling of humiliation and the need for cultural self-assertion central to the historical experience of subject populations in Europe's Afro-Asian colonies.

Other explanations of Indian nationalism have also been attempted. The collections of essays edited by D.A. Low, *Soundings in Modern South Asian History* (California, 1968) and *Congress and the*

Raj: Facets of the Indian Struggle 1917–47 (London, 1977) are based on a shared assumption that Indian nationalism was a real and powerful force in shaping the history of the period. The contributors explore the social bases of the movement in various parts of the subcontinent, the patterns and circumstances of mobilization, on the basis of very detailed archival research. Professor Low argues in an introductory essay that the conversion of the affluent peasant to the nationalist cause guaranteed its eventual victory. A somewhat different thesis on the class bases of Indian nationalism based on neo-Marxist analysis of India's 'colonial bourgeoisie' was projected by Soviet historians in Balabushevitch and Dyakov (editors), *A Contemporary History of India* (New Delhi, 1964). The role of particular social groups or classes in indigenous politics—the merchants in Bombay, the upper caste *bhadralok* in Bengal—is the theme of a number of monographs. Gyanendra Pandey questioned the received wisdom projecting a steady expansion in the social base of nationalist politics. He developed an alternative hypothesis: the Congress secured a strong and solid base among several social groups, including the majority of the Hindu population in U.P., but it lost or excluded others, the majority of the Muslims and the marginal peasants among them, who had at one time become its supporters and allies. Both the inclusion and the exclusion resulted from the developing politico-economic realities of colonial rule. The nationalist rituals, institutions, propaganda (often xenophobic in tone and content) and spectacular acts of martyrdom were important components of that reality.[9] We have a very different explanation in Sumit Sarkar's study of the *swadeshi* movement in Bengal. He underlines the very limited *bhadralok* base of the agitation but suggests, in Gramscian terms, that this narrow social group sought to act as a 'substitute' for the absent popular support.[10] The emphasis on the distinctive linguistic cultures of India has been carried farthest in the United States where conferences on Punjab, Maharashtra, Bengal and other zones act as channels for multidisciplinary studies including history.

Biographies of pro-consuls and imperial administrators was at one time the very stuff of Indian political history. Lord Ronaldshay's two volume *Life of Lord Curzon* (London, 1928) is a classic example of this older approach to colonial history perceived as the arena for the unfolding of great lives. This tradition has more or less died out after decolonization. There are some highly interesting studies like Lord Beveridge's biography of his parents, *India Called Them* (London,

1947) or Martin Gilbert's *Servant of India: A Study of Imperial Rule as Told through the Correspondence and Diaries of Sir James Dunlop Smith* (London, 1966) which have not attracted the attention of those interested in mainstream Indian history. On the other hand, the interest in the history of Indian nationalism has generated a large body of works on the lives of the Indian leaders—Tilak, Gokhale, Gandhi, Nehru as well as the lesser luminaries. These works focus almost entirely on their political career and as such form part of the growing corpus on the indigenous politics of colonial India. The Sahitya Akademi, the literary institute set up by the Government of India, has published a large number of short biographies of Indian writers which illuminate the cultural history of colonial India. Similar works in Indian languages are numerous, but these are of course only accessible to those who read these languages.

In a very important essay which has not attracted adequate attention Bernard Cohn (see his 'Is there a New Indian History? Society and Social Change under the Raj 'in his *An Anthropologist among Historians*, Delhi, 1987) underlined the problem of speaking in terms of large social categories as he saw it from the stand-point of an anthropologist. Unless one studied 'behaviour on the ground' in the context of the total social system, such categories could often be misleading. 'Bhadralok', 'non-Brahmins', 'Muslims' are terms which cover a wide variety of people whose interests and roles can be very different. The same institutions (the Indian durbar for instance) can perform very different functions at different points in time. Only a small number of monographic studies on the history of India since 1858 meet the requirement posited in Cohn's essay. Bayly's study of client-patron relationships as the basis of indigenous politics in Allahabad is one of the best known exercises which does so.

To repeat, the plea for disaggregrated studies as a prerequisite for aggregative statements covering large social categories has so far had limited impact. A number of papers published in the volumes entitled *Subaltern Studies* and monographs written by the historians who contribute to these do focus on specific instances of 'behaviour on the ground' which flesh out their grand category of subaltern class, a paradigm covering very disparate elements. Susan Bayly's monograph on Muslims and Christians in southern India questions, on the basis of detailed studies of particular groups of Muslims and Christians, the generally held view that conversions were a means of

escape from the inequities of Hindu society or that the popular forms
of religion were at odds with some imagined universal set of norms
rooted in Brahminical scriptures. Her study of 'behaviour on the
ground' unravels the interplay between 'pure worship' and 'demonic'
forms of divinity, the close links between religion and politics of
power and shows how the Hinduism we know to-day is largely a modern construct.[11]

While the impact of anthropological method on modern Indian
historiography has been limited, in the sixties several historians,
mostly based in American universities, introduced sociological perspectives in their work. Broomfield discussed the communal problem
in Bengal in terms of elite conflict and identified the 'bhadralok' as
a specific formation of elite status.[12] Irschick in his study of non-
Brahmin movements in South India similarly tried to map a particular
social category and their aspirations in the nineteenth century.[13] Paul
Brass tried to explain both nationalism and communalism as con-
centric circles of politicized ethnicity.[14] In India, M.N. Srinivas's
very influential contribution to the study of Indian sociology, his
concept of Sanskritization as a characteristically Indian variant of
acculturization and upward social mobility and the debate which
developed around this concept, had their impact on historical writings
of the period.[15] Historical studies also focused on the notions of
tradition and modernity, identified the fuzziness of boundaries between the two and discussed the modernizing role of tradition itself.[16]

Another human science which has had a limited but interesting
impact on the study of Indian history is analytical psychology. Erik
Erikson's monograph on 'Gandhi's Truth'[17] was received as a remarkable *tour de force*, but it has had few followers. Only Ashish Nandy's
essays on the mentality of the educated Indian, their ambivalence
and contradictions in relation to the dominant western culture and
his biographical studies of Indian scientists as also Sudhir Kakar's
work on the Indian family and childhood apply consistently the tools
of psychology to historical studies.[18] Studies of childhood which
marked the real beginning of psychohistory as a discipline is an
underdeveloped area in Indian historiography. An interesting
contribution is Judith Walsh's *Growing Up in British India* (New York,
1983) based on autobiographies written in English by men born in
different parts of India between 1850 and 1920. The links between
psychological development and the experience of political subjection

are explored in a more recent monograph, Mrinalini Sinha's *Colonial Masculinity: The 'Manly Englishman' and 'the Effiminate Bengali' in the Late-nineteenth Century'* (Manchester and New York, 1995).

A number of works by political scientists like Bhikhu Parikh[19] and Rajni Kothari[20] introduced another dimension to the study of India's recent past. Such works have brought to bear on Indian historical studies the evolving and varied approaches of a different discipline. Parikh has explored the indigenous cultural roots of Gandhian ideology while Kothari identified the behavioural and institutional determinants of Indian politics. An early contribution to political scientific approach to Indian historical studies is Francis G. Hutchins' *The Illusion of Permanence: British Imperialism in India* (Princeton, 1967) which makes the important point that there was close interaction between the politics of England and that of her Indian dependency. Most studies of imperial rule in India treat the subject as something self-contained or merely refer to the British background without exploring its relevance in any detail. Hutchins point out that India, ruled by Britain's 'middle class aristocracy' was the shining hope of British reactionaries. Their governing idea of permanent subjection 'exerted a strong pressure on British life and thought'. Robin Moore's studies of the last decades of British rule in India confirms the truth of this insight. His *Crisis of Indian Unity 1917–40* (Oxford, 1974) shows how the only continuity in British policy towards India immediately prior to decolonization derived from the concern to stay on. Hence a series of *ad hoc* measures which did not even pretend to be mutually consistent.

Perhaps the most influential movement in the field of modern Indian history in recent times is represented by the volumes entitled *Subaltern Studies* and the monographs written by the historians, anthropologists and political scientists who have contributed to the movement. Its beginnings go back to Ranajit Guha's *Elementary Aspects of Peasant Insurgency in Colonial India* (Delhi, 1983) and his introductory statement in the first volume of the series published in 1982. The protagonists of this school include scholars from India, UK, USA and Australia. Their monographic studies, articles and papers build around the core concept of 'subaltern class' formulated by Gramsci, the notions of domination and subordination as key features of social-political relationship (which by-pass the Marxist analysis of relationship between classes, especially the emphasis on the means of production) and the post-modernist technique of deconstruction of 'texts' in terms of the analysis of dominant discourses.

One object of the project is to move away from Indian historiography's preoccupation with the elite, both the colonial ruler and the privileged in Indian society. The underprivileged were to be studied not simply as passive mindless victims or camp-followers incapable of autonomous consciousness, but 'as the subject in their own history'. The studies concentrate heavily on the moments of rebellion which helps one to move away from the usual concern of the anthropologist with the structures like family and kinship in everyday life and focus instead on 'the forms of domination belonging to the structures of modernity' like western law, medicine and bureaucracy. They also question the Weberian 'over-determination of man as a rational actor'.[21] One monograph on the history of popular agitation among the forest dwellers of the Himalayan foot-hills sets out to construct a sociology of domination and resistance.[22] The sources for such studies include neglected series of official documents like forest, medical and judicial records as also fieldwork. Conventional sources are analysed as 'texts' in the context of 'themes in the dominant discourse'. The end products include a remarkable reconstruction of the way in which paradigms take shape in the official mind.[23] Shahid Amin's monograph on the Chauri Chaura incident—the massacre of policemen in a UP village which led Gandhi to suspend his Non-cooperation movement in 1922—explores in depth the way in which the rural population interpreted the message of Gandhian non-cooperation.[24] The movement has also generated a fair amount of theoretical debate regarding the validity and limitations of its approach.

The debates centring on the *Subaltern Studies* and the post-modernist critique of western perceptions of Asia, allegedly determined by the equations of power inherent in imperialism, have pushed to the periphery the controversy over the economic nexus between Britain as an imperial power and her Indian dominion. That controversy goes back to the nineteenth century when publicists like Dadabhai Naoroji, and later, R.C. Dutt traced the roots of colonial India's poverty to economic exploitation in the form of drainage of resources through unrequited exports, home charges, the heavy cost of deploying the Indian army for imperial purposes and so on.[25] This view was challenged by the defenders of the imperial record who posited the theory of a positive transformation of the Indian economy through infrastructural investments, development of modern industry and the impact of international trade.[26] Estimates of national income, agricultural output and trends in India's international trade in the fifties and sixties provided a quantitative basis for such studies,[27] but did not really terminate the controversy which had strong ideological overtones. The views that per capita income suffered a decline or at least stagnated after 1921 and that the percentage of the work-force employed in agriculture remained unchanged over time were questioned in estimates which raised serious doubts regarding the reliability of the relevant statistics. Monographs on regional agriculture emphasized the fact of sustained growth in certain parts of the country. On the other hand, a study of private investment in India suggested that the differential rates of industrial growth in the different regions of India were casually linked to the differing patterns of colonial domination. Race was identified as a potent factor in determining the patterns of economic policy which favoured the white over the native investor.[28] A recent study has explored the complex nature of the relationship between Indian entrepreneurs and their British counterparts: it subsumed collaboration and competition just as the Indian entrepreneurs' relationship with the government had elements of resistance as well as co-operation.[29] The other side of the story consists in the economic concerns of Indian nationalism, far more radical than its political agenda in the early days and the very influential role of the Indian industrialists in the shaping of nationalist politics in the Gandhian era.[30]

As other contributors to this volume have also emphasized, the developments in Indian historical studies in recent years have been too rich and varied to be covered adequately in one medium-length essay. I have tried to discuss only some major trends leaving out others which are perhaps no less important. To touch briefly on some of these, women's studies, especially from a feminist perspective, are a growth area of considerable importance. The effort focuses on 'the recovery' of women's authentic voice, the patterns of patriarchy which informed the agenda for reforms affecting women and the false idealization or perceptions concerning the position of women in ancient India.[31] A substantial part of the relevant literature is produced as literary, rather than narrowly historical studies.[32]

In fact much of the work in one relatively neglected area of modern Indian history—the impact of the west—has also been done by students of literature. The histories of literature published by Delhi's *Sahitya Akademi* are interesting contributions to cultural history. The output in Indian languages in this field is far more extensive. While *mentalité* of non-elite groups is central to the concerns of the *Subaltern Studies*, recent work has also focused on the mental world of the educated middle class.[33]

Closely related to these themes and the post-modernist analysis of discourse is a highly influential work by a literary scholar whose interest in India is at best peripheral. Edward Said's *Orientalism* (London, 1978) projects a thesis which informs a great deal of current discussion on colonial India. Its central argument concerning Europe's exploration of Asian cultures being linked to equations of power and the consequent projection of these cultures as a homogeneity, one of Europe's several 'others' quintessentially inferior to western civilization, has undoubted value as an explanatory paradigm of both popular stereotypes and many scholarly formulations. Its credibility has suffered because of the tendency to reject exceptions to and variations within the 'Orientalist' perception of Indian and other Asian cultures.

An interesting development in modern Indian historiography is the recent concern with the history of modern Indian art. The two major contributions to the subject, both published in the 1990s—Partha Mitter's *Art and Nationalism in Colonial India 1850–1922: Occidental Orientations* (Cambridge, 1994) and Tapati Guha-Thakurta's *The Making of a New 'Indian' Art: Artists, Aesthetics and Nationalism in Bengal, c. 1850–1920* (Cambridge, 1992)—go beyond the usual scope of art history and locate the development of modern Indian art firmly within the context of cultural development. The overarching importance of nationalist consciousness and the complex responses to western art are central to the argument of both the studies. Guha-Thakurta concludes her account with a highly interesting development—the gradual deliverance from the cultural compulsions of nationalism, the movement towards expressions which ceased to be self-consciously 'Indian'.

Current social and political concerns are expressed in a new genre of historical writings. Ecological changes, mostly of a negative character, are projected in these studies as a by-product of colonial policies. The imperialists' need for the products of the forest, nineteenth-century ideology which glorified the extermination of 'ferocious animals' and the insensitive intrusion into the primeval rights of the forest dwellers generating their struggle for survival are central themes in these works.[34]

It is almost superfluous to emphasize that it is not possible to cover within the limits of one essay all the varied and rich developments in the field of modern Indian historiography. I have reluctantly abstained from discussing the development of Muslim consciousness and identity partly because the theme is covered to some extent in the essays on partition and transfer of power in this volume. There are other significant areas of current research, like the history of religion, missionary activities, and princely states which I have also left out of this discussion.

No study of historiography is adequate unless it relates the developments to the intellectual and cultural history of the relevant time period. As is well known, politics and ideology have been major influences on the historiography of modern India. In some instances, like the writings of the unabashed imperialists of an earlier epoch or the overtly nationalist writings of Mazumdar *et al.*, the political concerns are obvious. The same is true of the *Subaltern Studies* whose initiator sees his work as a contribution to the reversal of relationship between the dispossessed and the dominant. The feminist contribution to Indian historical studies is also informed by agenda for empowering women. At less obvious levels one encounters an impatience with the inheritance of Third World nationalism, a belief that the current facts of corruption in political life has historical roots. This enhances inherited doubts regarding the *bona fides* of the Indian political elite shared by radicals and conservatives alike. There is also an extreme sensitivity regarding any critique of the imperial record which comes out more in reviews and seminars than in monographic studies or research papers. *Honi soit qui mal y pense!* The other side of the picture is the tendency to label 'pro-imperialist' any positive statement on England's work in India. Assessments of the historiography of modern India which ignore such brash undertones would be less than accurate.

NOTES

1. See for example, M.N. Das, *India under Minto and Morley* (London, 1964); S. Gopal, *The Viceroyalty of Lord Ripon 1880–84* (Oxford, 1953); *The Viceroyalty of Lord Irwin 1926–31* (Oxford, 1957); *British Policy in India, 1858–1905* (Cambridge, 1965); R.J. Moore, *Crisis of Indian Unity 1917–40* (Oxford, 1974).

2. R.C. Mazumdar (ed.), *British Paramountcy and the Indian Renaissance* (Bombay, 1974); *Struggle for Freedom* (Bombay, 1969).

3. See John Strachey, *India* (London, 1888); V. Chirol, *Indian Unrest* (London, 1910); Verney Lovett, *A History of the Indian Nationalist Movement* (London, 1920).

4. R. Coupland, *The Indian Problem 1833–1935* (London, 1942); *The Goal of British Rule in India* (London, 1948).

5. See Judith M. Brown, *Modern India the Origins of an Asian Democracy* (Oxford, 1985); *Gandhi's Rise to Power—Indian Politics 1915–22* (Cambridge, 1972); *Gandhi and Civil Disobedience: The Mahatma in Indian Politics 1928–34* (Cambridge, 1977).

6. See K. Ballhatchet, *Race, Sex and Class under the Raj: Imperial Attitudes and Policies and Their Critics, 1793–1905* (London, 1980). Also see S.N. Bose, *Racism, Struggle for Equity, and Indian Nationalism* (Calcutta, 1981) and Sumit Sarkar, *Modern India 1885–1947* (Delhi, 1983), 22–5.

7. Nirad C. Chaudhauri, *Thy hand, Great Anarch* (London, 1988).

8. The theses so sumarized are developed through a large body of articles and monographs some of which are listed below: J. Gallagher, G. Johnson and A. Seal (eds) *Locality, Province and Nation* (Cambridge, 1977); C. Baker, G. Johnson and A. Seal (eds), *Power, Profit and Politics: Essays on Imperialism, Nationalism and Change in 20th Century Politics* (Cambridge, 1981); C.A. Bayly, *Local Roots of Indian Politics: Allahabad 1880–1920* (Oxford, 1975); D.A. Washbrook, *The Emergence of Provincial Politics; Madras Presidency 1870–1920* (Cambridge, 1976) and C.J. Baker, *The Politics of South India, 1920–27* (Cambridge, 1976).

9. See G. Pandey, *The Ascendancy of the Congress in Uttar Pradesh 1926–34: A Study in Imperfect Mobilisation* (Delhi, 1978).

10. See S. Sarkar, *Swadeshi Movement in Bengal 1903–8* (New Delhi, 1973).

11. See Susan Bayly, *Saints, Goddesses and Kings: Muslims and Christians in South Indian Society 1700–1900* (Cambridge, 1989).

12. J.H. Broomfield, *Elite Conflict in a Plural Society: Twentieth Century Bengal* (Berkeley, 1968).

13. E.F. Irshchick, *Politics and Social Conflict in South India: The Non-Brahmin Movement and Tamil Separatism 1916–29* (California, 1969).

14. Paul R. Brass, *Language, Religion and Politics in North India* (Cambridge, 1979).

15. M.N. Srinivas, *Social Change in Modern India* (Berkeley, 1966).

16. Susan and Llyod Rudolph, *The Modernity of Tradition* (Chicago, 1967).

17. Erik H. Erikson, *Gandhi's Truth: The Origins of Militant Non-violence* (New York, 1969).

18. A. Nandy, *The Intimate Enemy: Loss and Recovery of Self under Colonialism* (Delhi, 1983); S. Kakar, *Intimate Relations: Exploring Indian Sexuality* (Delhi, 1989); *The Inner World: A Psycho-analytic Study of Childhood and Society in India* (Delhi, 1978).

19. See B. Parekh, *Gandhi's Political Philosophy: A critical examination* (Notre Dame, Indiana, 1989).

20. Rajni Kothari (ed.), *Caste in Indian Politics* (Delhi, 1970).

21. For an assessment of this school's specific contributions, see Veena Das, 'Subalternas Perspective' in *Subaltern Studies, VI* (Delhi, 1989).

22. Ramachandra Guha, *The Unquiet Woods: Ecological Change and Peasant Resistance in the Himalayas* (Delhi, 1988).

23. See the chapter entitled 'The Bigoted Julaha' in G. Pandey, *Construction of Communalism* (Delhi, 1993).

24. S. Amin, *Event, Metaphor, Memory: Chauri Chaura, 1922–92* (Berkeley, 1995).

25. Dadabhai Naoroji, *Poverty and Un-British Rule in India* (London, 1901); R.C. Dutt, *Economic History of India*, 2 vols (London, 1901, 1903).

26. See L.C.A. Knowles, *Economic Development of the British Overseas Empire* (London, 1901); V. Anstey, *Economic Development of India*, 3rd edn. (London, 1928).

27. For estimates of national income, see S. Sivasubrahmoniam, 'National Income of India, 1900–1 to 1946–47' (Mimeographed, Delhi University, 1965). For agriculture output, G. Blyn, *Agricultural Trends in India, 1891–1947: Output, Availability and Productivity* (Philadelphia, 1966). For a critique of his views see Alan Heston's chapter in *Cambridge Economic History of India*, II (Cambridge, 1983). Neil Charlesworth was among the severest critics of the view which projected a negative picture of economic changes under Raj. Also see B.R. Tomlinson, *Economy of Modern India 1860–1970;* 'The Historical Roots of Indian Poverty: Issues in the Economic and Social History of Modern South Asia 1880–1960', *Modern Asian Studies,* 1988.

28. See A. Bagchi, *Private Investment in India 1900–39* (Cambridge, 1972).

29. B. Chatterji, *Trade, Tariffs and Empire: Lancashire and British Policy in India 1919–39* (Delhi, 1992).

30. See Bipan Chandra, *The Rise and Growth of Economic Nationalism in India: Economic Policies of Indian National Leadership 1880–1905* (New Delhi, 1966). C. Markovits, *Indian Business and Nationalist Politics from 1931–39* (Cambridge, 1984).

31. A major contribution to these studies are the essays published in K. Sangari and S. Vaid (eds), *Recasting Women: Essay in Colonial History* (Delhi, 1989); also see M.Borthwick, *The Changing Role of Women in Bengal 1849–1905* (Princeton, 1984). The journal, *Samya Shakti* published from Delhi contains a large number of articles on the history of Indian women from a feminist perspective.

32. See S.J. Tharu and K. Lalita, *Women Writing in India from 600 B.C. to the Present* (London, 1993).

33. See for instance, R.K. Ray (ed.), *Mind Body and Society Life and Mentality in Colonial Bengal* (Calcutta, 1995).

34. See, for instance, R. Grove, *Green Imperialism, Colonial Expansion, Tropical*

Edens and the Origins of Environmentalism, 1600–1860 (Cambridge, 1994);
M. Gadgil and R. Guha, *This Fissured Land: An Ecological History of India*
(Delhi, 1992) and M. Rangarajan, *Fencing the Forest: Conservation and
Ecological Change in India's Central Provinces 1860–1914* (New Delhi,
1995).

12

Re-reading *Divide and Quit**

I

Historical studies as well as contemporary narratives of historic events rarely have long lives, so far as readers' interest is concerned. Sir Penderel Moon's *Divide and Quit* is among the fortunate exceptions. Hardly any study of decolonization in South Asia and the partition of Britain's Indian empire published in course of the last four decades has failed to use this extraordinarily perceptive book. Sir Penderel's complex explanation of the long and short term developments leading to the partition of India and his empathic yet hard-headed narrative of the holocaust as it was experienced in one part of the Punjab, the princely state of Bahawalpur, are still of interest. The lay reader, seeking to understand events which seemed unlikely even a few weeks before they actually took place, continues to find here a combination of objectivity and intelligent analysis rare in the writings of people actually involved in those happenings. It was a wise decision to republish the book which is no longer easily available.

Sir Penderel, like some of his famous predecessors in the Indian Civil Service, was even more successful as a professional scholar and historian than as an administrator: arguably, he lacked the 'flexibility' expected of imperial bureaucrats who aspired to reach the top. His preoccupation with discovering the truth and, worse, telling it to the world could not have helped. Yet he evidently made a worthwhile bargain: lasting fame as a scholar of integrity for some higher rung in the bureaucratic ladder or cheap popularity as a writer. His judgements are not comforting to either the believers in imperial righteousness or the champions of Indian nationalism. Quite surprisingly, the varied and intensive research over the last thirty-five

*Published in the New Edition of Penderel Moon, *Divide and Quit*, OUP, Delhi, 1998.

years on many of the themes discussed in his book confirm his judgements far oftener than one might expect.

Yet, *Divide and Rule*, unlike the author's other works (excepting
the semi-fictional *Strangers in India*) is not a scholarly tome. It omits
all critical apparatus, cites very few sources of information and is
not based on archival research. It simply records the considered
judgement of an insightful participant-observer who had earned his
living as a responsible official in the British Indian administration in
the 'thirties and' forties. While doing so, he had also done his best
to try and understand the bewildering and tragic reality taking shape
under his eyes using both commonsense and scholarship. His conclusions offer a curious mixture of imperial stereotypes, profound
analysis and some highly idiosyncratic notions.

The list of long-term factors he identified as the ultimate cause
of the partition of India begins, unpromisingly, with an old familiar.
It was first evoked by Sir Syed Ahmad and used to great purpose in
generating a mass movement to achieve Pakistan: 'two nations—
Muslim and Hindu—could not sit on the same throne'. He considers
and rejects the other familiar stereotype—*divide et impera*—as a con-
tributory factor, but perhaps not entirely. The British, in his view,
certainly did not generate the communal problem; yet, they were
happy to make use of the existing divisions in Indian society. As
Linlithgow's constitutional adviser put it somewhat blandly, 'That
such divisions and conflicts should be used as practical aids to imperial government was only to be expected.'[1] The British were worried
when there were signs of Hindu–Muslim unity and certainly did nothing to resolve the conflict. Communal conflicts, Moon points out,
occurred almost exclusively in the British Indian provinces. The
princely states were for the most part free from this plague.

In his opinion, the most fundamental cause of the communal rift
and its final end products—the partition, massive violence and mass
exodus affecting the lives of millions—was not religion, but a more
modern preoccupation—nationalism. The struggle was not about
faith but power and the material gains which it might bring. Hindus
and Muslims were not interested in converting one another. If such
were the concerns of the ambitious elite, the Pakistan demand accorded with the 'blind impulses' of the Muslim multitude. The British
had contributed to these negative developments by introducing the
Westminister style of electoral process, something totally alien to

India's political traditions and entirely unsuitable for her non-literate masses who got caught up in processes of which they had no understanding.

Then there were the more proximate causes. The strategies and aspirations of the Indian National Congress and the Muslim League and the leaders of the two organizations led inexorably to a situation where no compromise was possible any longer. Gandhi and the Congress were determined to win freedom for a united India and claimed to speak for all Indians, even after the elections of 1937 and 1945 showed quite conclusively that the vast majority of Muslims were not with them. Mr Jinnah stood forth as the 'sole spokesman' for the Muslims and claimed that the League alone should represent the Muslims even at a time when there were non-League ministries in the Muslim majority provinces. Virtually autonomous regions in the Muslim majority areas, their boundaries and degree of autonomy defined vaguely to begin with, was his stated object. Initially viewed with scepticism, if not horror, by most Muslim leaders, the idea of an autonomous Muslim homeland acquired its own inevitable momentum until the road to a free and united India was firmly blocked. The British, anxiously concerned to preserve the unity they had created, tried to avoid partition far too late in the game.

With apologies to their followers and admirers, Sir Penderel insistently laid the blame at the door of the leaders—Gandhi, Nehru, Jinnah, Khizr Hyat Khan, Master Tara Singh and Baldev Singh—for the relentless descent into chaos and misery. He blamed the British for doing nothing to stop the journey to disaster when there was still time and even taking some pleasure in the disarray of the nationalists. He traced how it all happened step by step—the Congress refusal to form coalitions with the League in 1937 which finally alienated Jinnah, Nehru's Muslim mass contact programme which directly induced Jinnah to try the same game bringing communal politics to the Muslim masses, Linlithgow's uninspiring call for co-operation in the war effort with no inducement offered to the Indian nationalists, the resignation of the Congress ministries which was not unwelcome to the British bureaucracy, the failure of the Cripps Mission for which Moon held Gandhi responsible, the 'Quit India' movement which only helped neutralize the Congress for the duration of the war leaving Jinnah free to consolidate his power among the Muslims and the final negotiations for transfer of power in which Jinnah insisted on the League being the sole representative of the Muslims and Gandhi was adamant that the Congress Muslims should be represented in the interim government. This long litany of unfortunate decisions explains the circumstances leading to partition.

But, in Moon's view, they were less important than the fact that the aspirations of the nationalists and the politicized Muslims had become fundamentally incompatible: the Congress leadership, Gandhi excepted, came to find divided India a more acceptable solution than a loose federation with its two major partners always at loggerheads. Along the road there had been many alternative possibilities which could have led to a different outcome. An effective transfer of power before there was any serious demand for a partition of India, say around 1929, was one of these. But once Pakistan, however defined, had become the cherished object of Muslim aspirations, partition in fact, if not in name, was an unavoidable result. The wranglings over the precise interpretation of the Cabinet Mission's three-tiered constitutional proposals and the non-cooperation between the Congress and the League ministers in the interim government were symptoms rather than causes of irrecocilable agendas.

If partition had become inevitable after a point in time, the holocaust which accompanied it was the product of contingent rather than long-term factors. Moon's analysis is slightly ambivalent on this issue. He records Sir Sikander Hyat Khan's opinion that 'Pakistan would mean a massacre': the tribesmen and the Baluch, for instance, would be least concerned with the lethal consequences of their orgy of violence for their co-religionists in Hindustan. His not very satisfactory comparison between the communal violence of 1947 and the Indo-British conflict ninety years earlier also suggests a substratum of faith in a colonial stereotype—the historic and undying hatred between Hindus and Muslims. But his emphasis in explaining the tragedy is on immediate circumstances. The Muslim League which had the overwhelming support of the Punjabi Muslims in 1946 was prevented from forming a ministry by an unacceptable coalition of Khizr Hyat's Unionists with the Akali Sikhs and sundry Hindus. The League's protests were fought with prohibitory orders which could not be imposed leading to the first massacres of Hindus and Sikhs. The seeds of a terrible vendetta were thus sown.

The inclusion of the Punjab in Pakistan would mean the subjection of the Sikhs, a cohesive community, to Muslim domination. Nothing was done to make the prospect attractive or acceptable to them. And the Sikh desire to hold together as a community in one state meant that the partition of the Punjab which divided them did not solve their problem. Revenge for the events of March, 1946 and the desire to expel all Muslims from eastern Punjab to find *lebensraum* for Sikhs who would necessarily migrate from the west explain the massive violence which followed. In short, the Punjab tragedy was the end product of events which took place in the last year of British rule. It was a preventable disaster.

But once the cycle of horrors had begun, it had to run its course. The Border Security Force of 50,000 was inadequate to deal with the outbreak. The loyalty of the police, reluctant to fire on their co-religionists, could not be depended on. Many of the British officials, like the Governor of Bengal who had done little to stop the carnage in August 1946, failed to do even what was possible. One inexperienced official marched his British troops up and down the streets of Amritsar without firing a shot. Others advised the Hindus who sought their protection to go to Gandhi, Patel and Nehru who were not exactly in charge in Western Punjab. Even where they were, like Eastern Punjab, Delhi, Bihar and West Bengal, they had a hard struggle bringing things under control. On one point, however, Moon is quite emphatic. The events in the Punjab were in no way triggered off by the bloodshed in eastern India.

II

How far has Moon's analysis of the causes of the Partition and the horrors which accompanied it been confirmed by the very extensive research of the last three decades? One has to remember that his remarkably independent spirit notwithstanding his perceptions could not entirely shake off the ambience of the colonial discourse which coloured his views on Hindu–Muslim relationship. His own writings are full of examples of varied patterns of understanding between Hindus and Muslims depending on local circumstances. In the two largest Muslim majority provinces coalition governments including non-Muslims ruled until 1943 and 1945 respectively while in the North-West Frontier with its over 90 per cent Muslim population a Congress government held sway till 1946. The League secured the loyalty of the majority of the Muslims only in the last few years of British rule. Moon himself projects several alternative scenarios in which Hindus and Muslims could have co-operated in working a federal polity. Yet in his final conclusion he falls back on Sir Syed's simple dictum— that the two could not sit on the same throne. Moon goes further and sees in the policies of the Congress—with its claim to represent all

Indians and the demand that the Muslim League in U.P. should virtually merge itself in the Congress as the price for coalition—simply a reflection of the alleged Hindu tendency to absorb all and sundry.

The implication that there are two monolithic communities from time immemorial who inevitably pursued their separate political paths is accepted by only a handful of historians today.[2] The view that Hindus and Muslims as two distinct political constituencies and hence all-India communities with separate and competing political aspirations are the products of constitutional arrangements and executive policies of the colonial state is now widely accepted.[3] This view is not to be equated with the thesis that communal conflicts derived from a policy of divide and rule. The new thesis implies only that the politicization of communal identities and overarching solidarities covering the entire subcontinent emerged because 'Hindus' and 'Muslims' were the basic categories in the formulation of constitutional and executive policies of the British in India. As Ayesha Jalal pointed out in her monograph on Jinnah, the thesis that the 'myriad splits and fissures in Indian society had now somehow resolved into a simple line of division between Muslims and Hindus . . . is an unacceptable simplification'.[4] Support for the view that communal solidarities, rather than any pan-Indian nationalism, were somehow 'natural' foundations for political integration comes from an unlikely quarter, the radical writers who contribute to the volumes entitled *Subaltern Studies*.[5] They attribute to the unlettered masses an 'autonomous consciousness' rather than the totally 'blind feeling' manipulated by the elite. Communal loyalty is seen to be a major component of that consciousness.

Moon's view that the introduction of an alien system—constitutional processes based on the Westminister model with its elections and political parties to a society with a totally different political tradition—had a lot to answer for is indirectly confirmed by recent research, though on terms very different from his. Modern scholars do not share his view that the constitutional structure introduced by the British was a disaster which vitiated the body politic, but acknowledge that it was a major influence on the shape and course of indigenous politics. The constitution of 1919 with its emphasis on autonomy for the provinces and communal electorates opened the road to eventual partition: the fact that Hindus and Muslims would no longer require one another's support in order to get elected virtually meant the creation of two mutually distinct political bodies and the power which the Muslims now enjoyed in the provinces where they were in the majority gave them a vested interest in perpetuating provincial autonomy within a loose federal structure. These provinces thus became the future building blocs of Pakistan.[6] This line of argument, however, leaves unexplained the reasons why the idea of Pakistan was at first unacceptable to the leadership as well as their mass following in the Muslim majority provinces and their eventual conversion to the ideology of a separate Muslim state. Arguably, the substantial literature on the subject based on careful analysis of documentary evidence which were not accessible to the author of *Divide and Quit* do not really invalidate the basic line of his argument.

Questions do arise regarding some details of his narrative covering the specific circumstances which led to the transfer of power to two sovereign states. Documents made accessible to scholars in more recent years have disclosed facts which were not known to him. Some of his judgements regarding the unfolding of British policy are also not entirely acceptable.

There is an implied, and at times explicit, assumption in Moon's book that Dominion Status was the accepted goal of British policy in India—at least from the thirties—the hesitation to give up power and profit in the highest circles notwithstanding. The recruiters from Whitehall who went to his school and induced the idealistic teenager to plan a career in the ICS had appealed in terms of the white man's ultimate burden—training Indians for that stated goal. Lord Irwin's famous declaration intended to avert the threatened Civil Disobedience movement did state that Dominion Status in some unstated future was Britain's constitutional plan for India. Yet the expression occurs nowhere in the Simon Commission's Report published *after* the said Declaration nor does it appear in the pages of the 1935 Constitution. The federal proposals in the said document, it is now clear, were intended to neutralize the nationalists in the federal legislature with the help of the separately elected Muslim legislators and the large number of representatives nominated by the princes. They were not meant to set the scene for a dress rehearsal preceding the institution of Dominion Status.[7] Contrary to Moon's assumption, it was not obvious to all the decision-makers at the beginning of the Second World War that the empire would disappear at its end. Linlithgow, writing to the Secretary of State for India, Amery in 1940 opined that the likely date of British departure from India was still 'very remote' and meanwhile 'it would be a pity to throw too much cold water' on the Pakistan proposal which was welcomed in official circles as a means of checkmating the Congress.[8]

Moon's view that the Cripps proposal was rejected through Gandhi's influence has also proved to be incorrect. The Congress, it is now known, was willing to accept quasi-cabinet government without any change in the constitution for the duration of the war on the basis of an informal understanding given by the Viceroy. But Linlithgow would not stand for the convention of Cabinet government. In a letter dated 21 January 1942 he informed Churchill that Burma and India were conquered countries which were in the empire because they were 'kept there by force' and, unknown to Cripps, appealed to the Prime Minister for support on a policy of 'standing firm'. And the reasons why the Mission failed are summed up by Moore as follows:

Against his long and fiercely held imperialist prejudices, Churchill was forced by the pressure of Cripps, his Labour colleagues, and the Americans to acquiesce in the offer of post-War independence and wartime association of the Indian parties with the central government . . . Aided by the like-minded viceroy, Lord Linlithgow, a reaction among his Conservative Cabinet colleagues, . . . and a certain American hesitancy, Churchill was able to abort the negotiations.[9]

As an enthusiastic recruit to the ICS, Moon had sought to discuss with some Whitehall mandarins his ideas regarding reform and development in India. He was pointedly told that the British were not in India to teach Indians the art of self-government but to safeguard British investments in the country worth some thousand million pounds.[10] Evidently every British official and politician was not in a hurry to quit India. The reason why power could not be effectively transferred at a time when the conflict between nationalist and Muslim aspirations could still be resolved was that the decision makers in Britain wished to prolong their hold on India as long as possible. It certainly was not in their interest to seek a resolution of that conflict and hence it was no part of their political agenda. Their anxious efforts to prevent partition came much too late in the day.

III

The second part of *Divide and Quit* (chapters v–xiii), especially the chapters dealing with events in the West Punjab state of Bahawalpur where Moon served as Revenue Minister at the time of Partition, is almost unique in its importance as an eye-witness account of one of the greatest tragedies in human history. Such accounts have a relevance which goes way beyond the limited interest of historical narrative. Our capacity as a species for evil—the mindless infliction of monstrous suffering on fellow creatures—is something we are apt to forget. Records which help remind us of this potential, of what man can do to man, are hence essential props for the maintenance of our moral sanity.

Accounts of the holocaust in Germany and the suffering of the Soviet people under Stalin can be numbered in hundreds. By comparison, narratives of the mass killings and migration in the Punjab at the time of the Partition in India are indeed very few. And Moon's objective account of the tragedy based on the day to day experience of a responsible and highly perceptive official is perhaps the only one of its kind. The fact that it is limited to only a small part of the affected territory does not reduce its importance.

Alan Campbell-Johnson has described 'the scale of the killings and the movement of refugees' in the Punjab as 'even more extensive than those caused by the more formal conflicts of opposing armies' and the two-way migration as 'one of the greatest movements of population in recorded history.' On 21 September 1947 he looked down from the Governor-General's Dakota on two streams of refugees moving in opposite directions. He estimated one to be over fifty miles in length and the other at least forty-five.[11] Moon estimated the total number of casualties at below 180,000 for the Punjab and 200,00 for the subcontinent excluding eastern India (p. 293). Moore, in a later estimate puts the figure for those killed and maimed at 500,000.[12] To these figures one has to add the estimated 4,000 killed and 15,000 maimed in Calcutta in 1946.[13] As Hodson pointed out, it was impossible to be sure of the number of casualties because for much of the time in question there was no effective civil authority to report death. Besides, as Major-General Rees in command of the Punjab Border Force reported on one occasion, '. . . it was impossible to count the victims properly in the confused heap of rubble and corpses'.[14]

The estimates for the scale of the migrations similarly vary. The relevant figures as calculated by Moon are 4 million Hindus and Sikhs migrating from West Pakistan and 6 million Muslims moving in the opposite direction (p. 268). The geographer O.H.K. Spate, put the total number of refugees at 17 million.[15] According to Campbell-Johnson, in August 1947 some ten million people were on the move in an area 'about the size of Wales'.[16] V.P. Menon estimated that the relevant figures were 5 million each way besides 1 million from East Pakistan. R. Jeffrey, on the basis of detailed calculations arrives at the figure of 12 million for the Punjab.[17] Yet, as Campbell-Johnson pointed out, these horrors affected the lives of only 3 per cent of the subcontinent's population and were not comparable in their impact to the Bengal famine of 1943.

Bahawalpur, the region covered in *Divide and Quit*, was only the size of Denmark with a population of 1 to 2 million of whom 190,000 were Hindus and 52,000 Sikhs. It was unique in being the only Indian state ruled by a Musiim prince in which the majority of the population were Muslims. It had no record of communal violence and the nawab took pride in the loyalty of his Hindu subjects. As rumours of communal violence in Eastern Punjab reached the state and refugees with their tales of horror began to arrive, the scene changed. Muslim villagers started pillaging and killing Hindus and Sikhs, especially in the urban areas. Women were abducted as a matter of routine. Killing Sikhs, who were leaving the State in a body and were reported to be up in arms against the Muslims in East Punjab, became a legitimate blood sport. By September, the number of casualties had mounted to a thousand. The state police, never very effective, were reluctant to fire on co-religionists. Even if they could be disciplined, the army was not to be trusted. Several thousand Sikhs from the district of Rahim Yar Khan were treacherously attacked by the army unit who were to escort them to the border. They had taken the precaution of robbing them first. Their women had also been separated for 'reasons of security' and were later distributed among the soldiers. The commanding officer was arrested, but managed to escape to Pakistan of which Bahawalpur was not yet an integral part. Extradition was refused, allegedly through the influence of a highly placed British officer. Elsewhere Moon encountered a long column of Hindu women marching to a mosque to seek conversion. No reassurance would stop them. Their menfolk had probably been killed already. V.P. Menon, on hearing reports of such happenings in the State commented that it was 'a paradise compared with East Punjab' (p. 177).

Moon's dead pan description of the said paradise is capped by a comment of great moral significance:

. . . I found myself in a 'through the looking-glass' world of moral conventions. There was a complete breakdown, or rather reversal, of the ordinary moral values. To kill a Sikh had become almost a duty; to kill a Hindu was hardly a crime. To rob them was an innocent pleasure . . .; to refrain was not a mark of virtue but of lack of enterprise.

Some years ago, a leading Indian sociologist studied some Punjab villages in the grip of both Khalistani and police terror. She found that all the expectations of normal existence and the associated values had disappeared. The only concern was survival and that *anyhow*.[18] The world of mass hysteria described by Moon has a similar ambience. Yet all human values had not collapsed. Majority of the State officials did their duty conscientiously. Rich Muslims offered shelter to Hindus and Sikhs. At the railway station there were moving scenes of Muslims bidding farewell to their Hindu neighbours whom they would never see again. But the twin syndromes of fear and vengeance were the dominant emotions of the day. The present writer was a witness to the Calcutta riots of August 1946 and remembers how people, whom one had known to be gentle and peaceable, stood forth as great avengers and killed innocent men, women and children on the plea that offence was the best means of defence in the circumstances.

The question as to whether this tragedy could have been averted has been answered in the negative by virtually everyone who has written on the subject. For one thing, no one had anticipated violence on such a scale. The civil administration, crippled by the Partition, could not cope with the pervasive defiance of law. East Punjab had lost 7000 Muslim policemen. Neither soldiers nor the police could be relied upon to restrain their co-religionists. A force at least four times the size of the BSF was required to cope with the crisis. The people had defied their leaders and taken charge.[19] In fact it was surprising that things returned to 'normal' by the end of that fateful year. The circumstances of the Partition rendered the holocaust inevitable. Moon puts the blame mainly on two persons, Gandhi and Jinnah—their inflexible attitudes regardless of consequences. But his own account shows that the responsibility was far more widely distributed and that Britain's reluctance to quit when there was still time was a prime factor in the tragedy. The holocaust in the final analysis was the end result of human errors, committed in the very last days of colonial rule rather than of long term trends in the Indian polity. But once these had occurred, the tragedy was not preventable.

IV

Divide and Quit has to be read in the wider context of Moon's perception of British rule in India and of Indian society. That perception was informed by a remarkable degree of objectivity, intellectual honesty and a high-mined view of Britain's duty to India. They also reflect very idiosyncratic opinions which are curious variants of the colonial discourse.[20]

Moon had no doubts regarding the greatness of the British achievement in India—the unification of a vast territory, peace, the massive infrastructural developments and an usually mild rule. He considered it a joint achievement of the British and Indians which future generations would hold in admiration. Admiration for the imperial past was highly and openly popular in England until the end of the Second World War. Academic and intellectuals who still share that enthusiasm would be more hesitant to declare it today, though there are notable exceptions. The blasts of anti-colonial criticism from the Third World and western liberals have induced a measure of circumspection. It is worth noting, however, that the dominant ideology in the early days of Indian nationalism, in fact as late as 1918, acknowledged the grandeur of the British achievement in India, its many failings notwithstanding. That admiration has no resonances in the intellectual or popular culture of contemporary India. In Britain, expectedly, there is a persistent nostalgia for the imperial past and this is not confined to the politically conservative only. As to how future generations will assess England's work in India, any prediction is likely to prove premature.

Moon's admiration for the British achievements in India was tempered by serious criticisms of that record. He accused his fellow countrymen of treating Indians 'like scum', of heaping social insults upon them and excluding them from higher ranks of offices.[21] He accepted that pre-colonial India had enjoyed relative advantage as compared with the West in economic terms and that she had suffered relative rather than absolute decline. He denied that Britain had a deliberately exploitative policy after the first decades of the post-Plassey era, and affirmed that Indian poverty was the result of population growth which far exceeded the rate of growth in income and resources. But he did not absolve Britain of responsibility for the situation. He considered developmental strategies possible and the grounds on which these had not been adopted entirely spurious; in this sphere the Raj made 'difficulties instead of trying to overcome them'.

British policy, in his view, was directly responsible for keeping the Indian peasants in absolute poverty and reducing them to a state of bondage. The introduction of the English legal system, with its emphasis on the inviolability of contract, into a society where the majority were illiterate meant a subjection of the peasant to the moneylender. Introduction of legally guaranteed proprietory rights in land in an economy where such rights were rudimentary in the past ensured ruthless exploitation by the landlord. The new legal system which replaced the older practice of consultation with local worthies by the new requirement of evidence from sworn witnesses guaranteed denial of justice and massive corruption. The lower ranks of the colonial bureaucracy were mostly corrupt. The police habitually used torture and were left undisturbed in their practice because it was convenient for the British to do so. And the worst mistake of all was to try and introduce the parliamentary system which was totally alien to the traditions of the country. Of course the Indians were perfectly capable of governing themselves but not in terms of an alien system and its unfamiliar standards.[22]

Curiously enough, Moon's critique of the economic consequences of the empire had much in common with the views of the nationalists though he rejected their thesis of absolute impoverishment and deliberate exploitation: he does not even refer to the thesis of drainage of wealth from India, central to the nationalist critique. The debate on the implications of the colonial economic nexus is still far from concluded. There are doughty defences of the imperial record which suggest that India did well economically under *pax Britannica*. The opposite view now emphasizes statistical evidence for decline in per capita agricultural output and executive policies which actually hindered industrial development and contributed to over all structural stagnation in the economy.[23]

Not a great deal of work has been done on the implications of the judicial and police systems for India's rural society, but it would be difficult to reject the findings of this astute participant–observer. The allegations of racism in both social relations and executive action have been confirmed by later research.[24]

Moon's perception of Indian society and prognostications for its future were not based only on his observations. It *was* informed by colonial stereotypes however much he might disapprove of his countrymen's attitudes. 'Hindus', 'Muslims', 'Sikhs', 'Punjabis' *et al.* appear in his writings as monolithic and timeless categories and so do 'Indians'. Parliamentary government was totally unsuitable for the said Indians who had a healthy respect for authority and hence the institution of princely states was a welcome feature of its polity which would prove useful in the future. Indian qualities of leadership, especially in matters military, were inadequate and hence marriages between the Princes, natural leaders of the people, and English women might produce the right kind of human material.[25] In the event, princely states have disappeared from the Indian scene without anyone shedding tears for this particular loss. The progeny of the princes, even those born of British mothers, have not been prominent in the ranks of India's leaders. Over time, the people of the subcontinent have developed a stake in the parliamentary system of government and, arguably, some understanding of it. Two of the successor states have returned to it after periods of military dictatorship which had the blessings of the western democracies.

Moon believed that Independent India would need British military protection for some time to come, but was sure to fall under the influence of one of the Great Powers—Britain, Russia or China. Hindu India would have a natural affinity with China or, given the predilection of her intelligentsia, they might fall under Russian influence. U.S.A., oddly, is not mentioned in his list of Great Powers. Writing in 1945, he does not anticipate the Cold War and hence neutralism as a possible option. He warmly recommends Soviet-type planning for industrialization, especially massive investment in irrigation and hydroelectric projects and was strongly in favour of co-operative farming. In all this his pragmatic preferences came close to Nehru's socialist ones. He accepted the latter's invitation to work as an adviser to the Planning Commission and helped shape its policies.

His relationship with Indian nationalists had a quality of ambivalence. He evidently shared the British officials' impatient incomprehension of Gandhi, but acknowledged his honesty of purpose and the element of true saintliness in the man. He distrusted the nationalists' preoccupation with parliamentary government. He disapproved even more of high-handed methods in dealing with them, even when they were in open and, in his view, pointless rebellion. Expression of such disapproval nearly cost him his job.

He was not one to hide his true feelings whatever the situation. During my brief tenure as an official of the National Archives of India, I had to deal with a devastating review he had written of Maulana Azad's introduction to S.N. Sen's *Eighteen Fifty-Seven*. The review was meant for a publication of the Education Ministry and the Maulana was the Minister of Education. I went to see Sir Penderel and asked if he would modify the more trenchant comments. He offered to withdraw his review. We were saved further embarrassment when the Minister asked us to publish the piece without changing a word. I met Sir penderel for the last time when he came to give a talk at our weekly South Asian History seminar at Oxford. At question time he dropped a sizeable brick—referring to the alleged deficiencies of a certain Indian community. Three members of the said community were sitting in the front row. The speaker was exceptionally quiet later that evening. When we invited him again to speak to our seminar, he declined. He said he no longer felt very confident as to what he might say. There is no lack of confidence in his written words. Even his idiosyncratic views detract little from their abiding importance.

NOTES

1. V. Hodson, *The Great Divide*, quoted in G. Rizvi, *Linlithgow and India : A study of British Policy and Political Impasse in India, 1936–43* (London, 1978), p. 105.
2. See for example Chaudhri Muhammad Ali, *The Emergence of Pakistan* (New York and London, 1967). R.C. Majumdar's *History of the Freedom Movement*, 3 vols (New Delhi, 1973) also basically accepted the two nation thesis.
3. See Anil Seal's introductory essay in J. Gallagher *et al.* (eds), *Locality, Province and Nation* (Cambridge, 1973).
4. A. Jalal, *The Sole Spokesman: Jinnah, the Muslim League and the Demand for Pakistan* (Cambridge, 1985), p. 223.
5. See R. Guha, editor, *Subaltern Studies*, vols 1–6 (New Delhi, 1982–93). This thesis is presented quite powerfully in Partha Chatterji, *The Nation and Its Fragments* (Princeton, 1991). Gyanendra Pandey is currently working on the popular consciousness expressed in the conflicts and violence which attended the partition in the Punjab.
6. See David Page, *Prelude to Partition* (New Delhi, 1976).
7. For a full discussion of British policy in India in the late twenties and thirties, see Robin J. Moore, *The Crisis of Indian Unity* (Oxford, 1974).
8. See Rizvi, op. cit., p. 119.
9. R.J. Moore, *Churchill, Cripps and India 1939–45* (Oxford, 1979), pp. 1, 53, 115–25.
10. See typescript of interview with Sir Penderel Moon deposited at the India Office Library.
11. See Alan Campbell-Johnson, *Mission with Mountbatten* (London, 1951), pp. 178, 200–1.

12. R.J. Moore, *Escape from Empire: The Attlee Government and the Indian Problem* (Oxford, 1983), p. 327; R. Jeffrey, 'The Punjab Boundary Force and the Problem of Order, August, 1947', *Modern Asian Studies*, VIII, 4 (1974), pp. 491–520.

13. See A. Jalal, op. cit., p. 46.

14. H.V. Hodson, op. cit., p. 418.

15. O.H.K. Spate, *India and Pakistan: A General and Regional Geography* (London, 1954), quoted in A. Jalal, op. cit., Introduction.

16. A. Campbell-Johnson, op. cit., p. 175.

17. V.P. Menon, *The Transfer of Power in India* (Orient Longman, 1968, first published, 1957), p. 439; R. Jeffrey, op. cit.

18. Paper presented by Veena Das at a seminar on *Subaltern Studies* in Calcutta, 1991.

19. See A. Campbell-Johnson, op. cit., pp. 355–7.

20. See his *Strangers in India* (New York, 1945) and typescripts of his interview given to David Blake deposited in the India Office Library.

21. *Strangers in India*, pp. 22, 30.

22. Ibid., chapters 1–3.

23. For emphasis on the positive aspects of the imperial record, see *Cambridge Economic History of India*, vol 2 (Cambridge, 1983), D. Fieldhouse's chapter in P.J. Marshall (ed), *The Cambridge Illustrated History of the British Empire* (Cambridge, 1996) and Neil Charlesworth, *British Rule and the Indian Economy 1800–1914* (London, 1982). For the opposite point of view see, *Private Investment in India, 1900–39* (Cambridge, 1972); M.D. Morris *et al.*, *Indian Economy in the Nineteenth Century: A Symposium* (New Delhi, 1969).

24. See for example K. Ballhatchet, *Race, Sex and Class under the Raj: Imperial Attitudes and Policies and Their Critics, 1793–1905* (London, 1980).

25. This idea of Sir Penderel Moon was mentioned by S. Gopal in his lecture, 'All Souls and India' delivered at All Souls College in 1993.

III

Colonial Legacies:
Post-colonial Conflicts

13

Shadows of the Swastika: Historical Perspectives on the Politics of Hindu Communalism

A valedictory lecture is usually an anodyne statement—at its best a summing up of one's life-work, rich in wisdom and scholarship. The present exercise does not belong to that category, not merely because the speaker lays no claim to wisdom or scholarship, but because the present moment is unsuited to anodyne statements on India. Besides, the concern of this lecture has only peripheral links with my areas of professional expertise. It is addressed to a political-cum-cultural phenomenon in contemporary India which, in the opinion of many, portends a grievous threat to the cherished values on which the Indian democracy is based. We also believe that this threat, if not neutralized in time, may yet destroy the structure of polity and society which the Indian nation-state has sought to nurture and done so, despite its many failures, with at least a modicum of success. A struggle is on for the hearts and minds of the Indian people. The present exercise is meant to be a modest contribution to the debate which is at the very heart of that struggle.

The title of my lecture identifies my sympathies in the on-going conflict. I do not speak as a dispassionate observer. Yet, I claim objectivity for my statements with regard to selection of data as well as the analysis of the problem in question. I do so in the belief that any effort to eradicate a poison must identify it correctly without reference to one's hopes, fears and preferences.

On 6 December 1992 a sixteenth-century mosque in the mediae-val town of Ayodhya was destroyed in broad daylight by a fanatical Hindu mob. This was the culmination of a campaign launched by

*Valedictory lecture delivered at the University of Oxford in June 1993.

the Sangh Parivar, i.e. 'the family' (incidentally, the term has a delightful Sicilian resonance) of organizations built around the Rashtriya Svayamsevak Sangh, ostensibly a cultural organization meant to propagate and nurture Hindu values. The RSS was banned for some time after the assassination of Mahatma Gandhi because it was suspected of complicity in the crime. Its leader, Golwalkar was imprisoned but had to be released eventually because the evidence in the hands of the state prosecutor was not enough to prove his responsibility for the assassination in a court of law. The assassin, Godse, was long a member of the organization and though he had left it to join the overtly political Hindu Mahasabha, he went to the gallows with a prayer prescribed by the RSS on his lips.

The Sangh Parivar projects the belief that a Rama temple once stood on the sacred spot where the incarnate deity was born. Further, according to their canon, it was destroyed by Babar, the founder of the Mughal empire whose general, Mir Baqi constructed a mosque in its place. Replacement of the mosque with a Rama temple, an enterprise to which all good Hindus, it was hoped, would contribute has been given top priority in the Sangh Parivar's agenda. There are other mosques standing on the site of ancient temples which have to be similarly replaced. The full list is said to cover some three thousand items. The Tajmahal, a Hindu monument according to Dr Oak, a 'historian' much respected by the Parivar, is one of these. But the immediate focus would be on three mosques starting with the one at Ayodhya.

The destruction of the Babri mosque has been interpreted in sections of the western press, when they have bothered to notice it, as one more episode in the timeless conflict between two mutually antithetical monoliths, the Indian Muslims and their hereditary enemies, the Hindus. More concerned observers have commented on the absurdity of secularist aspirations in a society as illiterate and as committed to the *vita religiosa* as the Indian. Expectedly the root of the folly has been traced to the one person who, we now know, with the blessings of the IMF, is responsible for most of India's current ills. Incidentally, there is a happy consensus between right wing and radical observers of the Indian situation on the matter of Jawaharlal Nehru's original sins, of which more later.

The destruction of the mosque and the movement for reclaiming Rama's birth-place for the Hindus, have produced a substantial body of concerned writings by Indian journalists and scholars. The copious evidence collected by them prove beyond reasonable doubt that the mass hysteria over the Babri mosque–Ramjanambhoomi controversy is not a symptom of religious revivalism or any spontaneous resurgence of Hindu concern for the honour of their ancient faith. It was in effect the successful end result of a sustained organizational and propaganda campaign launched by the Viswa Hindu Parishad (VHP), its parent body the RSS, the latter's political front, the BJP and many affiliates such as the activist youth organization, Bajrang Dal, the association of sadhus known as the Sant Sabha, etc. A local dispute going back to the century which had aroused little interest in the rest of the country was adopted by the VHP as a national cause of the Hindus in 1985. The long campaign of mobilization was structured around newly invented rituals, such as the laying of a foundation stone, the call to every Hindu village for the contribution of a brick for the projected temple, motorized chariot journeys by the (BJP) leader Advani in an attempt to raise consciousness, a barrage of propaganda, including some of exceptional virulence in their anti-Muslim rhetoric and using the most advanced technology available to mass media and, of course, mobilization and recruitment of RSS cadres whose current strength is estimated at 2 to 3 million. This sustained campaign has succeeded in converting an issue of no relevance to the multiple problems of contemporary Indian life into the central concern of Indian politics.

Statements like the one I have just made is ascribed by the supporters of the movement to the westernized pseudo-secularist's total incomprehension of Hindutva, the essential content of the Hindu ethos, all that makes a good Hindu tick. If such ascription is correct, one would like to ask why Hindu passions on this issue lay dormant until VHP adopted it as the central plank in their programme. Mosques built on the sites of destroyed temples are not very rare in India and the country also has an unfortunate record of communal frenzy, at times without provocation from outside. Yet we know of no incident where Hindus, eager to restore the glory of their faith, have tried to destroy such mosques and replace them with temples. After all even Ramlalla, baby Ram (a new addition to the Hindu pantheon) allegedly manifested himself at the temple site as early as 1949. Yet until 1985, good Hindus have shown no excessive anxiety to replace the Babri mosque with a Rama temple. Why?

The answer is provided in an anecdote recorded by the young Harvard scholar, Nico Blank, in his report of dialogues with the people of Ayodhya. A wrestler turned ascetic who had tended to one of the many Rama temples in the town for a period of years told him that a holy place was not a suitable site for conflicts in any form. Mrs Sahi, the tea vendor had a very different view of the matter. She confessed to a deep hatred of Muslims and gratefully acknowledged that the VHP's campaign had first made her aware of the misdeeds of that hated community.

One central object of the entire exercise was made explicit by Mr Advani in a statement recorded by a young journalist, Smita Gupta: 'We always refer to the disputed structure in Ayodhya as Ramjanmabhoomi (the birthplace of Rama). On the two occasions that the building was stormed we said that saffron flags had been hoisted on the Babri Masjid. You see, there is no triumph in planting a saffron flag on a temple.' After the destruction of the mosque, the RSS mouthpiece *Organiser* published a photograph of the Pakistan flag flying at half mast at the High Commission in Delhi. The caption read: 'Mourning liberation of Ramjanmabhoomi'. The party intellectual Seshadri described the act as 'a tremendous morale-booster for the Hindu psyche', 'a symbolic self-assertion of the nation's Hindu identity'. Such evidence leaves one in very little doubt as to the real object of the entire campaign. An issue highlighting alleged historic insults inflicted by Muslim rulers on the Hindu faith had been chosen to whip up anti-Muslim sentiments as the basis for forging a Hindu identity. Hence the destruction of a mosque is not a cause for shame but instead a tremendous morale booster for the Hindu psyche, in effect an act of liberation. The Pakistan flag flying at half-mast is a token of victory, a just retribution for ancestral misdeeds.

The attitudes reflected in such statements and projections are not sudden aberrations. These have been the basis of an organization and its ostensibly non-political cultural programme going back to the late twenties. That organization, the RSS and its many affiliates have spread their tentacles through six and half decades of sustained effort. Their quiet growth had gone unnoticed for the most part until it was reflected in the very recent electoral gains of the Hindu party BJP and the spectacular extra-parliamentary activities of the Sangh Parivar since 1985. The said gains and activities have been rendered possible by a specific and dangerous historical conjuncture, a theme to which I shall return later. They do not derive from the devotional concerns deep rooted in the Hindu psyche, otherwise such concerns would have been manifest powerfully at a much earlier date. Besides, the very real phenomenon of Hindu devotionalism is expressed traditionally in a quietist nonconfrontational idiom. And the alleged spontaneous revival paradoxically seeks exclusive expression through the Parivar's carefully orchestrated campaign for the destruction of mosques and their replacement by temples. The central focus is on alleged historic wrongs and the fomenting of hatred against a religious minority.

A group of Indian scholars has recently published a tract tracing the history of the RSS and its affiliates. It projects in brilliant detail a sinister record of ideology and organization structured around xenophobia, the project for a nation state which would relegate non-Hindus to the status of a subject population. Savarkar first spelled out this new notion of Hindutva in 1923 when he declared that only those who thought of India as the Holy Land as well as the Fatherland could be true patriots. Since this joy was inaccessible to Muslims, their patriotism should always be suspect. In 1925, in the wake of extensive communal riots on a scale without precedent Dr Hedgewar established the RSS in direct response to the new quest for disciplined cadres of Hindu communalism. The founder's analysis of the political situation which necessitated the new organization is illuminating: 'the yavan-snakes reared on the milk of non-cooperation were provoking riots with their poisonous hissing'. The riots were Muslim riots because in every single case 'it is they who start them'. Thus 'it became evident that Hindutva was Rashtriyatva' i.e., Hinduness was the same as nationalism. It was hence necessary for dedicated Hindu youths to organize in self-defence. Golwalkar, who succeeded the good doctor to the leadership of RSS, developed the notion of cultural nationalism as distinct from territorial nationalism. The idea that those who lived within the geographical boundary of a country constituted the nation was rejected.

He defined his notion of cultural nationalism along following lines:

German national pride has now become the topic of the day. To keep up the purity of the nation and its culture, Germany shocked the world by purging the country of the semitic races—the Jews. National pride at its highest has been manifested here. Germany has also shown how well-nigh impossible it is for races and cultures, having differences going to the root, to be assimilated into one united whole, a good lesson for us in Hinduism to learn and profit by. . . . From this standpoint sanctioned by the experience of shrewd old nations, the non-Hindu people in Hindustan must either adopt the Hindu culture and language, must learn to respect and revere Hindu religion, must entertain no idea but the glorification of the Hindu nation . . . in one word they must cease to be foreigners or may stay in the country wholly subordinated to the Hindu nation claiming nothing, deserving no privileges, far less any preferential treatment, not even citizen's rights.

He went on to castigate the minority treaties laid down by the League of Nations on the ground that these would confer unlimited rights on the minorities and Hindu national life would 'run the risk of being shattered'. Of the five criteria of nationhood he laid down, race was the most important. Hence the need to equate Hindus with Aryans and claim that Aryans did not come from outside the holy land of Bharatavarsha. The latter belief is central to the version of Indian history taught in schools which were controlled by the BJP state governments. Interestingly, Guruji Golwalkar rejected all western ideologies as alien. Fascism was the one exception. And perhaps inspired by the ideal of greater Germany, the map of Hindu India on the jacket of his book included Afghanistan, Burma and Sri Lanka.

In recent RSS propaganda there have been attempts to explain away such ideas and suggest that Guruji actually revised his earlier opinions. In fact, the minor verbal changes in later editions do not modify the pristine purity of Guruji's ideals and these have never been directly repudiated by the RSS or BJP leadership. As the BJP leader Malkani helpfully explained in a television interview, many Indians admire Hitler. He did not explain if he shared that popular Indian preference.

In effect the RSS ideology implies a total rejection of the composite nationalism enshrined in the constitution of India. In 1949 Golwalkar criticized the Indian constitution as unBharat anticipating the VHP's more explicit description, unHindu. Earlier, Guruji had interpreted swaraj, the stated goal of the movement for India's independency, as 'our Raj'. But who were we? His answer, expectedly, was only the Hindus. The animosity to the national movement and its vision of unity transcending ethnic boundaries, so prominent in Hedgewar's statements, was intensified when the All India Congress Committee announced in 1931 that free India would be a secular democratic republic. The RSS was virtually absent from the mass movements of the 1920s and '30s, a fact underlined in the otherwise sympathetic history of the organization by Anderson and Damle.

These movements for the achievement of national independence under Gandhi's leadership were unacceptable, because they were unlikely to lead to the establishment of a Hindu Rashtra, their central objective. As already noted, Hedgewar unequiocally condemned the Non-cooperation–Khilafat movement because it had encouraged 'the yavana-snake'. The enemy of the nation, as perceived by the RSS, was not colonial rule, but the Muslims of India. Absent from the Quit India movement, the RSS cadres were very prominent in the riots of 1946–7.

The core doctrine of the movement today can be summed up as follows. It is stated succinctly in the slogan their cadres shout every morning at the branch of *shakha* meetings, 'Hindustan Hinduka, nahi kisika baap ka'. Hindustan belongs to the Hindus, not to anybody else's father. Hindus constitute the nation. Their faith, in its unique catholicism, is superior to all other religions. All other cultural traditions in India survived by Hinduizing themselves. Oxbridge trained pseudo-secular and deraciné nationalists like Nehru had introduced a pseudo-secular constitution and the country was now ruled by pseudo-secularist traitors to the Hindu nation who appeased Muslims as vote banks. The truly secular Hindu Rashtra would offer true protection to the non-Hindus. RSS cadres often explain that as the followers of the world's most tolerant faith they of course love Muslims; in fact they love even insects. Bhandari, one of BJP's top ranking leaders, pointed out that even Muslims have their gentlemen. I doubt though if he would let them marry his sisters. Unfortunately Islam being a proselytizing religion, all Muslims were necessarily intolerant. And India was in danger of becoming a Muslim majority state. They will soon outnumber Hindus by means of their highly fecund polygamy. Less legitimately, being lustful by nature they would rape Hindu women, and thereby add to their own numbers, which will be further augmented by migrations from Pakistan and Bangladesh. Pakistan will eventually invade and conquer India aided by the majority Muslim population of the once Hindu land. The pseudo-secularism of the Oxbridge trained pseudo-Hindus—the *Organiser* delights in underlining that unfortunate academic link—is a part of this treacherous grand design.

The joint authors of the track *Khaki Shorts, Saffron Flags* were told by two leaders of the BJP that the ideal Hindu Rashtra had to be an absolutist state in which the individual must merge his/her identity. Back in 1981, when the Janta alliance broke up, Nanaji Deshmukh attacked parliamentary politics as opportunistic. Much earlier, in 1946 Mahatma Gandhi described the RSS as a 'communal body with a totalitarian outlook'. Its declared principle of allegiance to one leader, '*ek chalak anuvartita*' and the insistence on total obedience validates this assessment. The cadres when asked what they would do if asked by their adhikari, the officer in command, to jump into a well is expected to answer, 'We shall do so immediately.'

This uncompromising ideology is dispensed through the *shakhas* or branches. The recruits are boys of twelve to fifteen. Indoctrination takes the form of handing down simple messages of Hindu glory, tales of resistance to Muslim tyranny. Discussion or complex ideas do not form any part of the *bauddhic* or intellectual sessions. An educational programme was initiated to complement the training of cadres as far back as the 1950s. There are provisions for primary and secondary schools as well as informal schooling for slum children. The total number of these institutions is about 4000. Students listen to frequent lectures on the duty to die for one's own religion. Indian culture as dispensed in these schools again emphasizes Hindu resistance to Muslim tyranny. Non-Hindu heroes are no part of that culture or the iconography of Indian heroism displayed on school walls. This particular version of Indian culture has now penetrated schools and colleges run by older Hindu reform movements like the Arya Samaj. The emphasis throughout is on a thousand year old struggle for Hindu independence. That heroic tale virtually excludes the resistance to British rule and by pseudo-secularists. A new emphasis surfaces in the prescription for the Hindu's ritual duty of pilgrimage. Sites desecrated by Muslim rulers feature almost exclusively in the RSS list of holy places.

The RSS long remained quietly in the background as a purely cultural organization. Its gradually unfolding programme has been one of penetrating organizations who share their basic outlook and then create a number of affiliates encompassing many areas of Hindu social life and political action. In 1931, the youth wing of the Hindu Mahasabha merged with the RSS giving the latter, till then largely confined to upper caste Marhattas, a chance to penetrate the Hindi belt. In 1941 when Shyamaprasad Mukherji set up his new Hindu Party Jan Sangh, Guruji Golwalkar sent four trained cadres of the RSS to assist him. This committed band included the mild-mannered Advani and the liberal Vajpayee. Bhandari who has met gentlemen even among Muslims was a third member of the group. It is worth remembering that none of these gentlemen has repudiated their guru's high ideals or his professed admiration for Hitler. Jan Sangh reborn as BJP, a formidable mass party, borrows its cadres and ideology from the RSS. As Bhandari helpfully explained, RSS is the organizational, BJP the political and VHP the social wing of the same Hindu nation. Like Brahma, Vishnu and Siva they are three parts of one indivisible reality. It would be a serious mistake ever to forget the fact. The VHP which has spearheaded the campaign to reclaim Ramjanmabhoomi was born in 1964 when Golwalkar met a group of Hindu ascetics and heads of religious organizations in the quest of Hindu unity and a new legitimacy for the RSS. The Hindu Sadhu is now a political animal and their deliberations on the question of re-claiming the three holy sites at Ayodhya, Mathura and Kashi are projected in the VHP video cassettes as 'urgent devotional necessity'. Thanks to the VHP initiative, taped speeches of the firebrand fe-male ascetic, Ritambhra, who delights in referring to Muslims with an unmentionable epithet, are now broadcast in Hindu temples to gatherings of the often innocent faithful. The *sants* are not very easy to control. After their Ayodhya victory, an enterprise in which they were prominently visible, they demanded the immediate abrogation of India's pseudo-secular constitution. An embarrassed BJP repu-diated that demand. Evidently, they are willing to wait.

The VHP's Foreign Co-ordination Committee has projected the brilliant idea that the Hindus all over the world constitute a single country, divided for its purposes into thirty odd branches. The British Committee funded by very wealthy expatriates has established an association innocuously named Friends of India. At one of its recent seminars, to which some Hindu academics were invited, the VHP version of the Ayodhya temple's history was presented as proven truth. Attempt to question it were shouted down. At home, its de-partment looking after the Ramjanmabhoomi campaign has freely recruited sections of the urban poor without any regular means of livelihood and at the margin of subsistence who are known to have a very low flash point, into their youth wing, the Bajrang Dal. Admit-tedly, these sections of the urban population have had a role in all mass agitations, but they have also provided the fire power in the subcontinent's communal riots over the years. It was a clever idea to organize them for an aggressive campaign of communal hatred, but their ardour has been difficult to contain.

However, the chief concern of RSS/VHP is with the educated

middle classes. The student wing of BJP, Bhartiya Vidyarthi Parishad, wields considerable power in Delhi and other north Indian universities ever since the early 70s. And there are organizations working among women, tribals and importantly, factory workers. The last named organization is dedicated specifically to the task of fighting the pernicious doctrine of class war. Maharashtra's Shiv Sena, originally set up to protect Marathi interests against outsiders like the Tamil clerks in Bombay, has now jumped on to the Hindutva band wagon. Some of its leaders have claimed credit for the destruction of the mosque and smilingly acknowledged that their boys were very active in the anti-Muslim riots in Bombay which followed.

The many-pronged struggle for the eventual establishment of a Hindu Rashtra has produced the largest single organized movement in the country. The efforts spread over many decades are beginning to pay rich dividends. The number of *sakhas* went up from 8,500 in 1975 to 11,000 in 1977 and reached 20,000 by 1982. In 1982 RSS cadres had reached an estimated one million. The current estimates put the figure at about 2 to 3 millions. By 1981, the financial contributions amounted annually to 10 million rupees. The current figure is certainly much higher, with nonresident Indians contributing generously to the cause of Hindutva. All contributions, incidentally are anonymous. The BJP had two seats in parliament in 1984. Now it leads the opposition with 119 seats. Its extra-parliamentary power was manifest in the assaults on the Babri mosque.

The movement and the organizations I have discussed have been described, expectedly, as fascist by their radical critics. As Professor Trevor Roper (as he then was) pointed out in an essay, the term fascism has been applied to too wide a range of phenomena to have any clear identifiable meaning any longer. Unless the term was used simply as political abuse, it was in his view really relevant only in the context of an industrialized society in the grip of a political and economic crisis, especially after defeat in war. In Europe, to his understanding, it was closely linked to the fear of socialist revolution. Others have pointed out that fascism has mushroomed in industrially backward countries as well and the *fuhrerprinzip* has emerged even in the absence of an outstanding leader.

It is generally agreed that historically fascism has been marked by some common characteristics. It is a movement of aggressive nationalism with strong anti-intellectual or non-intellectual overtones. In industrial societies it was the movement of a frightened lower middle-class anxious to defend their interest without disturbing the existing social hierarchy. It emphasized the organic character of society and preached a gospel of racial superiority as well as the spoliation of a social outgroup. It has sought a break with the existing structure of power and to forge a wholly disciplined state to achieve a new preeminence based on past glory. Everywhere it has been marked by a deep nostalgia for return to a mythical past. In some instance it began in a disorderly way and retained that disorderly and nebulous character throughout its career. Weakness of parliamentary governments has contributed to its emergence. Structurally, it has been based on a coalition of classes, with industrialists generally willing to help, especially after the movement has acquired state power.

This inadequate summary of the shared characteristics of fascism in very different societies is not meant to provide an abstract model of the phenomenon or to explore its affinities with the Indian situation. My object is simply to indicate that in certain historical situations aggressive nationalism, invoking myths of past glory and racial superiority with strong overtones of xenophobia, has been projected by social classes who feel threatened. Such emotionally charged movements are usually illiberal, anti-intellectual and totalitarian in inspiration. Based on an alliance of a broad spectrum of social class they profit from the weakness of constitutional regimes and seek to construct a repressive political system and do so, *inter alia,* by exploiting any available seam of hatred against one or other ethnic minority identified as a threat to the nation's well-being. In the rest of this lecture I shall try to show that the striving for a Hindu Rashtra and the efforts at mobilization to that end is acquiring the features of such a movement. For a multi-ethnic, poor and at the moment weak parliamentary democracy like India, such a movement, whether it acquires total power or not, has disastrous implications.

To appreciate the nature of the threat, one needs to analyse the nature and origins of Indian nationalism—its political and ideological basis. The colonial discourse on India repeated *ad nauseum* the evident fact of India's ethnic diversity to assert the impossibility of nationhood for India. The ideological construction of Indian nationhood in the nineteenth century by the emerging politicized intelligentsia sought to challenge this colonial perception by emphasizing elements of cultural unity in the subcontinent and imagining a past of imperial unity based on a high and superior civilization. The early versions of this imagined unity focused almost exclusively on the Hindu elements of past glory. They also projected the conflicts between the medieval dynasties of Turkish or Afghan origin and the local Rajput or Maratha chieftains as a struggle for independence by their Hindu ancestors. At a more self-conscious stage in the development of nationalist ideology, the composite character of Indian society, the traditions of tolerance and co-existence, the claims to a unique pattern of unity in diversity, were projected as the basis of Indian nationhood. The Indo-Islamic past was proudly claimed as an integral part of the Indian inheritance. Throughout the years of the nationalist agitation for independence in the present century, this ideal of a composite nationhood was a central theme in nationalist mobilization. The efforts at mobilization also sought to create and sustain an alliance between all classes in Indian society as a basis for the future independent state. These efforts had achieved a measure of success by the time of independence.

As to the class basis of the newly-born Indian state, radical critics may be right in emphasizing its exploitative character, but the social revolution which accompanied the end to colonial rule also needs to be underlined. Within a few years, the centuries old princely India disappeared for good as did the world of great landlords. A very substantial class of upwardly mobile and increasingly wealthy farmers became a part of the social and political landscape. The intelligentsia benefited from a remarkably quick expansion of the tertiary sector and higher levels of education. There were seventeen universities in India in 1947. There are one hundred forty now and more than four thousand colleges in place of the two hundred in the year of independence. The absolute growth in the industrial sector was quite phenomenal. While some 300 million people are still below the poverty line, in percentage terms people in that unfortunate position have fallen from some 53 per cent to about 30 per cent in rural areas. The condition of the marginal peasant has not improved except in one or two states, but the tenant of yester-year now owns his land. And universal adult suffrage has meant a political revolution the full impact of which remains to be analysed. The poor and illiterate elector has since 1979 repeatedly exercised his power to throw out regimes unacceptable to them. The untouchable still remains where he was socially, but the statute book at least contains a law which renders the practice of untouchability punishable by rigorous imprisonment. More important, Nehru, the misguided socialist, laid the foundations of an infrastructure for agriculture and industry which made India self-sufficient in food probably for the first time in two hundred years and has helped create a relatively affluent class estimated at somewhere between 150 to 200 million.

The end result of the positive and negative developments, and the latter includes a phenomenal increase in population which eats up most of the benefits of economic growth, is the emergence of what Kalecki described as the intermediate state. Such states, according to his analysis, are marked by an unlikely alliance of wealthy farmers, the petty bourgeois, and the capitalists (to which one should add the intelligentsia) as the ruling class. At best, this is an uneasy alliance for it is difficult to reconcile the interests of these social classes. Besides, they also need to handle the tensions arising from the existence of a vast and ever growing class of the underprivileged, whose sense of deprivation is now continually exacerbated by their exposure to visual media such as television. One source of the present crisis has to be sought in this particular conjuncture of circumstances.

The urban petty bourgeois—shop keepers, small businessmen, clerks, lower level professionals and the like—are highly politicized by now and they share the multiple aspirations of their more fortunate fellow citizens. They also feel excluded from the higher echelons of political and administrative power, as well as social privilege by virtue of their relative disadvantage in matters of education and resources. Their children do not go to the English medium schools and can hardly even dream of education abroad. In the vast Hindi speaking belt where the standard of literacy and education is lower than elsewhere, this significant section of the electorate feel that they are excluded from the privileged world of the modern intelligentsia whose language of discourse is in effect English. The world of vernacular, especially Hindi media press and publications, on the other hand, is of little interest to the English speaking intelligentsia.

One interesting consequence of the expansion of university education has gone unnoticed. It would probably be true to say that in the great majority of university and university level institutions in India today the education dispensed to the bulk of the students is indifferent in quality. English, which remains the main avenue of access to the world of knowledge, is not really understood by the bulk of the university educated in India today. This deficiency has created a new hierarchy among the relatively privileged in India today, a clear division between those whose educational advantage gives them an access to careers with high income and status and the others who are excluded from these benefits. Much of the history of political conflicts in modern India is a story of rivalry between the more privileged and the less privileged among the elite groups at given periods in time. That pattern of conflict has acquired a new context and dimension through the educational and socio-economic developments of the last five decades. Political India now has two mutually unrelated worlds of intellectual discourse. When the Indian intellectual contemptuously refers to the Hindi-speaking region as the cow belt and its denizens as ignorant obscurantists, he aggravates the resentment of a politically conscious and powerful social group. He also sharpens the edge of their need for psychological self-assertion. Inflation, scarcity of urban housing and unemployment threaten their fragile hold on a genteel life-style. And the upper caste component of the urban petty bourgeoisie feel both socially and economically threatened by efforts at positive discrimination in favour of the lower castes, a magnanimity which the more secure elements in the intelligentsia can afford. We have here a fertile ground for ideologies of anti-intellectual nationalism, anger against the Oxbridge trained pseudo-secularist of RSS propaganda and their alleged protégés, the hated descendants of tyrannical conquerors one reads of in the Hindi text-books.

The constitution of independent India projected a federal state. In fact, however, the political contingencies of post-independence India produced a highly centralized government. The Nehruvian state has been described, up to a point correctly, as a mandatory dictatorship. Power was vested by popular will in the hands of a charismatic leader. The inheritance of the partition riots, the war with Pakistan and the task of integrating the Princely States rendered a concentration of authority at the centre virtually unavoidable. These were not tasks which State Governments could have handled on their own. As the National Congress had virtual monopoly of power in the States down to the early sixties, this centralization did not create insoluble tensions. Challenges to centralization were quantitatively speaking a marginal phenomenon.

The mandate for the Centre was gradually eroded by the debacle of the China war, the increasing corruption in politics, and the rising aspirations of the political leadership at the State level. In parts of the country, especially the North-east where people had genuine grievances in terms of unfair distribution of resources and power, politically ambitious leaders could mobilize mass support for their aspirations in the name of ethnicity. Much of the tensions which have been identified as centrifugal tendencies was no more than bargaining for a larger share of the national cake, at least to begin with. A classic example is the Sikh demand that a third of the Indian army should be recruited from their community. This does not exactly sound like a desire to break away from the Indian union. To take another example, the protagonists of the Tamil autonomy movement who rejoiced in burning the Indian constitution swore undying faith to the same constitution the day their party was elected to power in the State. Quantitatively speaking, the political consensus in favour of national unity has far outstripped the challenges to that unity in independent India. One reason for this was the structure of representation with the dominant party, which allowed conflicting aspirations to be accommodated. As non-Congress governments were formed in the States since the mid-sixties, the resolution of Centre–State tensions and the conflicting claims of the States have been far more difficult to resolve. The system has yet to develop the necessary resilience to tackle these problems. But it is worth noting that except in Kashmir and the Punjab, and there for very special reasons, the tensions have not reached anywhere a point of no return.

The true erosion of consensus really happened in the last phase of Mrs Gandhi's government. In her anxiety to retain personal power and establish a dynasty, she played short-sighted political games dangerously undermining the national consensus. This is how the Sikh demand for a greater measure of autonomy and a larger share of the national cake was transformed into an angry desire for total independence. She also closed the channels of political communication with the Muslims of the Kashmir valley, by rigging elections and throwing out the National Conference Government. Furthermore, to consolidate her personal power, she dismantled the structure of elections within her own party. How one single individual succeeded in doing so much damage is a mystery which still remains unresolved. The basic weaknesses in the political system which provided the opportunities for her cynical action has yet to be scrutinized. However the negative end results of a disastrous regime were accentuated by the final loss of credibility when after the Bofors scandal people came to believe that the very centre of authority was corrupt.

The erosion of confidence in the government at the centre accentuated another negative development in Indian political life.

Nationalist ideology and the politics of mobilization in the twenties and thirties had deliberately set about creating a nation based on a sense of unity which would encompass all ethnic elements among the people living within the geographical boundaries of India. That the effort had achieved a measure of success was evident in the electoral successes of the Indian National Congress (INC) since 1937 as well as the popular enthusiasm for the nationalist leadership. Indian nationalism, always a somewhat nebulous phenomenon, was powerfully expressed in that very evident enthusiasm. In the latter years of Mrs Gandhi's regime a disillusionment with the political system became an integral part of popular consciousness in India. *Sab Chor Hai*—they are all thieves, is an expression heard at every level of society as a description of the country's politicians. The extensive criminalization of politics which has a longer history stretching far beyond the latter years of Mrs Gandhi's rule suggest that the popular perception has a large element of truth.

Nationalism, the emotion based on a sense of belonging to a political community which one is willing to defend with one's own life, if necessary, has to be the ultimate foundation of a modern nation state. Anyone who has lived in India under colonial rule and in the early decades of independence knows that this sense of belonging was very much a reality among extensive sections of the population. It had been created, as already noted, by the words and deeds of the nationalist movement and sustained as well as developed further, through the experiences of representative democracy. The fact that the unlettered masses were not indifferent to the fate of political democracy was proved by the massive turnout to vote Mrs Gandhi out of power and again, two years later, to bring her back after the dismal failure of the Janta coalition. These events were surely the end product of complex processes and interplay of interests and not merely triumphs of a popular nationalist concern. But to overlook the anxiety of the Indian masses for the maintenance of acceptable norms at the centre of authority manifest in these events would be a misreading of the record. And that anxiety can only be explained in terms of some sense of belonging to a nation state.

There is a felt psychological need for the emotions of nationalism as a necessary underpinning of a nation state. That underpinning has been seriously damaged in India since the late-nineteen-seventies. The space vacated by the ideology of composite nationalism is being claimed by the doctrine of Hindutva and the Hindu state.

It is well to remember that construction of nationhood in terms of an all-India Hindu identity has been one of the alternative agendas in modern Indian politics. This was very directly fought with programmes based on the ideology of a composite nationhood especially from the mid-nineteenth-twenties onwards. The electoral records suggest that the popular mandate was in favour of the ideology of consensus and unity. Even in the wake of the disastrous partition riots, political organizations claiming to speak for Hindu interests secured only an insignificant proportion of electoral support. This may be due to a variety of reason and it is certainly true that the victory over Hindu communalism was secured by some concessions to its aspirations. The acceptance of Hindi as the national language to be written only in the Nagri and not in the Urdu script as well, as prescribed by the Mahatma, and the constitutional provision that the new national language should fall back primarily on Sanskrit for its vocabulary are instances in point. The prohibition of cow slaughter in the greater part of the country is another example. It is also known that the Hindu communalist has been prominently present, both in the leadership and among the cadres of the Congress party. Still, when they threatened to take over the organization, Nehru could carry out a purge in 1952 and it would be correct to say that the central agenda of the state has successfully emphasized anti-communal policies. It is the erosion of nationalism and the loss of credibility of the political party which projected that ideology as the basis of state policy that has opened the gate for an alternative nationalism based on the Hindu identity.

For historic reasons that identity in the colonial period and after has been built around xenophobia, more specifically, the hatred of the Muslims. The history of communal hatred as distinct from the aspirations of the subcontinent's Muslim elite which led to the formation of Pakistan, has yet to be written. There is little reason to doubt that it arose out of the conditions of colonial rule even though any exclusive emphasis on the consequences of imperial policy alone would be misleading. In pre-colonial days any struggle against 'Muslim tyranny', as projected in RSS propaganda, was probably no part of Hindu consciousness. The Marathi historical literature tracing the emergence of the Maratha empire does not talk about Muslim tyranny. In the late eighteenth century Sindhia, the leader of the confederacy was eager to convince the Hindu Rajput princes that he had no intension of overthrowing the Muslim Mughal emperor; he was in Delhi only to protect the emperor. The great rebellion of 1857 which involved Hindu soldiers, princes, and peasants, aimed at replacing the English East India Company's rule with that of a Muslim emperor. The spoliation of temples by Turkish and Afghan rulers is supposed to have generated a permanent hatred against Muslims in Hindu hearts. It is worth emphasizing in this context that India, unlike Europe, has no record of wars of religion involving the civil population. Further if memories of such wars do not sustain political conflict in modern Europe there is no reason to imagine that ancient wounds constitute a spontaneous basis for political hatred in modern India. Furthermore, it is not at all clear why the ardent Hindu has no special feelings of hatred towards the Turks or Afghans whose ancestors no doubt destroyed their temples from time to time. The fact that his rancour is focussed instead on often hapless Muslim slum dwellers who are almost certainly descendants of Hindu converts tells us much about the nature and origins of communal sentiments. Hindu as well as Muslim communalism as we know it today is the end product of historical contingencies of the colonial era. But there is little consolation today in that thought because the poison in question has by now a history of more than one hundred years. It is a part of our damned inheritance.

With the erosion of nationalist ideology, communal hatred which has long been a part of Indian social consciousness, began to move to the centre of the political stage. The process was helped by Mrs Gandhi's now notorious policy of playing the Hindu card. At the same time the Sikh rising and the massacre of innocent Hindus introduced a new component into Hindu xenophobia further sharpened by allegations of Pakistan's involvement in the Sikh movement for autonomy. The developments in Kashmir leading to the mass exodus of Hindus from the valley have provided more fuel for the fire. The protagonists of Hindu Rashtra have fully exploited these developments.

The Muslims in India are in a sense a decapitated community. The bulk of their elite migrated to Pakistan after partition. Consequently this large community has very little representation in the higher echelons of Indian political and economic life. Already by the thirties the national movement had lost the support of politicized Muslims, though there were some exceptions. The task of securing that support on an active basis in the aftermath of partition as an essential foundation of composite nationhood remained neglected.

Opportunist leaders have taken advantage of the community's withdrawal syndrome to try and fossilize a community-based politics. Political parties have willingly played their game justifying the allegation of treating the Muslims as a vote bank. The record of continual rioting after 1947 has stoked the fire of Muslim communalism. The two hatreds feed on each other. Only, the threat of absolutist politics based on hatred can be posed by the protagonists of Hindutva alone and hence they are the enemies the nation has to watch.

The doctrine of Hindutva and its subtext of communal hatred now enjoy widespread support across a wide spectrum of Hindu society. While its main base is the urban lower middle class, it has also the support of a substantial section of more affluent elements in urban society. A section of students and the upper strata of the professional classes including, very crucially, some journalists and academics, are active supporters of the RSS/VHP programmes. Interestingly and somewhat inexplicably, VHP posters picturing Lord Rama display in a corner the image of a Maruti Car, the symbol of Indian upper middle class aspiration. Industrialists encouraged by the Shiv Sena record of fighting class war and strikes in Maharashtra are also happy to support Hindutva. The affluent non-resident Indian who often leads an alienated and marginalized ghetto existence abroad is happy to be acknowledged as part of a world-wide Hindu nation. Most dangerously, the unemployed upper-caste Hindu youth scared by the policy of positive discrimination feels attracted by the saffron flag. The social trend towards consumerism and extensive corruption in administration and politics have generated an ambience of anomy in Indian society. A simple, direct and ethically correct political slogan which denounces the pervasive corruption and calls for dramatic actions of protest has obvious appeal to the educated young. Totally marginalized elements among the urban poor have always been in the forefront of agitational activity. They were conspicuously present when the mosque was destroyed.

This formidable coalition of mainly urban and upper-caste Hindu social groups may or may not produce an unchallengeable supremacy for the cause of Hindutva within the parliamentary system. But its penetration into the social and institutional life of India has already acquired threatening proportions. The paralyzed helplessness of the central government during the destruction of the mosque is an evidence of this danger. More significantly, the behaviour of the police both in Delhi and Bombay after the event was quite incredible. In both places they went on rampage in Muslim colonies and in Delhi actively harassed academics preaching communal peace. Then there are the judicial decisions which allowed Hindus to worship idols they had sneaked into the old mosque while denying Muslims the right to pray at the same site. The less tangible spread of communalist ideology among extensive sections of the Hindu middle classes including teachers and administrators is perhaps the most frightening feature of all. Over the years Indian civil society has developed to a remarkable degree a tolerance of violent repression by the state. If such official policies are now supplemented by an unofficial connivance at persecution of Muslims, the political portents for India may well be disastrous. The subjective consciousness of the Indian Muslim today is one of total insecurity.

Guruji Golwakar expressed his envious admiration for one experienced European nation about to solve its problem of a semitic presence. But Hitler and his cronies had one advantage. They had a mere twelve million people to deal with. We have one hundred and thirty million Muslims in India. The ultimate solution is hence likely to present a few logistic problems. Efforts in that direction, meanwhile may tear apart the fabric of the nation state. One has only to consider the fate of the island to India's south to appreciate the potentialities of xenophobic politics in a multi-ethnic society.

The Swastika painted straight in bright vermilion is a familiar symbol of bliss and well-being in every Hindu home. Tilted slightly to the right, it acquired sinister meaning on the world scene. A struggle is now on in India to prevent the threat of such a tilt. To repeat, the present lecture is an old academic's modest contribution to that effort.

POSTSCRIPTS

Since the Babri mosque episode, nearly six years have passed. India has seen the emergence of BJP as the main opposition in Parliament, then as the largest single party and finally as the successful contender for power at the centre albeit in coalition with a large number of small parties.

What does this portend for the future?

It would be paranoid to prophesy the immediate emergency of fascist rule in India. But certain signs are worth watching.

The BJP dependent for their survival in power on local parties and splinter groups with no interest in Hindutva, does not have a free hand. So the prophets of Hindutva are making secular noises. The savants who read into their rise the inevitable end to secularism should now explain why BJP has to court that discredited doctrine. Has the famous Hindu revival suddenly ended or BJP decided on a change of heart out of magnanimity?

But alas, there is no change of heart. First, the leaders of the party have repeatedly asserted their loyalty to their alter ego, the RSS. The latter has never repudiated their xenophobic doctrines. Singhal, the VHP chief has threatened Muslims with further humiliation if they do not hand over the other mosques where Hindu temples originally stood. Quietly, in Rajasthan, stone masons are busy hewing out different parts of the projected Rama temple. The Home Minister, Advani who led the campaign resulting in the destruction of the mosque has declared that whatever he has learnt is from the RSS, an organization of which he as well as the Prime Minister remain members. Advani, Joshi, Uma Bharati — all facing criminal charges in the mosque affair at the behest of the Supreme Court, are ministers of the central government. Uma Bharati is the minister of state and Joshi the cabinet minister in charge of education. It might help to remember that one of the main weapons in BJP propaganda was a distorted version of Indian history introduced in the school text boxes. The new government's education policy is worth watching.

Also worth watching is what they do at the executive level. All State Governors have been sacked. Some are to be replaced by RSS leaders who have no mandate. A constitutional head in normal times, the Governor exercises great power in uncertain political situations.

One of the main planks of the RSS–BJP agenda was intervention in the centuries old Muslim personal law. Have they given it up? The BJP, with their options limited, is showing signs of sweet reasonableness, except that they have placed far from reasonable men and women in positions of great power, assured the RSS that it has nothing to worry, laid the basis for executive action the nature of which is still not clear. There are no indications that they have abandoned policies at the heart of their political propaganda.

Their declared objective is total power at the centre. Whether they will make it without depending on a host of allies, is uncertain. One gimmic, the explosion of nuclear devices, has not produced quite the results it was expected to do. The sanctions and the protest of most sensible men have cooled the enthusiasm of the celebrants.

The by-elections have been generally disappointing. Yet it is too early to celebrate the demise of Hindu communalism. The disunity of centrist and radical forces may still open the door to BJP–RSS victory. If they do seize power at the centre, without depending on sundry allies, there is nothing to suggest that these leopards will change their spots. And if they fail, we can expect to see a return to the politics of the street in the name of Hindu honour, repetitions of the bitter episodes we have witnessed in the past.

Since names matter, let us be clear on one point. It does not help to refer to them as Hindu nationalists. It gives them an unwarranted legitimacy. They are no more Hindu nationalists than Le Pen's men are French nationalists or neo-Nazis are German nationalists. Describing Hindu fascists by their true names would help clarify the situation in India.

BIBLIOGRAPHICAL NOTES

This valedictory lecture is an exercise in historical analysis of a contemporary problem. It draws heavily on the secondary literature on the subject, especially the recent work of journalists and scholars, and is not based on any original research. Its only claim to originality is with reference to the conclusions and the arguments which lead to them.

The most convincing evidence in favour of the thesis that the movement to construct a temple at the site where the Babri mosque stood was the result of sustained campaign and organizational effort and not any spontaneous religious upsurge is provided in T. Basu, P. Dutta, S. Sarkar, T. Sarkar and S. Sen, *Khaki Shorts, Safron Flags* (New Delhi, 1993). Based largely on interviews with leaders and cadres of the Sangh Parivar, this brief study provides a graphic picture of the organization and activities of the Parivar. I have accepted the evidence presented there as true, partly because I have not come across any refutal thereof till now. The description of the Parivar's activities in this lecture is based to a large extent on this study. The report of dialogues in Ayodhya is in Nico Blank, *The Arrow of the Blue-skinned God* (Cambridge, Mass., 1993). Mr Advani's statement is quoted in an unpublished paper presented at a seminar in Oxford by Smita Gupta. The photograph of the Pakistan flag and interview with Seshadri was published in *The Organiser*, 20.12.1992. Golwalkar's statement occurs in his *We or Our Nationhood Defined* (Nagpur, 1939). Hedgewar's statement is quoted in S. Aiyachuri, 'Golwalkar and the Hindu Rashtra', *Frontline*, 12.3.93. For Savarkar's formulation of the same ideology, see his *Hindutva*, 4th edn. (Poona, 1949). For a history of Hindu nationalism, see Bruce Graham, *Hindu Nationalism and Indian Politics* (Cambridge, 1990).

The literature on Hitler and the origins of Nazism is vast. For a study of the affinities between the social and psychological bases of Nazism on the one hand and those of Hindu communalist politics on the other see the following works: T. Childers, *The Nazi Voter: The Social Foundations of Fascism in Germany, 1919–33* (Chapel Hill, NC, 1984); M. Kater, *The Nazi Party: A Social Profile of Members and Leaders, 1919–45* (Oxford, 1983); R.F. Hamilton, *Who Voted for Hitler* (Princeton, 1982). For striking similarities between the RSS techniques of propaganda and those of Hitler, especially the self-conscious appeal to fanaticism rather than interests or intellectual considerations, see Alan Bullock, *Hitler and Stalin: Parallel Lives* (London, 1991, 1993). The similarities are too great to be entirely accidental. Dr Andersen, who co-authored with Damle a fairly sympathetic history of the RSS, told me in course of a recent conversation that the leaders of the movement whom he knew in the 1950s were all great admirers of Hitler. For a brief analysis of the affinities with western fascism, see S. Sarkar, 'Fascism of the Sangh Parivar', *Economic and Political Weekly*, 30.1.93. For the psychological factors behind the support for Hindu communalism, see Sumanta Banerjee, 'Hindutva—Ideology and Social Psychology', ibid., 19.1.1991; G. Pandey, 'Hindutva and Others: The Militant Hindu Construction', ibid., 28.12.1991. For the behaviour of the police, see Sarkar's article, E.A. Gordon, 'After Bombay's Violence, Fear and Finger Pointing', *New York Times*, and Madhu Kishwar. 'Safety is Indivisible—The Warning from the Bombay Riots', *Bulletin, Committee on South Asian Women*, vol. 8 (1993).

14

Indo–Pakistan Relations: In Quest of a Silver Lining, Even a Smudged One*

I accepted the invitation to speak at this particular session of the conference with considerable misgiving. The organizers explained that I was to speak on Indo–Pakistan relationship, presumably from the Indian point of view. As I have no special expertise in this area of enquiry and there must be many present who have written on it with considerable skill and scholarship, I felt more than hesitant to accept the invitation, especially because if there is indeed a commonly accepted point of view on the matter in India, I certainly do not share it. Despite such hesitations I agreed to speak on the subject for one reason only. There seems to be no end to the saga of mutual bitterness between these two countries and this unhappy story is like a cancerous growth in the life of our peoples. Academics and intellectuals have had little influence so far on the course of the relevant events and there is little hope that they will do so in the foreseeable future. Yet it threatens so much that is of value in the life of the region that it is incumbent on the students concerned with its history to try and make some sense of the very dark picture. Perhaps one can even go a step further and explore possible ways out of the impasse, however quixotic the venture may seem. The non-specialist has a certain advantage in such exercises in that he can stand apart from the details of the unhappy story and try to unravel its meaning in the context of historical trends over a period of time. What follows is a tentative exercise, an impressionistic analysis with such aims in view.

After fifty years of independence, India and Pakistan remain two

*Lecture delivered at a Conference on Fifty Years of India and Pakistan at Madison, Wisconsin, 1998.

of the poorest countries in the world ranking twenty-seventh and thirty-fifth respectively in the league of poverty, according to the 1997 World Development Report. Pakistan's per capita annual income is 460 dollars. The corresponding figure for India is 340. The world's largest democracy also has the largest concentration of people below the poverty line with 52.5 of her population living on less than one dollar a day. By contrast, in 1995 India spent eleven dollars per head of population on defence; the corresponding figure for Pakistan was twenty-eight. In 1960, military expenditure as percentage of combined expenditure on health and education came to 393 in Pakistan and 68 in India. By 1990–91, the relevant figures have come down to 125 and 65 respectively. The much larger resource base of India explains the relatively modest percentage and also helps explain the hardly acceptable level of expenditure in the case of Pakistan. I am not suggesting that a country with over 52 per cent of its population living on less than a dollar a day is justified in spending 8,238 million dollars per year on defence. My object is simply to underline the enormity of expenditure on defence in two very poor countries. For Pakistan, with a narrower resource base, the burden becomes all the heavier. But with a neighbour, perceived to be hostile, having a defence budget some 2.25 times the size of her own and an army of 1.145 million compared to her 587 thousand, the grotesque imbalance in her budgetary priorities becomes understandable. In simple language, two of the world's poorest countries invest unacceptable proportions of their income and resources on unproductive expenditure which they certainly can not afford. In 1965, it was estimated that these two countries could afford the luxury of a modern war for a maximum of nineteen days. In fact the war that year between the two neighbours threw out of gear the entire planning process in India, a disaster from which it never entirely recovered. It is worth enquiring to what extent the slow growth in her economy was the result of such displacement rather than her alleged socialistic policies. The consequences of the three wars between them for the economies of India and Pakistan have not been examined. Such examiration might provide some salutary lessons.

Of course, it would be incorrect to suggest that the unacceptably high expenditure on defence in the two countries is only for their mutual benefit. India had to keep an eye on her northern neighbour and that necessity may not have entirely disappeared even now. Pakistan too had to watch her border with Afghanistan especially after the Soviet intervention. Besides, both countries have unhappy records of using their armies to deal with domestic insurgenies. Yet there is little doubt that but for their mutual hostility and suspicions, the unproductive expenditure on defence would have been far less spectacular.

There are less calculable costs of mutual hostility which, in the long run, may prove to be more disastrous. It is conceivable that with enhanced rates of economic growth both countries, especially India with her much larger base, may be able to afford the high cost of defence with less damage to her economic and social programmes than at present. But it is exceedingly doubtful if they can do so without undermining their democratic institutions and values which have been very fragile at the best of times. And in both countries xenophobia, focused on the Muslim community in the case of India and on the alleged threat from India in the case of Pakistan, has been a highly potent source of threat to sane politics. Fanaticism and democracy do not make very good bed-fellows and the slide down to highly illiberal and oppressive regimes can be much swifter than one imagines. Arguably, the most important factor in the rise of a right wing Hindu party from a position where they had only two seats in parliament to one where they emerged as the largest single party in the Indian legislature in a remarkably short time was the xenophobic campaign centred on the Babri mosque–Ramjanmabhoomi issue.

Since the party in question has acquired a measure of legitimacy even in the eyes of radical intellectuals, it might be useful to take a quick look at the nature of their propaganda. Incidentally, that propaganda illustrates the not so subtle links between communal hatred and Indo–Pak relationship. After the destruction of the Babri mosque one of the BJP–RSS leaders, Sheshadri, observed in an interview to the *Organiser* that the episode had been a 'boost for the national psyche' of the Hindus. The RSS daily added for good measure a photograph of the Pakistan flag flying at half mast in their High Commission in Delhi. The caption read, 'Mourning the liberation of Ramjanmabhoomi'. The creators of this line of propaganda saw an obvious link between the humiliation of India's Muslims and the sense of loss in Pakistan. Destruction of a mosque became thus a two-fold triumph—over Indian Muslims, the supposed descendants of hated conquerors, and over the country which symbolized their aspirations of yester year. The unofficial but ubiquitous slogans one heard during the campaign pin points the two-fold hatred: '*Musalmanon ke do sthan,*

Pakistan ya kabarstan'. There are only two places for Muslims: Pakistan or the grave. The two hatreds feed on each other and provide a very satisfactory base from where blind hostility can be transmuted into political advantage.

My familiarity with the internal developments in Pakistan is limited. But there too, it seems, such legitimacy as the military dictatorships acquired owed much to the bugbear of India. And it is worth enquiring in what measure the influence of extreme orthodoxy over politics and society derives from the perceived threat from a non-Muslim neighbour equated with a threat to the survival of the sub-continent's Muslims, their faith and their way of life. The struggle for autonomy in the Kashmir valley is frequently projected in the popular press as *jihad,* holy war. The extent to which the bitterness between the two countries spawns the politics of unreason was demonstrated by an opinion poll in Pakistan on the question of a nuclear war with India. Apparently, some 70 per cent of the respondents were in favour of using nuclear warheads in case there was aggression from India. I should add that I got this information from a Pakistani colleague and can not vouch for its authenticity. Pakistan's nuclear programme is understandable as a deterrent in view of her disadvantage in conventional forces and the assumption that India has nuclear capability. But popular support for the use of these weapons with Pakistan as the first user is equivalent to a mass death wish. It points towards a paranoid hatred which is evident to a dangerous degree on both sides of the Indo–Pakistani border. The literature on Indo–Pakistan relationship frequently uses a vocabulary which seems to suggest an unbroken continuity of policy and to present the relevant decision-making process as emanating from decision makers who represent monolithic solidarities over the entire half century. This may be my misreading of the said literature, but if it is stated that 'India' and/or 'Pakistan' did this or that without specifying the role of the relevant actors and the complex pressures and counter-pressures which produce particular decisions, one is left with an impression of uncomplicated unilinear developments probably not intended by the authors. Bureaucrats, military top brass and politicians shape the relevant decisions and they do not think alike or speak with the same voice either at particular moments or over time. Yet, there is a remarkable continuity in policy in this sphere which almost justifies the shorthand reference to the two countries which I have just mentioned.

As some commentators have noted, disputes and claims which referred to pragmatic issues like canal water or division of assets have been settled with relative ease, with no more than the expected amount of hard bargaining and acrimony. Bureaucrats and politicians enjoy a measure of autonomy in deciding such matters. But there are areas where the limits to choice in decision making are defined by popular will, not only in democracies but even in dictatorships because no dictator is omnipotent enough to consistently ignore people's sentiments, especially those rooted in strong feelings. Besides, very often the decision makers not only share such sentiments, but seek to enhance their own legitimacy or gain advantage over their rivals for power by fomenting or manipulating such passions. Hence the continued intractability of certain problems between the two countries which sustain policies of mutual hostility. The matters which remain insoluble are the ones which are rooted in passion and ideology. The chief among these is Kashmir and the question of plebiscite in that state. Except for the brief departures like the Simla Agreement and the faint hope of improved relationship when Benazir met Rajiv, this dispute seems to be imprinted in granite for all eternity. And so long as it persists, one may tinker with the edges of mutual hostility, with annual meetings of the SAARC and liberalization of visa rules for judges and parliamentarians, but the mutual bitterness will persist unabated. There is a catch twenty-two situation in the relationship of the two countries. The outstanding issues will not be resolved until there is real abatement in mutual hostility which is for the most part autonomous of specific circumstances. And there will be no abatement in mutual hostility until the outstanding issues are resolved.

The ideological roots of that hostility are to be found in the history of conflict between Hindus and Muslims in the twentieth century. With the creation of Pakistan that conflict has been raised to the level of inter-state relationship which in its turn helps vitiate Hindu attitudes to Muslims in India. The fear of Hindu domination which engendered the first seeds of the demand for Pakistan is now translated into fears regarding the Indian threat to Pakistan's survival and the perception that India has a hegemonic agenda in South Asia. Both fears are aggravated by the experience of the 1971 War. Furthermore, the Indian state is seen to be persistent oppressors of Muslims in India (to wit, the record of communal riots and the destruction of the Babri mosque). And reneging on the international commitment to hold a plebiscite in Kashmir, a Muslim majority state which would have and should have acceded to Pakistan but for the machinations of Nehru, Mountbatten and the Hindu maharaja, is India's ultimate act of perfidy against South Asia's Muslims. The gross violation of human rights in the attempt to repress the Kashmiris' struggle to break away from the Indian Union reveals the true agenda of Hindu imperialism. Neither Indian nationalists nor Hindu chauvinists (and there is little to distinguish one from the other) have ever accepted the legitimacy of Pakistan and are simply waiting for an opportunity to undo the Partition which all Hindus consider a tragedy.

The Indian counterpart of such negative perceptions subsumes the belief that Pakistan was the final consummation of an imperialist policy of Divide and Rule, a triumph of reactionary forces among the Muslims of India in leading the Muslim masses away from the ranks of nationalism. The end result is a theocratic and obscurantist state which has got rid of its minorities. Its political culture is opposed to all liberal and democratic values. On the international scene it played its expected role of toadying to neo-imperialists. In South Asia, it has done its best to help and generate disruptive forces within the Indian Union and actually abetted terrorism in Kashmir and the Punjab. India has no reason to be apologetic about Kashmir, because the State joined the Indian Union with the full support of the popular party led by Sheikh Abdullah and only after Pakistan had invaded the territory. As to the commitment to plebiscite, Pakistan's refusal to withdraw her armed forces from the territory under their control has rendered it obsolete. As for the conflict in Kashmir, it would have never got off the ground but for Pakistani sponsorship.

When opinions such as these dominate mutual perceptions the minutae of disagreements on specific issues become almost irrelevant. To change them as a necessary step towards creating the conditions for a stable peace and co-operation appears to be almost an utopian dream, surely beyond the power of academics and intellectuals. Yet, academics and intellectuals do have a role in this context. After all, the concept of Pakistan was first formulated by a poet and a young intellectual and Indian nationalism was first dreamed up by writers and publicists long before it emerged as a mass movement. The analysts of the Indo–Pakistan conflict can perhaps venture to try and educate public opinion by first sifting what is true from what is palpably false. To my understanding, some of the current trends in the study of South Asia serve exactly the opposite purpose giving a respectability to old and harmful myths under new names.

The intellectual in Pakistan could take a hard look at the murky reality of Indian politics and examine dispassionately the question as to whether any sane actor on that scene seriously thinks of undoing partition today. I believe he would find that this is not the case. And if educated public opinion in Pakistan could be convinced of the fact, that would be a great step forward. If some mandarins in South Block or hotheads in a particular political party have visions of Indian hegemony in South Asia, it is unlikely that the twenty-seventh poorest country treats it as the central plank in their policy. Individual actions, like the intervention in Sri Lanka, may spring from correct or incorrect understanding of the country's foreign policy needs. To string these together as evidence for hegemonic intent is probably a mistake. It would be a great step forward if the intelligentsia in Pakistan could be convinced of the fact.

On the Indian side, it would help if we could try and stop thinking of the events of 1947 as the much regretted Partition of India and learn to use a new vocabulary which would refer to the establishment of Pakistan with respect as the fulfilment of the aspirations of a very large segment of the subcontinent's Muslims. It is time to give a rest to the debate over the two nation theory, focus instead on the crystallized consciousness of nationhood in Pakistan and recognize it as a major fact of the political reality in South Asia. The traders in hatred who hope to profit from persistent conflict are unlikely to be enthusiastic, but anyone who desire peace in the region is committed to fight them. We also need hard research in both countries on the cost of on-going conflict and quantified contrafactual analysis of what peace between the two neighbours might mean in terms of positive growth. Presentation of these results through the less fanatical section of the popular press might have some impact over time.

I have suggested that the mutual bitterness between India and Pakistan is ultimately a projection of the Hindu–Muslim conflict to the level of inter-state relations. In India, faced with the rising threat of Hindu chauvinism, radical academics have made serious efforts to understand the nature and sources of communal hatred. The general consensus seems to be that the communal problem as we know it to-day is a development of the colonial era, especially the inter-war period. It owes much to the complex workings of the colonial nexus in which state policy was certainly a factor though not the only one. Nothing on the scale of the communal riots of the 1920s and 1940s has been traced in pre-colonial times despite considerable efforts in that direction. I have underlined elsewhere the often ignored implications of the rising in 1857 when upper caste Hindu sepoys and feudatories fought alongside Muslim princes and peasants to bring back the long dead Mughal empire, the rule of a Muslim king. This does not suggest that communal identities had hardened into mutually exclusive and hostile monoliths in the political consciousness of traditional India. One could cite many such evidence to contradict the view of one historian that communalism then was the same as communalism now. My questioning of this emerging orthodoxy has caused considerable mirth and one American scholar has seen in this a laughable revival of the obsolete Divide and Rule theory.

Whether the problem in question arose in the colonial or precolonial times makes little difference to the current reality of ferocious hatreds. But since our perceptions of the past influence powerfully our attitudes in the present it is essential that we examine those perceptions with great care. Projection of the Indian middle ages as an age of Muslim tyranny and the oft-repeated theory that Indian civilization is a seamless web in which the Islamic element alone refused to get absorbed, standing out like a sore thumb, are powerful instruments in the ideological training of cadres of Hindu and Muslim chauvinism alike. As one Indian Muslim scholar put it, whether his son will return home safely from school depended on what his neighbour believed about the country's past.

There are certain current views of our history and society which legitimize highly disruptive an xenophobic political postures. If these are objectively valid views of South Asia's past and present, one would of course need to accept them. But are they? Of course one can start from the position that objectivity is a mirage. One can only take up positions. If so, I submit, some of the positions taken up in practice justifies politics of extreme intolerance for which ultimately the dispossessed, more than anyone else, pay with their lives.

The views I refer to have two interrelated components. First, it is suggested that secularism as state policy and social ideology is irrelevant to the social culture of South Asia and hence political parties which speak in terms of communal identities reflect social reality more than those which at least speak in terms of agenda transcending such identities. Secularism in the Indian context has meant two things: first, state policies which aim at neutrality between communities and ethnic groups as the only viable way of managing the problems of multi-ethnicity; second, programmes of education, health, economic development which project the world view of modern science based on that much derided human faculty, reason. For example, Darwinian theories are preferred in school curricula to creation myths of varied provenance and to combat epidemics, inoculation is preferred to the public worship of disease deities. The notion that secularism of this variety is alien to the cultures of South Asia harks back to the old imperialist view of the inherent backwardness of Indian civilization centred on religious beliefs and ideology. The falsity of this perception and its irrelevance to political reality is proved *inter alia* by the history of the Pakistan movement. There were Muslim political parties deeply committed to religious ideologies and hostile to the idea of Pakistan. When the crunch came, they were swept aside in favour of Muslim League representing the very secular interests of Indian Muslims. And for nearly half a century, the Indian electorate under universal adult suffrage have voted to power political parties which do not speak in terms of particular interests. Even in the aftermath of the whipped up frenzy which led to the destruction of the Babri mosque, the communalists forces have not quite made it yet. To suggest that politics of communal hatred are the only politics natural to the people of the subcontinent is a travesty which has ominous implications for the people of the region. An American savant dubbed me a neo-Nehruvian nationalist for expressing this opinion. I am grateful to him for his kind help with discovering my identity: genus nationalist, species neo-Nehruvian, an undesirable life form on both counts.

Closely linked to this perception of quintessentially anti-secular nature of South Asian societies, is the view that nation states are unnatural and oppressive structures especially for South Asia. Echoes again of colonial projections—the impossibility of nationhood for India which was no more than an aggregation of societies. The natural socio-political forms, we are told, are the communities and political salvation lies in empowering them. Two things are not explained. First, what are these communities of new radicalism, Hindus, Muslims, Sikhs etc. classified on the basis of confessional faith? Or, the numberless castes and tribes so dear to the colonial publications? And how are they to be empowered? Are their writs to run in space devoid of territory since they so frequently inhabit the same locality or do we envisage a vast confederation of communities, a sort of United Communities of South Asia presided over by priests, mullahs, granthis and the like? Disillusionment with the political record of independent India and Pakistan is perfectly understandable. But if that frustration generates chimera unrealizable even in theory, it is time to stop and take thought. And the net contribution of such analysis is to create among our intelligentsia, sections of people who find unlikely champions among the most reactionery and at times most vicious elements of our society. If understanding of our society can contribute to strategies of harmony, here we have prescriptions for sure disaster.

I conclude this talk on a note of very feeble hope. Today, the external circumstances are more favourable to reduced tension. A fear of US presence in South Asia was one important factor in determining Indian attitudes. The dissolution of the Soviet Union has reduced US interest in the region and Indian attitudes to USA are more relaxed now. Temporarily at least a new ideology dominates our planet—the pursuit of profit as the supreme goal of human life. And profit-seekers prefer methods other than old fashioned gun-boat diplomacy to secure their goals. The new slogans favour unrestricted trade and they are popular in both India and Pakistan. Informed economic opinion in Pakistan is now in favour of open trade with India and India has already accorded Most Favoured Nation status to Pakistan. Pakistan's new trade policy has allowed imports of new items from India even though there are fears in the former country that their infant industries will be threatened by India with her diversified industrial base. If the free marketeers are right, such fears will not persist and mutual self-interest may open the way to reduction in hostility.

There is one peculiar fact about Indo–Pak relations. It is unlike Arab–Jewish relations a love-hate rather than a hate-hate relation. Visitors from one country to the other feel that they are among friends rather than enemies. As enemy, Pakistan and India are grand abstractions somehow dissociated from their individual citizens. This has not helped in solving any problems so far. But if Arabs and Israel have been able to start a process of détente and blacks and whites in South Africa today jointly rule the country even though the problems in either area are in no way at an end, may be there is some hope for Indo–Pakistan relationship. The academics and intellectuals can contribute to the process by honestly projecting analysis which do not encourage them to launch nuclear wars or, at home, slaughter their neighbours' children returning from school.

POSTSCRIPT

Since I wrote this paper, India has a government at the Centre in which the BJP in the major partner. That government has thought it fit to explode five nuclear weapons opening a new phase in the sub-continent's arms race. Pakistan has matched the Indian achievement and the defence budget in India has been increased by 14 per cent. The rattling of nuclear weapons was greeted with unholy glee by sections of the population, evidently in the belief that the relevant achievement has enhanced India's military might and taught the arrogant western nations a lesson they richly deserve. In Pakistan, the popular celebrations were punctuated with shouts of 'Hindustan Murdabad'. The formal agenda of the new Indian government include rectification of the frontiers which means, *inter alia,* a new affirmation of claim to sovereignty over Azad Kashmir.

In short, if there ever was any sign of a badly smudged silver lining peeping through the dark clouds of India's relationship with Pakistan, it has now been erased with a firm hand. All the more reason for the intelligentsia in both countries to say 'no' to this persistent madness. Indian intellectuals have raised their voice in criticism of the arrant stupidity which informs the country's nuclear policy. Their Pakistani counterparts have drawn attention to the economic disaster their political bosses have brought upon their country. The short-sighted stupidity of politicians has opened the way for a dialogue across the unfriendly frontier. Little is to be hoped from such a dialogue in the foreseeable future, but it has to start—to forestall another half-century of avoidable waste and misery.

Index

abortion 78
Age of Consent Bill 13, 124
Ahmad, Sir Syed 189, 192
al-Bīrūnī 23, 45n9
Amery 194
Amherst, Lord *see* Roy, Rammohan
Arnold, Mathew 61
Aryabhatta 30, 60
Arya Samaj 16, 214
Ayodhya 207, 208, 210, 215
    Ramjanambhoomi 209, 210,
        215, 232
    see also Babri mosque

Babri mosque 208, 209, 226, 232,
    238
    Mir Baqi 208
Bacon, Francis 29, 30, 56
Bhawalpur 197
Bajrang Dal *see* Sangh Parivar
Banerji, K.M. 80
Basu Rajnarayan 68, 81, 131
    and Muslims 131
    Society for the Promotion of
        National Feeling among the
        Educated Natives of Bengal
        131
    The Hopes of an Old Hindu 131
Basu, Shankariprasad 136
Bharatendu, Harischandra 15
Berkeley 31, 59
Bharatiya Janata Party (BJP) *see*
    Sangh Parivar
Bidyaratna, Girish 73, 76–7, 80–1
Blank, Nico 210

Brahmo Samaj 85, 99
    Brahmo ethos 85
    influence of Christianity 87, 106
    influence of Protestantism 105
    influence of Vaishnavism 106
    reformist tradition 102
    Sadharan Brahmo Samaj 16,
        61, 105
    see also Roy, Rammohan and
        Sen, Keshab
Bhutto, Benazir 234
Buchanan, Francis 23
Buddha/Buddhism 113, 114, 125
Burke, Marie Louise 118

Calcutta Medical College 54
Calcutta riots, August 1946 198
Campbell-Johnson, Alan 196, 197
celibacy 15, 88, 89, 117
    Anandamath 88
    platonic love 88
    Prakash Ray 88
        Aghorprakash 15
    Ramakrishna 89
Chaitanya 17, 106, 114
    Lord Chaitanya 108
    movement 98
    neo-Vaishnavism 108
Chakravarti, Sarat 112, 115
Chatterjee, Partha 126
Chattopadhyay (*also* Chatterji),
    Bankim Chandra 9, 11, 12,
    14, 26, 30, 38, 39, 57, 58, 59,
    60, 61, 62, 81, 82, 85, 86, 102,
    109, 132

Anandamath 62, 88, 109
Debi Chaudhurani 67
the *sharia* 132
Chaudhuri, Nirad C. x, 14, 88, 89, 158, 175
Chauri Chaura 181
child brides 70–3, 74–5
  Haimavati 71, 72, 73, 75, 78, 88, 90n6, 94n59
  Prasannamayi 71, 73, 90n7
  Rassundari 70, 71, 73, 75–6, 77
  Saradasundari 76
child marriage 67, 69, 81, 83
  and sex 72
  and Vivekananda 124, 130 *see also* female sexuality
Christian/Christianity 5, 12, 34, 35, 43, 104, 106, 113, 117, 118, 131
  Jesus Christ 7, 33, 34, 35, 101, 136
  and Jews 35
  and Romans 35
  dogma 33, 102, 169
  sectarianism 33
  Trinitarianism 7, 34, 51, 99
Churchill, Winston 195
Civil Disobedience 194
  see Irwin
Clive, Lord xi, 167
Combe, George 54–5, 56
  The Constitution of Man 54
consumerism *see* Swami Vivekananda and Sen, Keshab Chandra
Copernican theory 30, 60
Crawfurd, John 38
Cripps Mission 190, 195
Curzon, Lord 62, 156, 165

Darwin 58
Das, Durgamohan 84–5, 106
Das, Jnanendranath 86

Datta, Akshay Kumar 29, 30, 34, 54, 55, 57, 59, 60, 61, 79, 107
  Bahya Bastur Sahit Manaber Sambandha Bichar 103
  and George Combe 54–5
  and institutional religion 55–6
  rationalism 102, 103
Datta, Bhupendranath 133
Datta, Kaminikumar 79
Datta, Michael Madhusudan 12, 66, 80, 85
Datta, Ramchandra 87, *see also* sexual fantasy
Debi, Kailasbasini 83
Debi, Nistarini 74, 75
Derozio, Henry Louis Vivian 53, 79
  and Scottish Enlightenment 53
Deshmukh, Nanaji 213
Dev (also Deb), Radhakanta 7, 9, 52, 79, 80
Dewan Kartikeya 75, 76, 77, 83, 87
Dominian status 194
drunkenness 35
Duff, Rev. Alexander 53, 103
Dupleix, J.-F. 23, 82
Dutt, R.C. 13, 42, 82, 86, 146, 181
  and Christianity 35
  on European life 36
  on European women 36, 83
  Three Years in Europe 38

English East India Company 160–1, 165, 167, 224
Enlightenment 28
Ethnological Society 38

famine
  caused by Haider Ali 161
  of 1770 161
  of 1889 167
  of 1943 xi
fascism 216
  fuhrerprinzip 216

female sexuality 67
  women's sexual instinct 62,
    see also child marriage and
    sex
filial piety 12, 13
Fort William College 129

Gandhi, Indira 221, 222
Gandhi, M.K. 157, 175, 178, 180,
    181, 190, 192, 195, 198, 208,
    213, 223
  and European civilization 42,
    142–4, 145, 146
  and Indian civilization 146
  and married celibacy 15
  and modern civilization 142–4,
    145
  and modern technology 9
  and Tagore 141–51
  and the Raj 20, 157
  and Winston Churchill 157
  film by Attenborough 157
  Hind Swaraj 142, 144
Gandhi, Rajiv 234
Ghori, Mohammad 129
Ghosh, Aurobindo 62, 63
Ghosh, Sisir 108
  Lord Chaitanya 108
  see also Vaishnava/Vaishnavism
Godse 208
  see also Sangh Parivar
Gokhale 142
Golwalkar 208, 211, 214, 215
  and Fascism 212, 226
  and undivided India 211–12
  see also Sangh Parivar
Goswami, Bijaykrishna 86
Guha, Ranajit, *see* Subaltern
    Studies
Guizot 40, 144

Halbfass 4
Heber, Bishop 79

Hedgewar, Dr 211, 212, 213
  see Sangh Parivar
Hind Swaraj see Gandhi
Hindu College 20, 53, 79, 80
Hindu Mahasabha 208
Humboldt 29
Hussain, Ghulam 24, 161
Hussain, Musharraf 131
Huxley, Aldous 112

Ilbert Bill, 1833 172
Indian Association, The 131
Indian National Congress 131,
    174, 190, 191, 220, 222
  Extremists 174
  Moderates 174
individualism 9, 10, 61
Irwin, Lord 194
Islam 43
  and Swami Vivekananda 129–35
issues, social
  child marriage 82, 84
  polygamy 82
  widow remarriage 84
  women's education 82

Jambhekar 29, 30, 32
Jalal, Ayesha 193
Jesus *see* Christian/Christianity
Jinnah 190, 193, 198

Kalecki 219
Karve, D.D. 12
Kepler, Johannes 30, 60
Khan, Khizr Hyat 190, 191
  Unionist 191
Khan, Sir Sikander Hyat 191

Lawrence, D.H. 103
Linlithgow 189, 190, 194, 195
Lutfullah, Mirza 23, 24, 25, 26

Macaulay, Lord 29, 77, 122, 169,
    170

Macfarlane 6
Majumdar, Krishnachandra 87
Malabari, Behramji 37
Manusmriti 68
Menon, V.P. 197
Mill, James 31, 169
    Logic 31
Mill, John Stuart 58
Mitra, Kishori 104
Moon, Pendrel 156, 173, 188–202
Most Favoured Nation 239
Mountbatten, Lord 235
Mukherji (*also* Mukhopadhyay)
    Bhudev 40, 57, 61
    and Islam 131, 132
    Samajik Pravandha 39
Mukherji, Dakshinaranjan 80, 85
Mukherji, Shyamaprasad 214
    Hindu Party Jan Sangh 214
Muslim League 190, 191, 192, 193,
    238
Mysticism 98–9, 107
    Bauls 98, 106
    Christian 106
    Sahajiyas 98, 106
    tantra 77, 98, 121
    yoga 98

Naoroji, Dadabhai 37, 42, 157,
    181
    The European and Asiatic Races
    38
Narmad 15
nation/nationalism/nationalist 5,
    8, 18–19, 131, 165, 169, 174,
    176, 177, 178, 209, 211, 212,
    217, 218, 222
    and Tagore 145
Nehru, Jawaharlal 190, 192, 208,
    218, 223, 225, 238
    Nehruvian state 220

Orientalism/Orientalists 27, 145,
    148, 183

Orwell, George ix, 155

Pal, Bipin 66
Pandit Sasadhar 108
Panikkar, K.M. ix
Patanjali 116
    Yogasutra 116
philosophy
    Advaita 112, 113
    dualism 113
    Kanāda 56
    non-dualism 112, 113
    nyāya 48, 100
    Positivism 57, 61
    Sankhya 31, 46n38, 59
    smriti 48, 100
    Utilitarianism 39, 58, 61
    Vaiseshikā 56
    Vedanta 12, 31, 46n38, 59, 113,
    121, 122, 127, 130
Phule, Jotiba 14
Plassey 129, 199
polygamy 66, 69, 70, 73, 74, 75,
    81, 91n16, 126
    and Muslims 213
Prithiviraj 129
prostitutes 87
    prostitution 35, 88
pseudo-secularists 209, 214, 220
    pseudo-secular (constitution)
    213, 215
purdah 83

Rahim Yan Khan, district 197
Rajendraprasad 20
Ramakrishna 62, 87, 89, 108–9,
    111, 113, 114, 116, 119–20,
    139
    and celibacy 87
    Ramakrishna Mission 118–19,
    120
    Ramakrishna Order 112
    Ramakrishna-Vivekananda
    movement 125

Ranade 14, 120
Rashtriya Svyamsevak Sangh *see* Sangh Parivar
Rassundari 104 *see also* child brides
rebellion of 1857 161, 224, 237
  First War of Independence 160–1
  Kunwar Singh 161
  Mutiny 161
  Rani of Jhansi 161
Rees, Major-General 196
Religious cults and sexual practice 77
  Kartabhajas 78
  Tantricism 78
  Vaishnava 78
Renaissance 30
Roper, Trevor 216
romantic love 13–15, 76, 81–3, 85–7
  Bankim Chatterji 14
  Bijay Goswami 14
  Nirad C. Chaudhuri 14
  Romeo and Juliet 14, 82
Roy, B.C. (chief minister, Bengal) 15, 86
Roy, Rammohan 7, 20, 26, 32, 50, 51, 52, 56, 57, 58, 59, 106, 126, 142
  and Christianity 7, 32–3, 34, 99, 102, 106
  Gift to Monotheists 50
  institutionalized religion 55, 56
  Islamic education 100, 102
  letter to Amherst 53–4, 59
  monotheism 99
  Percepts of Jesus 33
  and sati 63, 81
  and tantra 101
  view of Europe and Europeans 28–9, 59

Salisbury, Lord 155

Sangh Parivar 206–16
  Bajrang Dal 209, 215
  Bharatiya Janata Party (BJP) 209, 210, 211, 212, 215, 216, 232, 240
  Bharatiya Vidyarthi Parishad 215, 226
  Rashtriya Svyamsevak Sangh (RSS) 117, 208, 210, 211, 212, 213, 214, 215, 216, 220, 225, 226–8, 232
    opposition to Gandhi 213, 214
    Organiser 210, 213, 232
  Sant Sabha 209
  Vishwa Hindu Parishad 117, 127, 208, 209, 210, 215, 225, 227–8
Sant Sabha *see* Sangh Parivar
Savarkar 211 *also see* Sangh Parivar
Sarada Devi 114
Sankaracharya 125
Sarkar, Akshay 103
Sarkar, Sir Jadunath 157–8
Sastri, Sibnath 16, 83, 84, 100, 106, 126
Sen, Amiya 124
Sen, Keshab Chandra 7, 16, 60, 61, 62, 72, 81, 106, 113
  and Christianity 33, 34, 35, 107
  and consumerism 37
  Nababidhan 105, 107
  Sadharan Brahmo Samaj 105
  Vaishnava devotionalism 107, 126
Sen, Krishnaprasanna 108
Sen, Nabin 15, 83, 85, 86, 87
sex 15
  sexual excess 15
  sexual fantasy 87–8
  sexual instinct 62
  sexual urge 67, 124
Sheikh Abdullah 235

Sheikh Waliullah 56
Shiv Sena 216, 225
Simla Agreement 234
Simon Commission Report 194
Singh, Baldev 190
Singh, Master Tara 190
Sister Nivedita 118, 132, 134, 138
Spate, O.H.K. 196
Subalternin Studies 178, 180, 181, 183, 184, 193
    Gramsci 180
    Ranajit Guha 180
suttee *also* sati 17, 50, 52, 63, 81
    see also Roy, Rammohan
Swami Vivekananda viii, 6, 7, 19, 38, 88, 111–28, 136–40
    Chicago Congress of Religions 111, 115, 116, 140, 142
    criticism of missionaries 33
    and Christian influence 109
    and modern Europe 42–3
    and western consumerism 37
    and western democracy 35

Tagore, Devendranath 57, 106, 107
    Praphullamayi (daughter-in-law) 75
Tagore, Dwarkanath 51, 71, 74
Tagore, Gyanendramohan 85
Tagore, Indira Devi 80, 85
Tagore, Rabindranath 13, 80
    and Gandhi 141–51
    and Gokhale 142

and Indian civilization 146–8
and modern civilization 143–5, 146, 147–8
and modern European culture 40–1
and nationalism 145
Chaturanga 62, 100
Gora 13, 97
Premer Abhishek 89
Smaran 80
Tagore, Satyendranath 80, 81, 83
Talib, Abu 24, 25, 26
tantra/tantricism *see* mysticism
Tata, Jamsetji 33
Tripathi, Govardhan 11

Unitarians/Unitarianism 33, 100
    see also Roy, Rammohan
Upadhyaay, Brahmabandhab 74, 88
Utilitarianism *see* philosophy

Vaishnava/Vaishnavism 81, 98, 107, 108, 126 *see also* Chaitanya
Vishwa Hindu Parishad (VHP) *see* Sangh Parivar
Vidyasagar, Ishwar Chandra 11, 31, 54, 59, 102
    and widow remarriage 78, 81

widow remarriage 17, 67, 81, 84, 85, 86, 126
    enforced widowhood 69–70 *see also* Vidyasagar
Wilson, Reverend 55